AN INTRODUCTION TO

TWENTIETH CENTURY MUSIC

George J. Zack

1963

The twentieth century is more splendid than the nineteenth century, certainly it is much more splendid. The twentieth century has much less reasonableness in its existence than the nineteenth century but reasonableness does not make for splendor. The seventeenth century had less reason in its existence than the sixteenth century and in consequence it has more splendor. So the twentieth century is that, it is a time when everything cracks, where everything is destroyed, everything isolates itself, it is a more splendid thing than a period where everything follows itself. So then the twentieth century is a splendid period, not a reasonable one in the scientific sense, but splendid. The phenomena of nature are more splendid than the daily events of nature, certainly, so then the twentieth century is splendid.

GERTRUDE STEIN

Peter S. Hansen

HEAD, DEPARTMENT OF MUSIC
NEWCOMB COLLEGE, TULANE UNIVERSITY

Allyn and Bacon, Inc.

BOSTON, 1961

AN INTRODUCTION TO

TWENTIETH CENTURY MUSIC

PHOTOS UNACCOMPANIED BY A CREDIT LINE CAME FROM THE FOLLOWING SOURCES:

PAGE 92 *Photographed by John D. Schiff, from the collection of Mrs. Frederick W. Knize, New York*
96 *Photo by Roger-Voillet, Paris*
97 *Columbia Records Photo*
98 *Photo by Roger-Voillet, Paris*
100 *Photographed for the Metropolitan Opera Company by Sedge LeBlang*
239 *Columbia Records Photo*
241 *Photographed for the Metropolitan Opera Company by Louis Mélançon*
242 *Boosey and Hawkes*
243 *Associated Music Publishers*
244 (left) *Boosey and Hawkes*
245 (top) *Oxford University Press*
(bottom) *Boosey and Hawkes*
246 (left) *Photo by Paul Moor, courtesy of Boosey and Hawkes*
(right) *Roy Harris*
247 (left) *Boosey and Hawkes*
(right) *Edward B. Marks Music Corporation*
248 (top) *Eastman School of Music, photographed by Louis Ouzer*
(bottom) *Music Press, Inc.*

FIRST PRINTING : AUGUST, 1961
SECOND PRINTING : JULY, 1962

Preface

THE PURPOSE OF THIS BOOK is to present the main lines of development of twentieth-century music through a study of selected compositions by its most influential composers. The author assumes that the student has some knowledge of the main stream of music and an understanding of its underlying principles (such as tonality, harmony, form, etc.), since the new style traits are presented as outgrowths of this more familiar music. On the other hand, extensive technical knowledge is not necessary to use this book. It is designed for college courses having no other prerequisite than an introductory course in music, such as Introduction to Music or Music Appreciation.

In surveying the era and attempting to evaluate its musical achievements, one finds that the first half of the twentieth century has as many shifting patterns and designs as a kaleidoscope. To impose a definitive pattern is impossible at this time and the different books devoted to the subject reflect various points of view. Some books supply us with a year-by-year recording of events while others describe musical activities within geographical boundaries. Still others discuss the period by writing biographies of composers, analyzing significant compositions, or by defining certain aspects of music theory. All of these approaches are valid and helpful to students.

This book seeks to treat the principal factors involved—personalities, chronology, style—in a manner that shows various interrelations as well as fundamental trends in the development of the art. The special problem of writing contemporary cultural history is the necessity of making judgments about persons, events, and works of art that have not yet stood the test of time—the only true criterion of aesthetic value. As a result it is inevitable that there will be differences of opinion concerning emphasis and proportion in such a book as this and that the final decisions will be more personal than if one were making a survey, say, of the music of the first half of the sixteenth century. The present author has been guided in his decisions by his experiences with and predilections for twentieth-century music and by the practical consideration of the amount of material that can be included in the one semester usually allocated to a course in contemporary music in our colleges and universities.

The underlying organization is chronological, as evidenced by the three main divisions: the turn of the century to World War I; the period between the wars; and the post World War II years. Within these large divisions, the contributions of individual composers are described against a background of their particular cultural environments. This is not the neatest possible plan, since some of the composers who have lived through all three periods are encountered in more than one chapter; yet it has the advantage of serving the author's broad purpose of showing large trends and period styles, as well as introducing key works of a period. The chronological charts spaced throughout the book will aid the student in associating simultaneous events sometimes described in widely separated chapters, and the chronological list of composers will show still other relationships to composers mentioned in no other place in the book.

The various approaches employed—chronological, cultural-historical, biographical, analytical—have but one aim, to give the student, whether he be a music major or not, insights, understanding, and increased enjoyment of twentieth-century music. All of the compositions discussed have been recorded. These recordings should be available, for nothing is more futile than to read about music unheard in performance.

The author is indebted to his students and colleagues in the Music Department at Newcomb College, Tulane University for many helpful suggestions. Special acknowledgements are made to the following individuals:

Mr. Lehman Engel, New York, for permission to quote from a letter written to him by Charles Ives.

Mrs. Frederick W. Knize, New York, for permission to include a reproduction of the portrait of Schoenberg painted by Kokoschka.

Mr. Rollo Myers, London, for permission to make citations from his translation of Cocteau's *Coq et Harlequin*.

Mrs. Gertrud Schoenberg, Los Angeles, for permission to make citations from Arnold Schoenberg's works.

Mr. Igor Stravinsky, Los Angeles, for permission to make citations from his published writings and for the revisions and clarifications of passages of his *Conversations* made for this book.

Acknowledgment is also made of the courtesy expressed by the Metropolitan Opera Company in supplying photographs of their productions, and to the various music publishers for permission to make citations from scores.

P.S.H.

Contents

1945 - 1960

AN INTRODUCTION TO

TWENTIETH CENTURY MUSIC

PART ONE

1900-1914

CHAPTER I

NINETEENTH CENTURY BACKGROUND

*Richard Wagner stands before my eyes suffering and great as
that nineteenth century whose complete expression he is.*

THOMAS MANN

Most of the people who heard the first performances of
Pelléas et Mélisande (1902), *Pierrot Lunaire* (1912), and
Le Sacre du Printemps (1913) believed they were witness-
ing a brutal assault on musical sensitivity, intelligence,
and morality. It seemed as if the continuum of music
history had been broken and that the rich beauties of the
past had been replaced by willful and capricious ugliness.
Impressed by what they considered a complete change in
style, critics spoke of *neue Musik*, new music, just as their
predecessors of 1600 and 1300, also times of style change,
had spoken of *nuove musiche* and *ars nova*.

Now that the midpoint of the twentieth century has
passed we hear this music with different ears. What seemed
to be unplanned cacophony we now accept without a
shudder, and the various idioms which were so shocking
have been analyzed and systematized in textbooks. Furthermore, we now realize that the continuum of history was not

broken: Debussy, Stravinsky, and Schoenberg each developed in a particular musical environment, and their music is as much a result of their having been born at a certain time and place as was Beethoven's or Palestrina's.

Because of this close connection with the immediate past, the discussions of the composers and styles of twentieth-century music will be preceded by a short survey of the music of the nineteenth. Because a comprehensive discussion of the nineteenth century is obviously inappropriate to this book, the purpose of this survey is only to reacquaint the reader with the musical environment into which composers of twentieth-century music were born and in which they developed.

Nineteenth-century music extends from Beethoven to Wagner. This period was, of course, the century of romanticism, and music, the most romantic of all the arts, assumed a dominating position and acquired a listening public far surpassing that which it had enjoyed in earlier times. Instead of being associated almost entirely with church or court, music became one of the most prized possessions of the new middle class. People of the day performed music for their own pleasure as never before, whether as amateur pianists playing the *Songs Without Words* or four-hand arrangements of Mozart symphonies, or as parlor singers rendering one of the hundreds of love songs that were published at the time, or as members of a municipal chorus. For listeners, too, an opportunity to hear symphonies and operas as well as glamorous virtuosos was provided by the public concerts that, for the first time, were given in large numbers.

THE POSITION OF BEETHOVEN

Beethoven is the great figure towering over all nineteenth-century music, and his influence was so enormous that it was felt by the most distant of his followers. Both Wagner and Brahms, for instance, no matter how different their ideals, could claim to be his heir. The composer of music dramas looked to the last movement of the Ninth Symphony as evidence that instrumental music needed words in order to be truly expressive, while Brahms, who had actually been hailed as the third "B," found it natural to write most of his works in Beethoven's favorite modes of organization, the sonata and variation forms.

Beethoven's technical contributions to the art of music can be summarized in the word *expansion,* for he pushed open all of the dimensions of music. He exploited extremes of pitch, both high and low, and extremes of dynamics, both loud and soft. His compositions are longer, his rhythms are stronger and more complex, and his palette of orchestral color is more varied than that of any composer of the eighteenth century.

As a result of this expansion, his music became a powerful expression of individual, personal feeling, and it is the development and exploitation of this function of music which is perhaps Beethoven's greatest legacy. We commonly speak of his music as being *noble, tragic, boisterous, dramatic,* and although the words are not the exact equivalents of the expression of the music, they continue to be used with meaning. Much of Beethoven's music is *serious,* and both he and Wagner censured Mozart for having written an opera based on so trivial and immoral a story as *Don Giovanni.* They believed that music was an art that should elevate and ennoble its listeners and therefore should not be used for lesser purposes.

Wagner, for instance, did not write his music dramas to provide an evening's casual entertainment. He insisted that the *Ring* should be performed not in a traditional opera house, but in a shrine of its own away from any commercial atmosphere, to which pilgrims would come for spiritual elevation, following the pattern of the ancient Greeks attending their annual rites. After the Festspielhaus was built in Bayreuth, for several years he restricted the performances of *Parsifal* to this sacred auditorium. It is significant that an enthusiastic audience which accepted Wagner's terms attended the opening performances in 1876. Many of those present had prepared themselves for the experience by memorizing the leitmotifs (the musical themes associated with characters and situations in the operas), and it is said that some devotees went so far as to fast before the performances in order to be in a sufficiently elevated mood.

IMPORTANCE OF WAGNERIAN MUSIC DRAMA

The fact that it was opera that demanded such respect (opera of the particular kind that Wagner wrote) points up another strong tendency of nineteenth-century music—its growing ties with literature.

Here the line of Beethoven (of the Ninth Symphony)-Berlioz-Liszt-Wagner is clear, for each added to the notion that music is somehow better if it tells a story, paints a picture, or describes a character. Although the symphonic poem, the character piece for piano, and the lied accomplished this very well, it was opera that provided the perfect setting for bringing together all the arts. The ideal of the *Gesamtkunstwerk* (collective art work) was to combine poetry, gesture, movement, and color with music in order to make a product greater than the sum of the parts. This breaking down of the boundaries of the arts was a typically romantic obsession.

OTHER TRENDS

In the preceding résumé of nineteenth-century music, only the more spectacular and progressive tendencies have been mentioned. Since the state of music is never entirely consistent at any time, it should not be forgotten that the ideals of absolute (nonprogrammatic) music persisted in the chamber works and symphonies of Schumann, Brahms, and Bruckner.

Toward the end of the century, another group of composers, called the nationalists—such men as Smetana, Dvořák, Grieg and the Russian "Five" (Balakirev, Borodin, Moussorgsky, Cui, and Rimsky-Korsakov), made strong contributions to music with their folk-inspired melodies, rhythms, and colorful orchestrations.

STYLE CHARACTERISTICS

Orchestration

Because of technical advances in the art, music became expressive in a new way. However, the converse of the statement is equally true; that is, the powerful feelings experienced by the composers demanded new sounds and technical advances for their expression. Among these was the vastly expanded and more richly colorful orchestra. Again the line is Beethoven-Berlioz-Liszt-Wagner, with some important side contributions from von Weber and Mendelssohn.

The change in sound from the orchestra of Haydn and Mozart is to be accounted for by the addition of new instruments—trombones, English horns, harps, bass clarinets—and by the greater number of instruments. For example, Wagner wrote for eight horns compared with Haydn's two, and Berlioz' dream orchestra consisted of 467 performers, compared with the 30-odd performers in Haydn's orchestra.

To think of nineteenth-century music is to think of expressive tone color—the oboe and clarinet duets in the second movement of Schubert's *Unfinished,* the horn call at the beginning of his Seventh Symphony, the same instruments in the overture to *Oberon,* the trio of horns in the "Nocturne" of the *Midsummer Night's Dream* music, the English horn solo in the third movement of the *Fantastic Symphony* and its duet with the oboe, the tympani in the "March to the Scaffold" —the list is endless. Wagner above all is particularly rich in moments of magical tone color—the cellos at the beginning of *Tristan,* the horns in Act II, the mournful English horn in Act III, the brilliance of the "Ride of the Valkyrie," the ebullience of Siegfried's horn call—again the list is endless.

Chromatic Harmony

Music became more colorful in another sense, too, with the growing complexity of its chords and chordal relationships. Here practically every composer of the nineteenth century made a contribution: Schubert, with his alternating and mixing of major and minor modes; Chopin, with his splashes of nonharmonic chromatic tones, sometimes unresolved; or Liszt, with his use of augmented chords and exploitations of augmented fourth relationships.

Once again, it was Wagner who developed this enriched harmony to the limits of possibility. *Tristan und Isolde* is generally accepted as being the apex of chromatic harmony; from its first measure to its last, the freely altered chords make a shimmering, amorphous, ever-changing tissue of sound, ideally suited to the expression of the surging passions of the drama. Freedom in modulation is also fully developed here, and in great sections of the opera there is no clear establishment of key. Fluctuation from key to key is the normal state of affairs, and final cadences usually occur only at the ends of acts.

Psychological Form

Through the process of evading cadences, Wagner was able to write music of unheard-of breadth, continuous for long periods. In these extended, continuous forms, which were used in the symphonic poem and romantic piano music as well, virtually no respect was paid to the forms of organization that had shaped so much of the music of the preceding century. Instead of sonata forms, rondos, or minuets and trios, a type of organization best described as *psychological form* came into being. By this is meant that the musical composition—be it a symphonic poem, a sonata by Liszt, or an act of an opera—is shaped by dramatic, rather than by strictly musical considerations. Unity was often achieved through the use of theme transformation. Whether it was called an *idée fixe,* a leitmotif, or a characteristic phrase, the theme that had special significance and was transformed as the composition progressed, became the means by which many musical compositions were held together.

ROMANTIC COMPOSER IN SOCIETY

The composers in the Beethoven-Wagner line played a role in society that was vastly different from the role played by their predecessors. As "free" artists, i.e. unemployed, they wrote as their inspirations dictated and not in fulfillment of contractual obligations. Bach, Haydn, and Mozart wrote most of their compositions to order; but Beethoven wrote nine symphonies and thirty-two piano sonatas, along with many other works, because he was inclined to do so. Bach's cantatas were written because he needed new music to perform, but Wagner's operas were written when there was little probability that they would ever be staged. As a result of this freedom from external conditioning, the romantic composer gave full rein to his musical imagination. Not stopping to ask if his composition were playable or not, he immeasurably enriched the vocabulary and dimensions of music.

Moreover, the "free" artist of the nineteenth century was able to indulge in personal idiosyncrasies. Beethoven could live in disorder and confusion; Schubert could live in a state of unashamed irresponsibility; Liszt could theatrically flaunt middle-class morality; Wagner, as the *grand seigneur,* could ride over everyone in egomania; these were prerogatives of romantic composers. The expression "long-hair" suggests that the artist-creator is somehow different from his fellow men, and in so far as these composers indulged in unusual idiosyncrasies, the expression does apply to them.

THE RELATION OF THE NINETEENTH CENTURY
TO THE TWENTIETH

Subsequent events have proven that the composers of the late nine-teenth century were the culminating figures of romantic music because their fulfillment of romantic ideals was so complete that a change in ideal and style would inevitably follow them.

To find the direction of this change was the task of the next generation whose leaders were Debussy, Stravinsky, and Schoenberg —all of whom were born between 1862 and 1882. These men were Janus-faced. Each had deep roots in his respective national heritage and each grew up in the heyday of Wagner and colorful nationalism, a heritage evident in their early works. As they matured in the new century they developed their own highly original and influential styles, partly as a continuation of romanticism, and partly as a reaction against it. Their contributions will be described in the chapters im-mediately following.

SUGGESTED READINGS

The best study of nineteenth-century music is Alfred Einstein's *Music In The Romantic Era* (New York, 1947). Three books showing the continuity of nineteenth- and twentieth-century music are *A Hundred Years of Music* by Gerald Abraham (New York, 1938), *A Century of Music* by John Culshaw (London, 1952), and *Romanticism and the 20th Century* by Wilfred Mellers (London, 1957).

CHAPTER II

PARIS

Music should humbly seek to please: within these limits great beauty may well be found. Extreme complication is contrary to art. Beauty must appeal to the senses, must provide us with immediate enjoyment, must impress us or insinuate itself into us without any effort on our part. CLAUDE DEBUSSY

Paris has always been more than a settlement of people living on the banks of the Seine, for throughout the ages it has symbolized many things—the vigor of the Middle Ages, the elegance of the Renaissance, the splendor of the Baroque, the enthusiasm of the Romantic Period, the *dernier cri* of our day. In period after period the artistic creators of the world have found Paris a congenial place in which to work, and since the days of Abelard it has been a mecca for students.

In the early years of the twentieth century Paris was in a very mellow mood. It was a time of peace—the scars of 1870 were forgotten and new friendship with Russia augured well for the future. It was a time of prosperity in general, and prosperity in particular for those who had stock in the Suez Canal Company or Russian railroads. Paris became a new symbol, this time one of luxury and sophisticated sensuality—a place where enjoyment of life, food, and the fine arts was of prime concern.

11

FIN DE SIÈCLE—
SYMBOLISM AND IMPRESSIONISM

The expression *fin de siècle*, originally applied to the 1890's, not only names a decade but also describes a mood or attitude toward life which prevailed until the outbreak of the First World War in 1914, when the nineteenth-century way of life finally came to an end. The term connotes an attitude of decadence and overrefinement, and suggests a time when youthful enthusiasm and striving to improve had been supplanted by exquisite sensitivity and self-indulgence. It implies ripeness rather than vigor, and pagan rather than puritan attitudes. Des Esseintes, the hero of Huysman's novel *Against the Grain,* is an exaggerated portrait, to be sure, but nevertheless he is the typical man of the time who lives only for the stimulation and gratification of his senses. He has no regard for his fellow man and no moral sense. Life for him is a matter of feeling textures, smelling fragrances, and hearing sounds. He is a superlatively refined animal.

Symbolist poets—especially Verlaine, Mallarmé, and Jules Laforgue—and impressionist painters such as Monet, Pissaro, Sisley, and Renoir helped to sharpen the senses of their contemporaries. The poets became increasingly sensitive to the sound of words, often at the expense of clarity of statement. They aimed primarily at establishing vague and evanescent moods through the sheer sound and rhythm of their verses and avoided all attempts to tell a story or underline a moral. The painters also avoided anecdotal or historically realistic subjects in order to concentrate on the effects of light in nature. Subject matter became unimportant, while color, broken up into small patches to achieve a vibrant quality, became the chief interest. Monet's successive paintings of a haystack and the portico of the cathedral of Amiens at different hours of the day, revealing the subtle changes of color, show wherein his interest lay. Formal composition in painting became as unimportant as subject matter in poetry.

DEBUSSY, 1862-1918

Debussy, the composer who expressed the impressionist-symbolist ideal in music, was no more interested in the grand gesture and the dramatic moment than was Monet in painting scenes of crisis. Because Debussy's aim was the creation of exquisite, evocative sounds, he sought the *ton juste* (precise sound) as diligently as Flaubert sought the *mot juste* (precise word).

Debussy was born in St. Germain-en-Laye, a suburb of Paris, to the wife of a shopkeeper. As a young child he took lessons from a neighborhood piano teacher who had been a pupil of Chopin. Debussy's talent and aptitude were so pronounced that, following the long-established route of the musically gifted in France, he entered the Conservatoire in 1873. Here he was known as a brilliant pianist and also as a disturbing element in the theory classes, because he was more interested in playing shocking chords than he was in writing conventional harmony exercises.

When nineteen years old he was engaged by Madame von Meck, the Croesus-rich Russian widow, the patroness and "unknown beloved" of Tchaikovsky, as musical tutor for her children and as a general house-musician. He lived with the family for a short time in Italy and later in Russia and Austria. In 1885 he won the coveted Prix de Rome and spent the next year and a half in Rome composing, and counting the days until he could return to his beloved Paris. He did this in 1887 and remained there until his death in 1918, except for short trips to London, Vienna, and Bayreuth, where he spent his time composing, writing music criticism, and editing piano music for Durand, the music publisher.

An intimate friend of symbolist poets and impressionist painters, he frequented the famous Thursday afternoon symposia at the home of Mallarmé, the poet. He collected Oriental *objets d'art* and was unusually fond of the color green. In his early years he showed his disdain for middle-class conformity by wearing outlandish clothes (including a western-style Stetson) and by his stormy personal life. He became more conservative, however, after his election to the Institut de France, the ultimate honor his country pays to her most distinguished citizens, and after his growing recognition as a composer. His last years were plagued by ill health and he died as the Germans were cannonading Paris in 1918. Not only did his life span two eras, but also his music served as one of the most significant bridges between the nineteenth and twentieth centuries.

MUSICAL BACKGROUND

What was the musical environment of a composer growing up in *fin-de-siècle* Paris? At the Conservatoire Debussy received a thorough, academic training based on eighteenth- and early nineteenth-century music. He was well grounded in Bach, Mozart, and Beethoven, and as a pianist he played Chopin, Liszt, and Schumann.

The successful French composers of the day were those who wrote operas. Gounod, Massenet, Delibes, and Thomas were the men who enjoyed acclaim and official recognition. Their operas were predominantly lyrical, tuneful, sentimental, and carefully scored so that the orchestra would not overpower the typically small French voices. The librettos of these works were frequently sophisticated and daring (*Manon* and *Hérodiade,* for example), which added to their popular appeal. They were written to provide an evening's entertainment, and because the music was lovely and unobtrusive their success was inevitable. Although Debussy did not write any operas in this vein, he was too much of a Frenchman not to be aware of the charm, grace, and elegance embodied in these scores.

Another of the sources strongly influencing Debussy's style was the music of the Russian nationalists that he heard at a series of concerts conducted by Rimsky-Korsakov at the Paris Exposition in 1889. This exotic, brilliantly orchestrated music was a revelation to the young French composer. The Exposition provided another sound world that stimulated him—the music of the Gamelan orchestra which played in the Far East pavilion. The intricate rhythms, the hypnotic web of sound, and the pentatonic scales left their mark on his compositions.

The music of Moussorgsky also had a powerful effect on the formation of Debussy's style. He had a score of *Boris Godounov,* a rather famous copy which had been brought back from Russia by Saint-Saëns. It passed from hand to hand among a small circle in Paris, making a deep impression on Debussy and others because of its great originality. Here he found rhythmic and harmonic freedom unlike anything he had seen before. Unresolved dissonances, modal melodies, frequent meter changes, pedal points, ostinatos, and bell sonorities in the orchestra—all of these made *Boris* a magic garden of fascinating, seductive sound.

Perhaps the strongest influence was "that old sorcerer" Richard

Wagner, whose conquest of France began in 1887 with the first performance of *Lohengrin* in Paris. In 1893 *Die Walküre* was given and a group of enthusiasts, including Baudelaire, became active propagandists; the Wagnerian ideal of combining the arts into a new synthesis was close to their aim of bringing words, music, and color into new intimacies. Many French aesthetes traveled to Vienna, Munich, or Bayreuth to hear the music dramas, and the scores were studied intensely by others who stayed at home.

Young Debussy shared this enthusiasm. He made his Bayreuth pilgrimages and many of his early works, such as the songs *Cinq poèmes de Baudelaire*, show unmistakable traces of Wagner's harmonic style. Later, as he developed a more personal idiom, he became increasingly critical of Wagner and held up the French ideal of *clarté et concision* (clarity and conciseness) against the opulence of the German's music. Nevertheless, the fact that he continued to write about Wagner in his critical essays shows that he was always aware of his adversary. In a letter written during the time he was working on *Pelléas et Mélisande*, he complained of his difficulties: "And worst of all, the ghost of old Klingsor, alias R. Wagner, appeared at a turning of one of the bars so I tore up the whole thing and set off in search of some more characteristic compound of phrases."[1]

This, then, was the background of the composer who opened the door to the new century. Firmly rooted in the tradition of French music, and building from the style of his immediate environment, he created a musical language of the highest originality and beauty, a language that was to leave its mark on many of the composers who were to follow.

DEBUSSY'S COMPOSITIONS

This language was not achieved all at once. The style of a composer is not fixed and static; it develops and changes gradually, much as a human personality passes erratically and imperceptibly from childhood through adolescence to maturity. Style periods are not rigid, watertight compartments sealed off from one another, containing strongly contrasting material. They are simply a convenience in discussing a composer's works. For the sake of convenience, therefore, Debussy's compositions will be discussed in three periods.

Period 1: 1884-1900

The most important of the early works are:

CANTATAS

  L'Enfant prodigue (*The Prodigal Son;* 1884)
  La Damoiselle élue (*The Blessed Damozel;* 1888)

ORCHESTRAL

  Prélude à l'Après-midi d'un Faune (*Prelude to the Afternoon of a Faun;* 1894)
  Nocturnes. I. Nuages. II. Fêtes. III. Sirènes. (1893-1899)

PIANO

  Deux Arabesques (1888)
  Suite bergamasque. I. Prélude. II. Menuet. III. Clair de Lune. IV. Passepied. (1890-1905)
  Pour le Piano. I. Prélude. II. Sarabande. III. Toccata. (1896-1901)

SONGS

  Cinq poèmes de Baudelaire (1889)
  Ariettes oubliées (1888)
  Fêtes galantes (1892)
  Chansons de Bilitis (1899)

CHAMBER MUSIC

  String Quartet (1893)

In these well-known compositions one can trace Debussy's transition from a talented young composer of salon pieces to his emergence as a composer with a highly personal and original style. The influence of Massenet is strong in the two cantatas and the *Suite bergamasque* for piano, which includes *"Clair de lune."* As this well-known piece testifies, Debussy's music at this time was delicate, charming, and occasionally sentimental.

  The String Quartet is more sharply chiselled. Organized in cyclic form, which attracted so many composers of this period, it is unified by a motto theme that undergoes numerous transformations. Of note are the pert syncopations in this theme, the flowing figurations, the pizzicatos and rhythmic complexities of the second movement, the muted sonorities of the third, and the dissonances and excitement of the last. It is a composition of strongly personal imprint.

Perhaps the most important piece of this early period is *L'Après-midi d'un Faune,* which is flawlessly executed. Many of the sounds of the impressionist orchestra are revealed here in the languid flute solos, the swirl of the harp, the pianissimo chords of the four horns, and the poignant oboe solos. The work does not show quite as much originality in its chords and chordal relationships as in timbre. The middle section in D-flat major faintly suggests the drawing room atmosphere of *"Clair de Lune."* The suite *Pour le Piano* is more courageous in its harmonic vocabulary. In the *"Prélude"* there are striking passages of parallel augmented chords and whole-tone scales, and in the modal *"Sarabande"* chords are "blurred" by the addition of unresolved seconds.

The songs that Debussy wrote before 1900 should not be overlooked, for they established a new type of art song as different from the dramatic and highly charged lieder of German composers as it is from the simple melodies of the earlier French composers. Debussy usually set the verses of the decadent poets, and like the poems, the songs are often fragmentary, elusive, erotic, and atmospheric. There are no melodies in the sense of tunes-to-remember, for the vocal lines rise and fall subtly with the words.

Chansons de Bilitis, a setting of three poems by Pierre Louÿs, a friend of the composer, will be described to show some of the characteristic features of his songs. The first and last, *"La Flûte de Pan"* and *"Le Tombeau des Naïades,"* have a pseudo-antique flavor reminiscent of the subdued murals painted by Puvis de Chavannes in the Sorbonne and the Pantheon. The strictly syllabic setting of the words and conjunct melodies immediately proclaim the style (see Example 1). The first song is unified by the Lydian scale, suggesting the syrinx of the poem, heard in the introduction and again in the middle and in the postlude. Arpeggio figurations, reflecting the words, appear from time to time. The harmonies are very rich, particularly in the middle section where chains of parallel ninth and thirteenth chords fluctuate beneath the voice line. The third song of the set is similar in style, although here the solemnity of the poem is reflected in the constant sixteenth-note figure of the accompaniment. The second song, *"La Chevelure,"* is more personal and dramatic in its depiction of an erotic dream. Its haunting, inconclusive ending has a more powerful effect than the usual high climactic note.

EXAMPLE 1*

Doux et soutenu

Pour le jour des Hy - a - cin - thies,

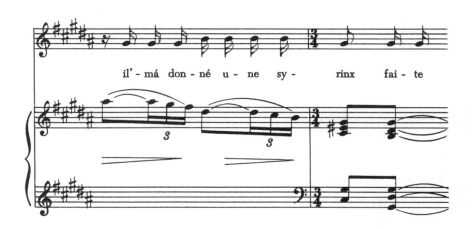

il' - má don - né u - ne sy - rinx fai - te

*Permission for reprint granted by Editions Jean Jobert, Paris, copyright owners; Elkan-Vogel Co., Inc., Philadelphia, agents.

18 / Part One: 1900-1914

de ro - seaux bien tail - lés, u - nis a -

These are songs that demand a particular kind of artistry on the part of the singer, and a particular kind of sympathy on the part of the audience. An understanding of French is necessary to appreciate them because of the close association of words and music. Furthermore, the poems are virtually untranslatable. Only in French can one say so little and imply so much.

Period 2: 1900-1910

The more important works of this period are the masterpieces of impressionist music which established Debussy as a major composer.

OPERA

> *Pelléas et Mélisande* (1902)

PIANO

> *Estampes* (1903)
> *Images* (1905 and 1907)
> *Préludes* (Book I, 1910; Book II, 1913; 12 compositions in each book)

ORCHESTRAL

> *La Mer:* I. De l'Aube à Midi sur la Mer. II. Jeu de Vagues. III. Dialogue du Vent et de la Mer. (1903-05)
> *Images:* I. Gigues. II. Ibéria. III. Rondes de Printemps. (1909)

Debussy's single opera *Pelléas et Mélisande* startled Paris with its originality and caused one of those scandals which would greet so many premières in the years to come. It is a marvelously subtle work, but it has never become popular because of its great restraint and constant understatement. The elusive characters move in a dream world, perfectly reflected in the quiet vocal lines and unresolved harmonies of the orchestra.

There are interesting, ambivalent relationships between this opera and the music dramas of Wagner. On the one hand, there are similarities in the musical structure. Debussy followed Wagner's lead in writing a continuous, recitativelike voice line, in treating the words of his libretto with great respect, and in avoiding arias and ensembles. Furthermore, he associates musical themes with characters and situations, and in choosing Maeterlinck's play as his libretto he chose a story very similar to that of *Tristan und Isolde;* both operas are concerned with the betrayal of an old king by his wife and a younger man.

But here the similarities end, for in other respects we see that the two operas are actually worlds apart. Their differences are epitomized in a comparison of the earth-shaking love scene in the second act of *Tristan* with Mélisande's timid declaration of love:

EXAMPLE 2a

EXAMPLE 2b*

*Permission for reprint granted by Durand et Cie., Paris, copyright owners; Elkan-Vogel Co., Inc., Philadelphia, agents.

Every element of *Tristan's* drama is expressed at length and with overpowering insistence, while in *Pelléas* everything is merely suggested or hinted. Isolde tells all; Mélisande, nothing.

In *Pelléas* and in the orchestral and piano music of this time a vocabulary of musical impressionism is established. Debussy is the most important composer of piano music since Chopin and Liszt, for he discovers new sonorities, pedal effects, and timbres in the instrument. His two books of *Préludes,* each containing twelve pieces, are important landmarks of twentieth-century music. Each piece has a poetic or descriptive title such as *"La Cathédrale engloutie,"* ("The Submerged Cathedral"), *"Minstrels,"* or *"Bruyères"* ("Heather").

"Feux d'Artifice" ("Fireworks"), the last composition of the second book, is typical and some of its salient features will be described here. It starts with the alternation of a three-note fragment suggesting the key of F with another suggesting G-flat.

EXAMPLE 3*

Modérément animé
léger, égal et lointain

*Permission for reprint for this and following Debussy examples granted by Durand et Cie., Paris, copyright owners; Elkan-Vogel Co., Inc., Philadelphia, agents.

Above this complex, tonally ambiguous sound, tones a diminished fifth apart are sounded. Everything is pianissimo until a sudden crescendo leads to a descending glissando on the black keys to the bottom of the keyboard. The motion starts again with a cluster of alternating minor seconds that lead to sweeping arpeggios under which a trumpetlike call is heard. One figure

EXAMPLE 4

is heard from time to time in rhythmic variants. It is the nearest approach to a theme in a piece that otherwise is a succession of pianistic figures of greatest diversity.

One particularly happy invention exploits the augmented fourth (C-F♯). With its ambiguous tonal relationship, this interval fascinated the progressive composers of the first decades of the century. Example 5 also shows the juxtaposition of chords unrelated by key.

EXAMPLE 5

The music becomes more frenzied until a shattering, two-handed glissando in minor seconds again drops to the bottom of the keyboard. Next there is a low background on the notes D-flat and A-flat. Above it, in C, a few notes of the *Marseillaise* are heard. The succession of these highly original, fragmentary effects marvelously evokes a celebration of the French national holiday, the fourteenth of July.

The compositions for orchestra written in these years are worthy of close study, for the sound and syntax of large-scale impressionist music were established through them. Among the unforgettable moments are the fragmentary English horn melody at the beginning of *"Nuages,"* the muted trumpets in *"Fêtes,"* and the transition between the second and third movements of *"Ibéria"* in which dance rhythms of a "Festival Morning" gradually supersede the exotic sounds of "Perfumes of the Night."

La Mer will be discussed in more detail. It consists of three sections, each having its own title. The first is called *"De l'Aube à Midi sur la Mer,"* and starts with a scarcely heard, low rumble, indistinct and fragmentary, a characteristic beginning for music of the 1900 period—so different from the clear-cut statements which mark the beginnings of earlier music. Tympani, harp, and low strings sound the background against which the oboes sing a plaintive fragment. Soon a theme is announced by the trumpet and English horn in octaves, an unusual combination of timbres, but one which shows Debussy's characteristic feeling for fresh and interesting colors.

EXAMPLE 6

This is used as a source theme from which much of the musical material of the entire piece is derived. It is tonally ambiguous, suggesting a pentatonic scale. The prominence of the interval of the fourth (melodic), both perfect and augmented, should be noted as well as the augmented fourths (harmonic) formed between the bass and the melody. The supple rhythm of triplet divisions of the beat against a duple background is also characteristic.

There is a change in tempo and key as the movement proper starts. Figurations are heard in the strings and woodwinds along with a new melody in the horns, which shows relationships with the source theme. When this section comes to a close, a more rhythmic, more definitely tonal section begins with the following motive:

EXAMPLE 7

The timbre is distinctive here since the composer calls for sixteen cellos divided into four groups. This section works up to a climax with sequences of ninth and augmented chords underlying the rhythmic figuration. When the motion quiets, the theme shown in Example 6 is again heard. There is a coda, and the last three notes of the movement refer once more to the source theme.

Paradoxically, there is interesting evidence of Wagner within this movement. The second measure of Example 6 is identical with the important Tristan motive of the opera, and the frenzied figuration of the middle section reminds one of the second act duet, with its diatonic ninth chords. Wagner was so powerful that many who denounced him could not entirely avoid his influence.

The second movement, *"Jeu de Vagues,"* is a marvelous example of impressionist, sensuous music. It is a catalog and textbook of orchestral devices, with its muted trumpets, harp glissandos, horns playing soft, close-voiced augmented triads, the celesta, and subtle cymbal sounds. As in the first movement, fragmentary melodies and ear-tickling effects alternate with a dancelike section in triple meter.

The principal theme also has a relationship to the source theme of the whole work:

EXAMPLE 8

The last movement, *"Dialogue de la Vent et de la Mer,"* again starts with a low rumble, built on a prominent augmented fourth. The source theme is heard in the muted trumpet playing *forte,* another unusual color effect. A new, warmly sentimental theme is heard in the oboe, and this, alternating with transformation of the source theme, is the thematic content of the movement. In the final measures the references to the source theme cannot be missed.

EXAMPLE 9

La Mer is an important achievement of twentieth-century music. The richness of its orchestral sound, the freedom and complexity of the harmony, and its firm structural devices make it a masterpiece.

Period 3: 1900-1917

Because of his failing health, the rich flow of Debussy's compositions slackened in the last years of his life. The principal works are:

Jeux (Play, ballet; 1912)
Twelve Études for piano (1915)
Sonatas for: Cello and Piano (1915)
            Flute, Viola, and Harp (1916)
            Violin and Piano (1916-1917)

A definite change in style is to be noted in these compositions, in which the lush, evocative sounds of impressionism give way to a new simplicity. A comparison of the titles of some of these piano pieces (e.g. "For the Five Fingers" and "For Double Notes" with "Gardens in the Rain" and "Pagodas") shows the change in orientation.

In the last set of sonatas Debussy returns to the formal types of organization he had neglected since the String Quartet. The third, for violin and piano, has a minimum of atmosphere. The harmonies are diatonic for the most part and concise themes are developed in the service of over-all design. In this, his last composition, he recalls the music-hall mood of *"Minstrels"* in the second movement, and at the end of the last, in his final final cadence, the bright key of G major is affirmed fortissimo. The enveloping fogs of impressionism have blown away.

STYLE CHARACTERISTICS

Debussy was one of the great innovators in the development of music. While he was not the sole inventor of some of the devices he used, as we have noted, he was the first to exploit them to such a degree that they became part of the vocabulary of music. Perhaps the most striking of his style traits was his preference for scales other than the familiar major and minor forms. Among these, the whole-tone scale is important, although he actually used it rarely. Two examples are to be found in *"Voiles"* and *"Le Tombeau des Naïades."*

EXAMPLE 10

p très doux

Whole-tone passages such as this, and those found in the following example, have become so associated with Debussy that when other composers employ the scale they inevitably and unfortunately sound "like Debussy."

Example 11*

Far more frequent are the modal scales. These are sometimes used programmatically to suggest medieval times, as in *"La Cathédrale engloutie"* and in *Pelléas*, but more often they are used for purely musical reasons. Debussy's interest in Oriental scales is well known. A pentatonic melody is to be found in *"Pagodes."*

*Permission for reprint granted by Editions Jean Jobert, Paris, copyright owners; Elkan-Vogel Co., Philadelphia, agents.

EXAMPLE 12

Modérément animé

pp delicatement

Debussy's melodies frequently consist of fragmentary motives joined asymmetrically; the repetitions, extensions, and developments found in romantic music are generally avoided. He once said:

> I should like to see the creation—I, myself, shall achieve it—of a kind of music free from themes, motives, and formed on a single continuous theme, which nothing interrupts and which never returns upon itself. Then there will be a logical, compact, deductive development. There will not be, between two restatements of the same characteristic theme, a hasty and superfluous "filling in." The development will no longer be that amplification of material, that professional rhetoric which is the badge of excellent training, but it will be given a more universal and essential psychic conception.[2]

Debussy's vocal melodies are remarkably close to the spoken word in both rhythm and inflection, and in general his instrumental melodies consist of short motives rather than extended lines. Some compositions, such as *"Poissons d'Or"* are without melody at all (in the usual sense) while others have but momentary allusion to tunes, as in *"Les Collines d'Anacapri"* or *"La Sérénade Interrompue."*

In matters of rhythm and meter, Debussy along with other French composers is fond of establishing compound meters (6/8 or 9/8) and contrasting duple subdivisions of the beats. *"Clair de lune"* contains many examples of this practice. Spanish rhythms, especially those of the tango and the habanera, are frequently found. *"La Soirée dans Grenade," "La Sérénade Interrompue,"* and *"Ibéria"* are examples. Syncopated rhythms associated with music halls and vaudeville are also found, inspired by the American minstrel shows which were touring Europe at the time. For examples see *"Golliwog's Cakewalk;" "General Lavine—Eccentric;"* and *"Minstrels."* In general, Debussy uses no strongly accented rhythmic patterns, but smooth, unaccented passages in which the rhythmic life flows gently in the background.

Debussy made his strongest contributions in the realm of harmony. Not only did he exploit new combinations of tones, but also he freed dissonant chords from the musical obligations they had carried for centuries. The principle that dissonance must be prepared and resolved, that moments of harmonic tension must be followed by moments of relaxation, was challenged by Debussy. The impact of this step upon music history was tremendous, for it attacked the foundations of tonality. In effect it was an attack on the morality of music, for the behavior of chords, established through the practice of hundreds of years, was suddenly freed from restraint. As in other matters, steps toward this freedom had been taken by certain composers who preceded Debussy, but they merely hinted at the newer practices.

If Debussy did not resolve his chords in the "proper" way, where did he lead them? Most often, to a similar dissonance on another level. Examples of this parallel treatment of chords can be found in *"Ce qu'a vu le Vent d'Ouest," "En Sourdine," "Le Tombeau des Naïades,"* and *"La Soirée dans Grenade."*

EXAMPLE 13

Ce qu'a vu le vent d'Ouest

Another example is found in the famous scene of the falling of Mélisande's hair.

EXAMPLE 14

Besides the parallel treatment of dissonance, the combination of two planes of chord progressions sometimes gives rise to very complex combinations. An example can be found in *"Les Sons et les Parfums tournent dans l'Air du Soir."* Debussy is also fond of deep pedal tones that add to the complexity of the harmonic moment.

In single chords there is also a special vocabulary. Augmented chords are frequent. The dominant ninth chord is also used very often, usually in parallel chains. (See Example 11.)

The "added tone" technique produces other combinations. Most frequent is the adding of seconds which makes for a blurred effect. Examples may be found in *"La Danse de Puck"* and *"Minstrels."* Chords without thirds are used sometimes to give an archaic impression. *"La Cathédrale engloutie"* offers many examples.

Debussy's treatment of dissonance changed its function. Heretofore dissonance had been used for its dramatic, expressive effect; that is, the intensity of the emotion was matched by the complexity of the chord. Now, however, very complex combinations were used not to create tension but simply to add color.

Another field in which Debussy made major contributions was that of timbre. Perhaps this is the outstanding characteristic of his music, since all of the other elements, including harmony, can be considered subservient to it. Debussy's piano writing follows the overtone displacement so beautifully exploited by Chopin—low pedal tones and dispersed chord tones spread over the entire piano with the more dissonant tones appearing near the top. Sometimes he leaves the middle area empty and combines extreme high tones with low tones, as for example in "*La Terrasse des Audiences du Clair de Lune.*"

In writing for voice he often exploits the lower reaches of the soprano or tenor range. This is a region that is not rich dramatically nor strong in volume, but completely right for whispering intimacies.

In general, he shows great sensitivity to the individuality of the woodwinds, as the melancholy English horn in "*Nuages,*" the warm clarinet in "*Fêtes,*" and the limpid flute in *L'après-midi* demonstrate.

Closely connected with timbre is the element of dynamics. Debussy is the great master of the whisper, and his scores abound in pianos and pianissimos. Seven of the *Préludes* of the first volume start *pp* and the other five are marked *p*. Stunning dynamic climaxes occur, but they are momentary flashes, soon to be replaced by quiet. Debussy's music is suggestive and insinuating. One cannot gain such effects by shouting.

From everything that has been said, it will be clear that the forms of classical music are rarely found in his music. He wrote sonatas only at the beginning and end of his life, and it has been already pointed out that the three last compositions are sonatas in name only. Debussy's innovations have been described at length because it was he more than any other composer who broke with the conventions that had governed music for the past three hundred years. Although some earlier composers had taken tentative steps in this direction, his loosening of the bonds of tonality and free treatment of dissonance, as well as his disregard for logical, formal processes of musical development, opened vistas for composers as disparate as Bartók, Schoenberg, and Stravinsky. The disintegration of the harmonic syntax of music, which was to characterize twentieth-century music, received its strongest impetus from Debussy.

SUGGESTED READINGS

The bibliography on Debussy is wide. Martin Cooper's *French Music from the Death of Berlioz to the Death of Fauré* (London, 1951) is an excellent survey of French music of the period. Perhaps the best biography and study of the compositions is Leon Vallas' *Claude Debussy, His Life and Works* (London, 1933), which contains a thematic index of all the works. Other books are by Oscar Thompson, *Debussy, Man and Artist* (New York, 1937), and Edward Lockspeiser, *Debussy*, 3rd Ed. (New York, 1951). An article by Marcel Dietschy, "The Family and Childhood of Debussy," *Musical Quarterly*, Vol. XLVI, No. 3 (July 1960), reveals some new facts about the composer's early years. Specialized studies are: *Piano Works of Claude Debussy* by E. Robert Schmitz (New York, 1950); Alfred Cortot's *French Piano Music* (London, 1932); and Lawrence Gilman's *Debussy's Pelléas and Mélisande* (New York, 1907). The critical writings of Debussy can be found translated in his *Monsieur Croche, The Dilletante Hater* (New York, 1928), and in Vallas' *The Theories of Claude Debussy* (London, 1929).

CHAPTER III

PARIS: OTHER COMPOSERS

Don't try to be a genius in every measure.   GABRIEL FAURÉ*

Debussy was by no means the only composer of importance in France during the period 1900-1914. Gabriel Fauré (1845-1924), the chief representative of a more conservative French tradition that existed side by side with impressionist music, was restrained, elegant, and economical in his compositions. He wrote many songs, music for piano, and chamber music. His setting of the *Requiem Mass* is noteworthy among the larger works. Never tempted by the "free floating" parallel dissonance of the impressionists, he developed instead a conservative, but at the same time highly original, harmonic syntax. Fauré's chords are chromatic and his modulations are frequently to remote keys, but because of his fondness for modal scales (with their lack of leading tones) the effect is one of serenity rather than one of feverish intensity that characterizes so much chromatic music.

A great deal can be learned about the styles of Fauré and Debussy by comparing the songs that they wrote to the same poems. For instance, in the two settings of Verlaine's poem, "C'est l 'extase," Fauré uses only the tonic chord in the two-bar introduction, while Debussy starts his song with a melodic motive built on the dominant thirteenth and

*Fauré's advice to a composition student.

33

uses rich chords throughout, with new accompaniment figures reflecting the changing thoughts of the verse. Fauré, on the other hand, does not vary his accompaniment figure from start to finish; although he modulates freely to remote keys, his harmonies are rarely more complex than seventh chords of various types. Because they are not so completely conditioned by the words with which they are associated, Fauré's melodies have a wider curve and a more regular profile than Debussy's.

EXAMPLE 15 (FAURÉ)

EXAMPLE 16 (DEBUSSY)

Fauré's contributions to the music of the early twentieth century are more important than these few paragraphs would indicate. However, since he was a conservative rather than forward-looking composer, we shall turn now to Maurice Ravel, his most distinguished pupil, who plays a more significant role in establishing the new idioms.

RAVEL, 1875-1937

Complex, but not complicated.

RALPH VAUGHAN WILLIAMS ON RAVEL'S MUSIC

Ravel was born in Ciboure in the French Basque country near the border of Spain. His father was a French engineer, and his mother was presumably of Basque origin. The family moved to Paris soon after the birth of Maurice and settled in Montmartre, at that time the habitat of many of the painters who were to revolutionize twentieth-century art. Ravel followed the path of most French musicians by entering the Conservatoire and receiving all his musical education there. His general education he received from Paris itself, and from the artists and writers who were his friends.

His life was outwardly uneventful. The controversy caused by his failure to receive the Prix de Rome and the newspaper debate as to whether he or Debussy was the first to write music of authentic Spanish flavor brought some prominence to his name, but it was not until 1911 and the production of his one-act comic opera *L'Heure espagnole* that he first achieved fame as a composer. He held no teaching posts and for the most part lived a quiet bachelor's life, enjoying the companionship of a small circle of friends. However, with the composition of *Boléro* in 1927 he did achieve world recognition suddenly. He found himself in great demand to conduct concerts of his music, and he made a tour of the United States. His health failed soon after, however, and he died after brain surgery in 1937.

RAVEL'S COMPOSITIONS

Ravel was a meticulous composer—a "Swiss watchmaker," his friend Stravinsky called him—and the list of his compositions is not long. Since there are fewer style changes in them than in other composers' works, division into style periods is somewhat arbitrary. However, a distinction can be made between earlier and later works. For the most part, the former group of compositions embodies impressionist, fin-de-siècle ideals as shown by their titles and their evocative sounds. It is interesting to note the similarity of genres found in the following list to those employed by Debussy at the same time. Both composers wrote a string quartet, an opera, songs, a ballet, orchestral music of strong Spanish flavor, and much piano music.

Period 1: 1900-1911

OPERA

L'Heure espagnole (1907)

ORCHESTRAL

Rapsodie espagnole (1907)
Daphnis et Chloé (1909-12)

CHAMBER MUSIC

String Quartet (1902-03)
Introduction et Allegro (for harp, flute, clarinet, and string quartet; 1906)

PIANO

Jeux d'eau (*Play of the Water;* 1901)
Miroirs (1905). I. Noctuelles. II. Oiseaux tristes. III. Une Barque sur l'océan. IV. Alborada del Gracioso. V. La Vallée des Cloches.
Sonatine (1903-05)
Gaspard de la Nuit (1908). I. Ondine. II. Le Gibet. III. Scarbo.

SONGS

Shéhérazade (1903)
Cinq mélodies populaires grecques (1907)
Histoires naturelles (1906)

As a composer of piano music, Ravel not only rivals Debussy but also actually anticipates him in certain areas. *Jeux d'eau,* is an example. Written in 1901 long before Debussy published the first book of *Préludes,* it exploits the treble region of the piano which was to be used so much by the older composer. It is very interesting harmonically, from its opening on a tonic ninth chord to its closing on a tonic seventh (Examples 17a and 17b).

EXAMPLE 17a

These chords are typical of Ravel's music, for he preferred diatonic dissonances to more tonally ambiguous chromatic combinations. The cadenza, built on superimposed triads of C and F-sharp is an intriguing swirl of sound. *Jeux d'eau* was the first in a long series of "water" pieces to be written by impressionist composers. His sets of pieces, *Miroirs* and *Gaspard de la Nuit,* are more involved and are among the finest piano works of the period. The lovely *Sonatine* might be cited as evidence of Ravel's interest in classical forms at a time when such an interest must have seemed reactionary.

One of Ravel's most popular early orchestral compositions is the suite arranged from the ballet *Daphnis et Chloé,* a key work of impressionist music which should be known by all students of the period. It starts in a characteristic manner, with a scarcely audible chromatic figure in the lowest strings while divided flutes and clarinets play murmuring figures. The horns sustain pianissimo chords behind the harp glissandos. "The Break of Day" (the title of the first section) is suggested by the flowing figure that starts in the double basses and eventually rises through the orchestra.

EXAMPLE 18*

A pastoral section follows, featuring the oboe and English horn.

EXAMPLE 19

The flute, the most favored instrument of the impressionists, is heard in the next section which consists of two dances, one slow and the other fast. The celesta and piccolo add to the color. After a

*Permission for reprint of this and the following Ravel examples granted by Durand et Cie., Paris, copyright owners; Elkan-Vogel Co., Inc., Philadelphia, agents.

pause, an exciting bacchanal starts and works up to a glittering climax. The meter is 5/4 and continuing triplets suggest the vigorous dance movement of the *corps de ballet*. The main theme shows an indebtedness to certain sections of Rimsky-Korsakov's *Scheherazade*.

EXAMPLE 20

Period 2: 1911-1931

OPERA

L'Enfant et les Sortilèges (*The Bewitched Child*; 1925)

ORCHESTRAL

La Valse (1920)
Boléro (1927)

CONCERTOS

Concerto for Piano (1931)
Concerto for Piano, left hand (1931)

CHAMBER MUSIC

Trio in A minor (1914)
Sonata for Violin and Cello (1922)
Chansons madécasses (*Songs of Madagascar;* for voice, flute, cello, piano; 1925-26)

PIANO

Valses nobles et sentimentales (1911)
Le Tombeau de Couperin (*The Tomb of Couperin*, i.e. In memory of C.; 1917)

The later works of Ravel become more austere in manner, and the warm, subjective expression of *Daphnis et Chloé* is not encountered again. The two large compositions for piano illustrate this trend. There is no elaborate figuration in the set of waltzes inscribed to the "eternally new and delicious pleasure of a useless occupation." In its place there is acrid, biting dissonance. This is the opening:

EXAMPLE 21

Le Tombeau de Couperin, a suite of eighteenth-century dances preceded by a prelude and fugue and followed by a toccata, employs a harpsichord style in which complex pedal effects are entirely absent. Each detail is sharply outlined in these tributes to the past. The same tendencies can be noted in other works; notably in the song cycles with instruments and in the piano concerto, although *La Valse* reverts to the rich sonorities of the earlier period.

STYLE CHARACTERISTICS

Ravel's fondness for modal scales, particularly the Dorian and Phrygian, is affirmed in many of his compositions from *Pavane* (1899) to the Piano Concerto (1931). He also uses pentatonic and six-tone scales.

   Although he occasionally writes in 5/4 meter *(Daphnis* and the *Trio)*, he more frequently uses the familiar ones. He is fond of dance rhythms, whether they be Spanish *(Boléro, Habanera, Malaguena)*, baroque *(Forlane, Rigaudon, Pavane);* or jazz *(Violin Sonata,* certain scenes of *L'Enfant et les Sortilèges,* and the Piano Concerto).

   He developed a distinctive vocabulary of chords, preferring complex diatonic structures on tones other than the dominant to Debussy's "juicy" ninth chords. He frequently adds to the pungency of a chord by sounding a chromatic appoggiatura along with its note of resolution. The following is one of his favorite chords.

EXAMPLE 22

The *Valses nobles* are a rich mine of such complex chords.

Ralph Vaughan Williams, the English composer, studied with Ravel for a short time in 1908. In his autobiographical sketch he reports:

> He [Ravel] was horrified that I had no pianoforte in the little hotel where I worked. 'Sans le piano on ne peut pas inventer de nouvelles harmonies,' he said [Without a piano one cannot invent new chords.][1]

Obviously Ravel regarded the invention of new chords as an important phase of composition. That he is one of the master orchestrators is evidenced by *Boléro* and by his transcriptions of his piano works and Moussorgsky's *Pictures at an Exhibition*. In common with Debussy, he favored the smaller forms and wrote sonatas only at the beginning and end of his career.

Although Ravel is sometimes thought of as merely a minor impressionist, this notion is far from true, for his impressionist works are of great importance. However, when he deserted impressionist ideals for a more precise language he returned to an older and more genuinely French tradition. Never reactionary, his original vocabulary of chords and his fine sense of orchestral color added much to French music of the time.

DIAGHILEV AND THE YOUNG STRAVINSKY

Ravel's ballets were written at the instigation of Serge Diaghilev, the famous director of the Russian Ballet and one of the key figures in twentieth-century art. In 1909 Diaghilev arranged a concert of Russian music in Paris, including the first performance there of *Boris Godounov*, with Chaliapin singing the title role. The next year he dazzled Paris by presenting the Imperial Russian Ballet, with such superb dancers as Pavlova, Karsavina, and Nijinsky in the company. The enterprise was so successful that he returned each year thereafter, and, with a wonderful combination of flawless taste and inspired showmanship, made these seasonal affairs the focus of Parisian social and artistic life. At first the repertoire consisted of such classical ballets as *Les Sylphides* and *Giselle*, as well as works of a strong Russian-Oriental flavor, such as the *Polovetzian Dances* of Borodin, *Cleopatra* by Arensky, and Rimsky-Korsakov's *Scheherazade*. However, with the European success of the Russian Ballet assured, Diaghilev began to commission new works so that he would have fresh and spectacular ballets to present each season. It was in this area that he showed particular genius, for he brought together the most prominent composers, choreographers, and painters to create the music, dances, settings, and costumes for the ballets he conceived. Until his death in 1929 he was without rival in presenting to the public what was new in the arts.

For the season of 1910 he brought together a new team—Fokine for the choreography, Bakst for the *décor*, and a 25-year-old Russian, Igor Stravinsky, for the music. This young composer, the son of an opera singer in St. Petersburg, was just beginning his career in music. After graduating from the University in law he studied for a short time with Rimsky-Korsakov. The only composition of his that Diaghilev had heard was a promising student piece, *Fireworks*. But Diaghilev made few mistakes, and the new ballet, *The Firebird,* was enormously successful and launched the career of one of the most distinguished composers of the century.

The Firebird is based on a fairy tale and follows the tradition of colorful, quasi-oriental ballets of the time. Musically it shows the heritage of the young composer—Rimsky-Korsakov, Borodin, Scriabine, and Moussorgsky. However, it is by no means entirely derivative, for it contains more than one hint of his mature style.

The suite that is most often performed at concerts consists of six sections. The introduction starts with mysterious sounds in the lowest strings. The interval of the diminished 5th which is outlined by the melody was one of the daring and fascinating sounds of the time. It is prominent throughout this work:

EXAMPLE 23*

*Permission for reprint granted by J. W. Chester, London.

Gradually the melody ascends to higher regions of the orchestra, interrupted from time to time by fantastic birdlike sounds from the violins, playing harmonics, and by chirping sounds in clarinets and bassoons. Muted horns and low flutes add to the impressionist effect.

The "Dance" that follows, suggesting whirling wings, is also full of magically evocative sounds. In the quiet section, "Dance of the Princesses," Stravinsky harks back to his Russian heritage. The melody is an adaptation of a Russian folksong, and the atmosphere is very close to that of the "Young Prince" in *Scheherazade*.

EXAMPLE 24

In the "Dance of Kastchei" the real Stravinsky appears. In its brusque rudeness and in the vigor of its syncopation, a new voice is heard. Once again the tritone is prominent.

EXAMPLE 25

The brilliance of the trumpet and lower brasses, the strident xylophone, and the glissandos in the trombones give it an excitement that is still powerfully felt.

The "Berceuse" shows Stravinsky's fondness for the bassoon in the high, poignant range, and the tritone is outlined in the main melody. The double ostinato in the harp and strings should also be noted, for pedal figures become a characteristic feature of the composer's mature style. Moussorgsky's sound-world is heard in the "Finale" where changes are rung on a recurring bell-like theme with constant variations of color.

This score is important historically in two ways. In the first place, it shows many of the influences that the sensitive young composer had experienced up to that time; secondly, it in turn has been a source of inspiration to many later composers, particularly when they've wanted to write magical, fantastic music.

With the success of *The Firebird*, Diaghilev lost no time in using his new composer again. The next year saw the production of *Petrouchka*, also a "Russian" work, but one far removed from the fairy-tale atmosphere of the first ballet. In this, the setting is a folk fair and the mood is earthy. The sound of the music is different also, for there are few impressionist colors here, since a more objective style prevails. Instead of concealing the sound of individual instruments in order to achieve striking new combinations, Stravinsky, in this score, exploits the individuality of the instruments. Chromaticism is abandoned and subtle melodies are replaced by vulgar street tunes. There is little mystery, and one can be sure that the stage lighting was much brighter for this work than for *The Firebird*.

The initial musical kernel for *Petrouchka* was a complex chord which attracted the composer—a C-major chord with a superimposed F#-major chord. Here we meet again that tritonal relationship which colored so much of the advanced music of the time. Stravinsky first planned to exploit this effect in a piano piece but Diaghilev persuaded him to use it in the new ballet. This accounts for the prominence of the piano in the score.

In listening to this music and to the other ballet music, one should not forget that it was written for dancers and that the demands of the stage conditioned the form of the music. The lack of continuity in the opening scene, for instance, reflects the wandering of the crowd at the fair. The "Russian Dance," with its striking paral-

EXAMPLE 26*

Tempo I (*Allegro giusto*)

ƒ sub.

*Copyright by Edition Russe de Musique; copyright assigned to Boosey & Hawkes, Inc., 1947. New version copyright 1948 by Boosey & Hawkes, Inc.

lel chords, has become one of the best known of Stravinsky's compositions. (Example 26). The prevalent peasant flavor is gained through imitations of accordions and hurdy-gurdies and parodies of street tunes.

The frequent meter changes reflect the variety of movement and the activity of the crowd but they also show the composer's interest in complex, irregular rhythmic patterns. This was to become one of his outstanding characteristics.

If *Petrouchka* showed many signs of increasing individuality over *The Firebird*, the next Diaghilev-inspired ballet, *The Rite of Spring* (*Le Sacre du Printemps;* 1913), startled the musical world with the certain knowledge that a new and disturbing composer had come of age. Few compositions have ever caused such a stir. *The Rite* had the same effect for Stravinsky as the publication of *Childe Harold* had for Byron—on the morning after the première he awoke to find himself famous.

This landmark of contemporary music was conceived and established by Diaghilev, in a characteristic blending of artistic sensitivity and calculated showmanship. Faced with the necessity of presenting a new and sensational ballet each year, and ever sensitive to what was new and "smart," he decided to capitalize on the current interest in primitive art. While Japanese prints had inspired the painters in the 1880's, African sculpture and masks had now captured the attention of the artistic world. The rude distortions and simplifications of the masks deeply stimulated German painters such as Kirchner and Marc, as well as Picasso and Braque, then young cubists in Paris. In addition, the publication of Frazer's *Golden Bough* pointed up an interest in a past far older than the Greco-Roman world which had been the source of so much art since the Renaissance.

The time was right, then, to exploit this dim past in the theater, and Diaghilev was the man to do it. He chose a new team, this time with Stravinsky for the music, Nijinsky for the choreography, and Roerich for the settings and costumes. The theme was the religious rites of prehistoric man in propitiation of Spring, culminating in a human sacrifice.

The reaction of the opening-night audience has been recounted by several eye-witnesses and participants. The audience soon took sides, those who were shocked at the ballet opposing those who were in favor of it. Soon duchesses were attacking their neighbors with their evening bags, and dignified, bearded Frenchmen were having fist fights. Those who were not physically engaged were screaming, either to show their disapproval of the ballet or to show their disapproval of those who were vocal in their disapproval. A few moments after the opening curtain, pandemonium reigned, and no one, not even the dancers on the stage, could hear the music. Nijinsky stood in the wings shrieking out the rhythmic pattern so that the dancers could have something to dance to.

What stirred this audience to such violence? They were repelled by the utter lack of charm and prettiness of the production. Ballet had been traditionally colorful and gorgeous, with beautiful dancers in magnificent costumes portraying characters in a fairy tale, all to the sound of charming music. There was none of this in *The Rite of Spring*. The dancers were dressed in dark brown burlap sacks and their gestures were rough and angular. The music was shatteringly dissonant and the rhythmic life of the score was brutal. It seemed as if the very foundations of music and all of the cultured refinements of ages were being attacked.

The Rite of Spring is in two acts, each preceded by an orchestral introduction. It is masterfully planned from the point of view of the theater, with its changes of pace and well-placed moments of climax. The first act, "The Adoration of the Earth," is concerned with the youth of prehistoric Russia reveling in games and dances honoring Spring. They pay homage to the Earth and the Sage, who reminds them of the ancient rites. In the orchestral "Introduction" there is an

EXAMPLE 27*

Lento *tempo rubato*

BASSOON I SOLO AD LIB.

*Copyright 1921 by Edition Russe de Musique; copyright assigned to Boosey & Hawkes, Inc., 1947.

evocation of the primitive forest. There are cackling, wailing sounds, suggesting the cries of birds and crawling things. Stravinsky achieves these sounds by depending almost entirely on reedy woodwind instruments. The opening notes, for instance, so poignant in their brutish sorrow, are played on the bassoon, but in a range far higher than that normally attempted by this usually jovial instrument. The effect is strange, pinched, dreamlike (Example 27).

In these opening notes many of Stravinsky's characteristics are to be heard—the narrow range of the melody, the meter changes, and the treatment of a melodic figure in such a way that when it is repeated its notes fall on different parts of the measure. The melodies are made up of little fragments, stopping and starting, with insistent repetitions, although the repetitions are never precisely the same. The buzzings and twitterings increase in volume and speed and then break off suddenly. Once again the lament of the bassoon is heard.

The "Dance of the Adolescents" follows. This is one of the most sensational pieces of music ever written, for while the "Introduction" exploited strange and original timbres, this section calls upon rhythmic resources hitherto unused in Western music. Its opening has become one of the classic passages of twentieth-century music. It begins with what sounds like a savage beating of drums (actually it is the strings repeating a very complex chord). Eight horns suddenly bark, and over the tom-tom of the strings this horn complex is repeated. The interval of time between the repetitions is not regular, however, and the jointed, rough effect is partially due to the fact that there are one, five, two, three and four beats between the horn chords. This is

EXAMPLE 28

not syncopation, which presupposes an underlying metrical pattern, but an irregular grouping of rhythmic units. These sections of great rhythmic complexity vary with others of almost mechanical regularity in which sing-song primitive tunes are heard.

EXAMPLE 29a

EXAMPLE 29b

EXAMPLE 29c

The second of these melodies is typical in its narrow range and its continual rearrangement in ever-changing patterns as though the notes were being played on a primitive flute that contained just a few tones, and the only variations possible were gained by changing the order in which they were played.

The next section, "Dance of Abduction," is the wildest yet encountered. There are several ideas—a dashing, chasing tune played first by the high wind instruments and an answering horn call. Toward the end there is a great deal of rhythmic complexity expressed in the frequently changing meter signatures, which sometimes vary every measure. Here is a typical sequence:

$$\frac{7}{8} \quad \frac{3}{4} \quad \frac{6}{8} \quad \frac{2}{4} \quad \frac{6}{8} \quad \frac{3}{4}$$

There are also examples of polyrhythm in which two or more rhythmic patterns are superimposed. The effect is deeply stirring.

"Spring Rounds," which follows, is a welcome relief after all this excitement. It moves at a slower tempo and opens with a clear wood-wind color, obviously introducing another set of dancers. There is a halting, syncopated string accompaniment and a primitive hymn in the flutes. It is a solemn, sweet melody, and when repeated later by the whole orchestra, it is as if a great chorus of people were singing a hymn of praise to a deity. Heterophony, the duplication of a melody at any interval, is a characteristic of primitive music. Stravinsky treats the hymn in this manner.

EXAMPLE 30

Vigorous action returns in the "Games of the Rival Cities" in which there are violent clashes of chords and keys and constant variety in meter. The idea of the competing cities is expressed through antiphonal writing (each city having its own music) and through a particularly astringent use of polytonality.

The same blatant tune is used as the main thematic material for the "Entrance of the Sage." The pages of the score become blacker with notes as more instruments are added.

"The Dance of the Earth" which concludes Act I is even more violent. Over an ostinato in the bass the instruments are used rhythmically, for individual timbre and individual melodic lines tend to be lost in the density of the sound. This section really needs the stage action to be convincing, for only as the accompaniment to a wildly rushing dance does it justify itself.

The second act is concerned with the sacrifice of a young girl, the Chosen One, to propitiate the God of Spring. The "Introduction" is a placid section, describing the pagan night. Here all flows quietly and another primitive, few-note melody is heard. The sound of the orchestra is reminiscent of Debussy and Ravel, with the prominent flutes, violin harmonics, and the three muted horns that close the section.

The same melody is used as the main thematic material of the first dance of the act, "The Circle of the Adolescents." A characteristic doubling is heard at Number 94 in the score:

EXAMPLE 31

CLARINETS

"The Glorification of the Chosen One," the next dance, is another wildly shrieking piece. The principal idea is a rush of sound upwards, followed by a resounding blow on the kettle drums and then a three-note figure descending. The whole theme expresses a choreographic idea, suggesting violent upward arm thrusts and spasmodic gestures.

In the short dance which follows, the "Evocation of the Ancestors," the texture is simplified somewhat and the tom-tom rhythms take over, calling the elders to participate in the ritual. They do so in the slow "Ritual Action of the Ancestors." Here the English horn and flute carry on an acrid dialogue over the driving beat of the rest of the orchestra until the horns take over in a proud theme.

The whole ballet comes to a climax in the final "Dance of the Chosen One," and Stravinsky's task of writing a climax to a work so extremely sensational must have been challenging, indeed. It is another cataclysm of sound in which everything is at the service of rhythm, and with little individuality of instrument or of melody. It is not surprising that Walt Disney used this section in *Fantasia* to portray the end of the world.

The effect is that of pandemonium, but Stravinsky has planned every effect and gives precise directions in the score for achieving each one. He tells the tympanist when to change from a hard, felt stick to a wooden one, and directs the gong player to describe an arc on the surface of the gong with the triangle stick. He instructs the horn players to play with the bells of their instruments pointing upward so that a particularly robust tone is achieved. For the last tone-cluster of the entire piece, the cellists are instructed to retune their A-string to G so that they can play their final chord savagely on open strings, a subtlety which might not be heard when at the same time four horns, tubas, four tympani, bass drum, and cymbals are playing fortissimo. Nevertheless, Stravinsky calls for precisely this sound and gives directions for obtaining it.

It is little wonder that the first performance of this piece ended in a riot. The audience apparently felt that violence had been done to the noble art of music. While Debussy had been puzzling and bizarre, at least his compositions were most often delicate in sound and almost precious in expression. But this was another matter. This was music of brutality and ugliness, not unlike the savage canvases being painted at the same time by artists of the Fauve—or "wild beast"—school. To condone this kind of expression was to attack the very basis of art.

While *The Rite of Spring* seemed like the last word in modernity to its first audiences, to one evaluating the work nearly fifty years later, knowing the course pursued by twentieth-century music since 1913, it seems rather to belong to the past—a product of late romanticism. In Chapter I it was pointed out that an important tendency of nineteenth-century music was its growing complexity and intensity in its role as collaborator with literature and drama in symphonic poems and operas. *The Rite of Spring* belongs to this tradition, since its novel and startling musical vocabulary was conceived to express the primitivism of Diaghilev's ballet.

Subsequent events have proved it to be an end point. After *The Rite* (and a few futile imitations by other composers) Stravinsky and many of the young composers around him turned to quite different ideals of composition. However, the powerful, irregular rhythms will be found in innumerable compositions of the following years.

The date of *The Rite of Spring*—1913—is significant. It was written just before the outbreak of World War I, and perhaps the violence of the music foreshadows the destruction and carnage which were about to begin. This war was the real end of the nineteenth century, for after it, the political, economic, and social life of Europe changed drastically. Not until the 1920's was the "brave new world" born.

Stravinsky's later compositions will be discussed in Chapter IX, where a summary of his style characteristics and a bibliography will also be found.

SUGGESTED READINGS

The best study of Ravel's life and music is Roland Manuel's *Maurice Ravel* (London, 1947). Other recommended books are *Ravel* by Norman Demuth ("The Master Musicians, New Series," London, 1947), and Victor Seroff's *Maurice Ravel* (New York, 1953).

Two fascinating books devoted to Diaghilev are Arnold Haskell's *Diaghileff, His Artistic and Private Life* (New York, 1935) and Serge Lifar's *Serge Diaghilev, His Life, His Work, His Legend* (New York, 1940). There are many books written by people who were connected with Diaghilev's ballet. Among them, *Nijinsky* by Romola Nijinsky (New York, 1934) is recommended for its pictures of backstage intrigue and insights into the complicated personalities of the important people involved in these crucial productions.

GERMANY AND AUSTRIA

The situation in Germany is serious but not hopeless; the situation in Austria is hopeless but not serious.   VIENNESE SAYING

In these rich years before World War I a musical tradition very different from that in France flourished in the German-speaking countries on the other side of the Rhine. Whereas France could boast of but one cultural center—Paris—scores of German, Austrian, Polish, and Bohemian cities enjoyed their own opera houses, orchestras, and conservatories. The Brahms-Wagner controversy, debated in Germany and Austria with the vehemence reserved for political discussions in France, shows how important artistic matters were to these people. The Germans were immensely proud of the long line of composers they could claim, and when Paris capitulated to the music dramas of Wagner in the 1880's they were as proud as they had been of Bismarck's victory over the French in 1870.

The turn of the century witnessed the complete victory of Wagnerian ideals which were carried forward in the works of Richard Strauss (1864-1949) and in those of a host of lesser talents. Strauss' tone poems, from *Don Juan* (1888) to *Ein Heldenleben* (1898), are extremely vital works that are still regularly performed. Around 1900 he turned to opera, and *Salome* (1905) and *Elektra* (1909) fascinated and repelled the musical world with their violence. These are overpowering works, completely devoid of "prettiness" or charm in the usual sense. Scenes such as the decapitation of John the Baptist were so sensationally neurotic that the performance of *Salome* was banned by several opera houses for some years. Musically, they are characterized by the use of rich dissonance (one thinks, for example, of the famous *Salome* chord heard at the climax of the opera), by an enlarged orchestra that continually threatens to engulf the singers, by leitmotifs that permeate the texture, and by cadence-avoiding continuity. In order to maintain dramatic and musical tension these operas are not divided into acts. Great demands are made upon the singers in the expression of their tortured emotions.

All of these traits are enlargements of Wagnerian principles, but *Salome* and *Elektra* are nevertheless far removed from the emotional world of such a work as *Tristan*. In the latter, the leading characters are highly moral court personages and the depiction of their fate is kept within conventional bounds. In *Salome* and *Elektra* restraint is cast aside and unrelieved starkness reigns.

Strauss himself went no further in this direction and his later operas reveal entirely different characteristics. *Der Rosenkavalier* (1909-10), *Ariadne auf Naxos* (1911-12), and *Arabella* (1930-32) are typical of his later works. They return to an atmosphere of warm sentiment and charm, and their musical vocabulary has little to do with the progressive tendencies of the twentieth century. For that reason they will not be discussed in this book—a fact which has nothing to do with their enduring value.

EXPRESSIONISM

The depiction of hysterical, larger-than-life emotion in *Elektra* was characteristic of much of the art produced in Europe in the early years of the century. Not only in music but also in painting, in the novel, and in drama, subjects heretofore considered off-limits were now exhaustively explored. In one sense, this development was actually no reversal from the art of high romanticism for that, too, was subjective, free in form, and relatively unrestrained. Rather, this new art enlarged these romantic traits to a higher degree in the service of a lower, or at any rate, different, order of subject matter.

This kind of art came to be called *expressionist* and embodied an artistic ideal which in one form or another became one of the poles of twentieth-century art. The term was apparently used for the first time to describe a group of paintings shown in the Paris Salon of 1901, as an antonym of the then popular term *impressionism.* Where the ideal of the latter was a fleeting impression of the outer world, expressionist painting emphasized the subjective emotions of the artist. Van Gogh's troubled canvasses soon defined the style, and other painters, such as the Norwegian, Edvard Munch, made important contributions. These men were followed in Germany by such painters as E. L. Kirchner and Schmitt-Rottluff of the group known as *die Brücke,* and by Marc and Kandinsky of the group called *der Blaue Reiter.* Expressionism came to the theater in the later plays of Strindberg and Wedekind, and in the next generation, in those of Georg Kaiser and Ernst Toller. These plays were antirealistic and dreamlike, and were rich in symbols. James Joyce's *Ulysses* and *Finnegans Wake* are the archetypes of the expressionist novel.

One of the best and most succinct definitions of expressionist art came from the German critic Herman Bahr, when he called it the "shriek of the soul."

VIENNA AND EXPRESSIONISM

Vienna, one of Europe's music centers since the beginning of the eighteenth century, developed its own variety of *fin-de-siècle* atmosphere. In contrast to the sensuous hedonism of the French, and the sometimes shocking brutality of the Germans, the Viennese enjoyed a curious and unique mood of carefree fatalism. Ernst Krenek has described it in these words:

> The feeling of the approaching decay was growing throughout the late 19th century, when the inability of coping with the increasing political difficulties on the part of the representatives of the imperial idea became more and more evident. A most particular attitude of hedonistic pessimism, joyful skepticism touching on morbid sophistication, became the dominant trait in Vienna's intellectual climate.[1]

Of particular significance to the over-all picture was the fact that Sigmund Freud lived and practiced in Vienna at this time. His discoveries in the realm of the heretofore hidden aspects of human personality greatly increased interest in the expression of subjective states—the main province of the expressionists.

Vienna quite complacently regarded herself as the capital of the music world. Her noble tradition of Haydn, Mozart, Beethoven, and Schubert was undoubtedly something to be proud of, but in their veneration of the past the Viennese had very little interest in newer trends. In the mid-nineteenth century they had been skeptical of such progressive composers as Schumann and Liszt, and their opposition to Wagner, crystallized in the writings of Edward Hanslick, their foremost critic, was diametrically opposed to the enthusiastic reception given the music dramas by the Parisian intelligentsia.

The most important composers active in Vienna at the end of the century were Brahms (died 1897), Bruckner (1896), and Mahler (1911). Among these Brahms held a special place. He was the composer who, without being reactionary, was firm in his allegiance to the ideals of absolute, nonprogrammatic music. His rich harmonic style and subtle rhythmic sense were employed not in operas and symphonic poems, but in symphonies, concertos, chamber-music, pieces for the piano, and in songs.

Bruckner, although "tainted" by his affinity with the large orchestral sonorities and the time-scale of Wagner, nevertheless held a position of dignity as professor of composition at the Vienna Conservatory. His most important compositions were his symphonies and religious choral works. He wrote no subversive, "modern" tone poems.

Because he was a conductor as well as a composer, Gustav Mahler did a great deal to make and disturb the musical atmosphere of Vienna. As music director of the Royal Opera he established new levels of perfection in his performances of Mozart and Wagner. As a composer he is remembered principally for his ten symphonies (1888-1910, the tenth unfinished) and his works for voice and orchestra, of which the most frequently performed are *Lieder eines fahrenden Gesellen* (*Songs of a Wayfarer*, 1883); *Lieder aus des Knaben Wunderhorn* (*The Youth's Magic Horn*, a collection of German folk poetry, 1888); and *Kindertotenlieder* (*Songs on the Death of Children;* 1904).

Mahler's compositions have always caused controversies; critical reaction to them seems to be either highly enthusiastic or unfavorable. His is an all-embracing style, typically late romantic in its joining of opposing elements. Heroic proportions and epic "messages" contrast with intimate genre pieces; massive forces (the Eighth Symphony, the "symphony of a thousand," calls for a large orchestra, two choruses, eight solo voices, and a boys' chorus) contrast with delicate combinations of solo instruments; and wide-intervalled, complex melodies contrast with folk tunes. Certain aspects of Mahler's later works—particularly the wide-spanned melodies and the use of guitar, harp, and solo instruments—left their traces in the works of Schoenberg, Berg, and Webern.

SCHOENBERG, 1874-1951

If a composer doesn't write from the heart, he simply can't produce good music. SCHOENBERG

Arnold Schoenberg, one of the giants of twentieth-century music, was born into the cultural milieu we have just described. Even though he was in no sense a prodigy either as a performer or composer, he nevertheless began to study violin at the age of eight, taught himself to play the cello, took part in amateur chamber music groups, composed a little, and avidly attended Vienna's concerts and opera performances. In order to augment his family's income, he became a bank clerk after the death of his father. It was at this time that he met the composer Alexander Zemlinsky and studied counterpoint with him for a few months; this was the only formal instruction he ever received. In a short autobiographical sketch, *My Evolution,* Schoenberg tells of these formative years:

> I had been a "Brahmsian" when I met Zemlinsky. His love embraced both Brahms and Wagner and soon thereafter I became an equally confirmed addict. No wonder that the music I composed at that time mirrored the influence of both these masters, to which a flavor of Liszt, Bruckner and perhaps also Hugo Wolf was added. . . . True, at this time I had already become an admirer of Richard Strauss, but not yet of Gustav Mahler, whom I began to understand only much later, at a time when his symphonic style could no longer exert its influence on me.[2]

Schoenberg started to compose in earnest and before the turn of the century had decided to make music his lifework. He spent two years in Berlin (1901-1903), where he was music director in a cabaret, but then he returned to Vienna and settled as a teacher, theorist*, and composer. World War I interrupted this way of life and he spent two years in the Austrian army (1915-1917).

SCHOENBERG'S PREWAR COMPOSITIONS

Because the works of Schoenberg show a gradual change in style, it will be helpful to group them into periods. It should be emphasized, however, that even when the musical vocabulary changes, the common core that runs through all his works is the musical personality of the composer who is at this time the expressionist artist—the deeply, sometimes excessively, emotional creator. This is important to emphasize, for much of Schoenberg's music has been completely misunderstood. Because of its complexity and difficulty it has been called mathematical or cerebral, but his own views on the function of art show how far this view is from his intent. He has written, "A work of art can produce no greater effect than when it transmits the emotions which raged in the creator to the listener, in such a way that they also rage and storm in him."[3] Another clear definition of his intention is found in this sentence: "In reality there is only one greatest goal towards which the artist strives: to express himself."[4] This is scarcely the credo of an "intellectual" composer.

Period 1: Chromatic

The first period extends from 1897 to 1908, Opus 1 through Opus 10. All of these compositions breathe the air of late romanticism.

Opus 1, 2, 3, 6, 8	Songs
4	*Verklaerte Nacht* (*Transfigured Night*; 1899)
5	*Pelleas und Melisande* (symphonic poem; 1902-03)

*His book, *Harmonielehre* was published in 1911; the English translation, *Theory of Harmony*, in 1948.

7	String Quartet #1 (1904-05)
9	*Chamber Symphony* (1906)
10	String Quartet #2 (1907-08)
No opus number	*Gurrelieder* (1900-01)

Verklaerte Nacht is the composer's most accessible and most frequently performed composition. Originally written for string sextet, this tone poem is usually heard today in a version for string orchestra. The poem that inspired the music describes the emotions of a couple walking through the woods. The woman confesses that she has been untrue, but on the man's assurance that he still loves her, her gratitude transfigures the night. This close association of man and nature is typically romantic; it permeates most of the art of that era.

If the "program" of *Verklaerte Nacht* is akin to that of *Die Walküre* (troubled love against a troubled landscape) the musical style is also Wagnerian. The themes, although untitled, have a leitmotif sound; furthermore, they recur constantly in rhythmic transformations and are therefore developed in the Liszt-Wagner-Strauss manner. In the essay already mentioned, Schoenberg speaks of the work:

> In *Verklaerte Nacht* the thematic construction is based on Wagnerian 'model and sequence' above a roving harmony on the one hand, and on Brahms' technique of developing variation, as I call it, on the other.[5]

This is precisely the kind of music against which Debussy was rebelling at the time. In 1899 he was a vastly more progressive composer than Schoenberg.

Other Wagnerian aspects are the texture, which is primarily homophonic, with clear melodies sounding against figuration, and the extensive use of chromatic nonharmonic tones. Only rarely does a chord occur on a strong beat without a decorating note. The form is that frequently found in symphonic poems—a long, one-movement structure of contrasting moods, unified by themes that recur from time to time.

That Schoenberg was deeply concerned with the emotional effect of the piece is proved by the numerous words of expression he wrote in the score. These are almost always preceded by the word *sehr* (very). On a single page one finds *sehr breit* (very broad), *sehr langsam* (very slow), and *sehr ausdrucksvoll* (very expressive).

The expressionist composer always deals in large denominations of emotion.

Closely akin to *Verklaerte Nacht* in style is *Gurrelieder* (the songs of Gurre, a castle in Scandinavian mythology) written, however, for a gigantic orchestra, and multiple choruses and soloists. It is a work that shows the influence of Mahler in its great length, size of the orchestra, and use of voices. The score calls for:

4 piccolos	10 horns	6 tympani
4 flutes	6 trumpets	bass drum
3 oboes	1 bass trumpet	cymbals
2 English horns	1 alto trombone	triangle
3 clarinets	4 tenor trombones	glockenspiel
2 E-flat clarinets	1 bass trombone	side-drum
2 bass clarinets	1 contra bass trombone	tambour
3 bassoons	1 tuba	xylophone
2 contra bassoons		tam-tam
5 solo voices		an iron chain
3 four-part male choruses		four harps
eight-part mixed chorus		strings

It should be pointed out, however, that although this mammoth orchestra is used, there are many passages that are delicately scored.

It is small wonder that *Gurrelieder* is scarcely ever performed, since this massive combination of symphony, song cycle, and cantata is very expensive and difficult to produce. The work shows the composer's almost total disregard for any practical considerations and his refusal to curb his musical ideas for any external reason.

Following these large-scale pieces, Schoenberg turned to writing for smaller groups of instruments, as demonstrated by the first two string quartets and the *Chamber Symphony* for 15 instruments.

The First String Quartet is also close in spirit to *Verklaerte Nacht*. Although it is without a published program it sounds as if it might have one, with its emotionally charged themes and clearly defined sections. It is a huge, one-movement work, lasting almost 45 minutes, gaining unity through transformations of the main themes. Its emotional gamut is wide, ranging from the headlong strength of the opening section, to hesitating "Viennese" charm in 3/4 time, to Schumann-like syncopations. There are climaxes that tax the resources of the four instruments and long sections of tremolos and of special effects such as *ponticello* and harmonics.

With the *Chamber Symphony* and the Second Quartet important changes in Schoenberg's style take place. Both show his growing interest in contrapuntal devices and in treating his material with great economy. In the last movement of the quartet a soprano joins the strings to sing a setting of Stefan Georg's poem, "I hear the breath of other planets," and the complex harmonies reach moments of atonality. In the *Chamber Symphony* there are also sections that go beyond conventional tonality; and the theme on which it is written, composed of a series of fourths, gives rise to a complex harmonic idiom of non-tonal implications.

Period 2: Atonal

Schoenberg's second period of composition extends from 1908 to 1912, from Opus 11 through Opus 21. The most important works are:

Opus 11	*Three Pieces for Piano* (1908)
15	*Das Buch der hängenden Gärten (The Book of the Hanging Gardens,* 15 poems for high voice; 1908)
16	*Five Pieces for Orchestra* (1909)
17	*Erwartung (Expectation,* a one-character opera; 1909)
18	*Die glückliche Hand (The Lucky Hand;* 1910-1913)
19	*Six Little Pieces for Piano,* (1911)
21	*Pierrot Lunaire* (1912)

In these compositions Schoenberg achieved a highly personal idiom, of the utmost importance to the whole of twentieth-century music, for in them he made the significant step that took him beyond major-minor tonality. Music "beyond tonality" is usually called *atonal* music, and in spite of the negative connotation of the term and the fact that the composer did not approve of it, it is generally used.

Considered from one point of view, the change between Opus 10 and Opus 11 was but a small one, for with the increasing use of chromatic tones all through the nineteenth century, the boundaries of the classical key system had already been vastly broadened. The continuously modulating, cadence-avoiding style of Wagner or Franck, for example, had definitely undermined clear tonal definition. Nevertheless, in such music, no matter how devious and adventurous the journey from opening to closing tonic chord, there was always a tonal goal toward which the composition progressed. The underlying principles were the same as those which had governed music since the time of Bach.

When a composer rejects these tonal principles he is faced with tremendous problems. The main one concerns organization, for without tonality—a tonal goal—how does one "go" anywhere and how does one "arrive" any place? When is one finished? It is not unlike the problem faced by completely nonobjective painters. When a painter frees himself from any attempt to portray objective reality he is faced with a terrifying freedom of choice. If any shape or color may be used without reference to the visible world, how does one start, organize, or complete a canvas?

This analogy to painting is especially meaningful in connection with Schoenberg, for he became very interested in the visual arts at this time and was a friend of Kandinsky, one of the founders of non-objective, expressionist painting. In writing of these years Schoenberg said, "With great joy I read Kandinsky's book, *On the Spiritual in Art*, in which the road for painting is pointed out."[6] The composer started to paint and even had one-man shows in Vienna, Berlin, and Munich.

What takes the place of tonality as a structural principle in atonal music? The compositions of Schoenberg's second period show various answers to the question. The composer himself has described the problem:

> The first compositions in this new style were written by me around 1908 and, soon afterwards, by my pupils, Anton von Webern and Alban Berg. From the very beginning such compositions differed from all preceding music, not only harmonically, but also melodically, thematically, and motivally. But the foremost characteristics of these pieces in *statu nascendi* were their extreme expressiveness and their extraordinary brevity. At that time, neither I nor my pupils were conscious of the reasons for these features. Later I discovered that our sense of form was right when it forced us to counterbalance extreme emotionality with extraordinary shortness. Thus subconsciously, consequences were drawn from an innovation, which, like every innovation, destroys while it produces. . . . New colorful harmony was offered; but much was lost.

Formerly the harmony had served not only as a source of beauty, but more important, as a means of distinguishing the features of the form. For instance, only a consonance was considered suitable for an ending. Establishing functions demanded different successions of harmonies than roving functions; a bridge, a transition, demanded other successions than a codetta; harmonic variation could be executed intelligently and logically only with due consideration of the fundamental meaning of the harmonies. Fulfillment of all these functions—comparable to the effect of punctuation in the construction of sentences, of subdivisions into paragraphs, and of fusion into chapters—could scarcely be assured with chords whose constructive values had not as yet been explored. Hence, it seemed at first impossible to compose pieces of complicated organization or of great length.[7]

The *Three Piano Pieces*, op. 11, are somewhat transitional, in that elements of tonality are still present. The first piece, so darkly expressive, is at the same time taut and economical in construction, a state of affairs often prevailing in Schoenberg's compositions. It is built on manipulations and developments of this melody heard at the beginning:

EXAMPLE 32*

The accompanying chord in the third measure consists of the same intervals (a third followed by a second) sounded together. The chord in the previous measure is similar, except that the third has been expanded to a fourth.

A traditional transposition of the material a fifth higher occurs a few bars later. After a short cadenza-flourish, motives from the theme are heard over a chord in piano "harmonics," showing Schoenberg's interest in unusual color effects. The effect is gained by depressing the notes *f, a, c*-sharp, and *e* in the central octave of the piano and then sharply striking the same notes low in the bass. The released strings sound in sympathetic vibration.

The rest of the piece consists of continuing references to the basic motive, sometimes inverted, sometimes expanded with larger intervals or with interpolated notes. But in one form or another, the theme-shape is almost always present. After a climactic fortissimo statement, the theme returns in its original form at the same pitch level as at the beginning. There is no doubt that this gives a feeling of tonality, although the final chord, a structure in fourths, is not related to any tonal center.

The second and third pieces of Opus 11 show family resemblances to the first. Thus, in the second, thirds are replaced with augmented fourths and fifths, but the descending minor second is still prominent, and there are many reappearances of the original series of intervals. The key of D minor is established by the accompaniment figure that appears at the beginning and end of the piece, which as a whole is divided into sections, defined in the traditional manner by recurrences of motives.

The third piece, the most violent, starts with an expanded version of the basic theme.

EXAMPLE 33

Extremely complex chords are employed, such as that in Measure 4 which contains ten different notes.

This important opus, one of the first of Schoenberg's atonal compositions, is worthy of close analysis because of the insights it gives into his methods of composition. The tightness and economy of structure, the continuing variations and development of a basic theme-shape, and the intense expression are features that will characterize many of his later works.

Five Pieces for Orchestra is one of the most important compositions of the time, startling and beautiful in its originality. Written for a large orchestra, the instruments are used more for their individual color than for mass effects. Tuttis are rare, and when they occur are short. The first piece, *Vorgefühle (Premonitions)*, is based on two ideas. The first is stated immediately by the muted cellos:

EXAMPLE 34*

while the second is an ostinato figure:

EXAMPLE 35

The contradiction between the length of the figure with the meter expressed by the barline shows that Stravinsky was not the only composer interested in the device at the time. The piece is violent and strident.

The second, *Vergangenes (Yesteryears)* is characterized by delicate color and delicious sound. It is permeated with a theme

EXAMPLE 36

that is heard in many rhythmic variants, and the shimmering sound of flutes, celesta, and the staccato bassoons give it a sheen as colorful

*Permission for reprint granted by C. F. Peters Corp., New York.

as anything written by a French composer. Nevertheless, the third piece, *Sommermorgen an einem See* (*Summer Morning by a Lake*), surpasses it in its dependence on tone color. In this piece Schoenberg employs a concept he called *Klangfarbmelodie* in which changes of orchestral color take the place of changes in pitch. This is one of the most static pieces ever written; much of it is merely the substitution of one instrument or group of instruments for another sounding the same note. Harmony, melody, and rhythm are sacrificed to timbre in this unusual composition. The score is loaded with dynamic indications, every note receiving its exact degree of loudness.

Music such as this, and particularly music written later by followers of Schoenberg, has been called *pointillistic*. This is a term associated with a technique of painting employed by Seurat, the French painter, and others. These men painted by putting thousands of vari-colored little dots or points on the canvas, which, when seen from a distance, seem to represent the outlines of solid shapes and objects. The term *pointillism* is used in music to describe a similar technique of avoiding solid, continuous musical lines and textures and, instead, employing a fragmentary style. The ear makes connections between the tones much in the same way as the eye constructs outlines that really do not exist in the paintings.

The fourth piece, *Peripetia* (a term associated with Greek drama, referring to a sudden reverse of circumstances), alternates rude sonorities and wide-interval melodies with passages for muted horns, while the last, *Das Obligate Rezitativ* (*The Obbligato Recitative*), is a slow waltz, redolent of Viennese nostalgia.

These pieces for orchestra furnish further insights into Schoenberg's musical personality. They are the works not of an ascetic but of a hypersensitive colorist, and their emotional gamut is wide, from moments of terrifying force to almost immobile lassitude.

Erwartung is another fascinating work. It is a monodrama, an opera for one character, and portrays the actions, reactions, and reflections of a woman who goes in search of her lover in a forest at night. As she is in a highly emotional state, her moods range from joyful expectation to fear of the forest with its insects and animals, to anguish and hysteria when she does not find the man she seeks. Exhausted, she sinks down on a bench. Feeling something with her foot, she discovers it to be a corpse—the body of her lover. She lies beside it and kisses it. Her mood changes as she reviles her dead

lover for having been untrue to her (Death being the "other woman").
She kicks the body. Later she makes love to it again, and as dawn
approaches she sings her irrational farewells.

This grisly work shows Schoenberg's fascination with morbid
and unhealthy emotion. It also shows him as the direct descendant of
Wagner and Strauss, as they too created heroines, Isolde and Salome,
who found love and death to be indivisible. However, this unhappy
woman with her unhinged behavior and frequent references to the
moon, which always lights such scenes, is much closer to Salome than
to the noble Irish queen.

Musically, *Erwartung* is also in the Wagner-Strauss tradition,
shown in the start-to-finish continuity and in the relation of the voice
to the orchestra. The voice line resembles a highly charged recitation
of the words and calls for musicianship and vocal range not often
found. Here are two characteristic phrases:

EXAMPLE 37a*

Herr Gott   was   ist   Hil -   fe

EXAMPLE 37b

für   mich   ist   kein   Platz   da

The orchestra accompanies, or rather proceeds simultaneously with
the voice in the timbre-rich, pointillistic manner of the *Five Pieces for
Orchestra*. The brief interludes that connect the scenes are striking,
and the last measures of the work, quoted here from the piano score,
show the great originality of the opera (see Example 37c).

Along with these resemblances to Wagner and Strauss, there is
one important difference. *Erwartung* is *athematic* in that there are no
themes or motives that are repeated, developed, or transformed.

*Copyright 1923, renewed 1950 by Universal Edition A.G., Vienna.

Debussy's ideal of a "music free from themes, motives . . ." is achieved in *Erwartung.**

Die glückliche Hand is close to *Erwartung* in feeling and technique. The general atmosphere of the work can be gathered from the stage directions for the opening scene:

> The stage is almost dark. Towards the front lies the Man with his face to the floor. On his back sits a cat-like fantastic animal (Hyena with large feather wings) which apparently has bitten the man's neck.[8]

It is another "nightmare" opera.

The *Piano Pieces,* op. 19, are examples of the miniature forms mentioned by the composer. Three of the pieces are but nine measures long; the longest has seventeen measures. Each is a highly expressive statement that is neither extended nor developed. The effect is not unlike that of a Japanese *Hai-kai,* a brief poem, of which the following is an example:

> Although it is not plainly visible to the eye
> That autumn has come,
> I am alarmed
> By the noise of the wind!
>
> FUJIWARA NO TOSHIYUKI[9]

Poems such as these were the models of the group of poets known as the imagists who were writing at this time. Their motivation was the same as Schoenberg's—to avoid rhetoric, preconceived patterns, and the elaborate structures of the nineteenth century, and to intimate by imagery rather than to describe concretely and directly.

Pierrot Lunaire is another important work of the prewar period. This is a composition for a speaker and a small group of instrumentalists—pianist, flutist (who also plays piccolo), clarinetist (who also plays bass clarinet), violinist (who also plays viola), and cellist. A setting of twenty-one short poems by the Belgian poet Albert Giraud, translated into German, the flavor of the poems is artificial and sophisticated, "arty" perhaps, typically *fin-de-siècle.* They are concerned with the familiar figures of Pierrot and Columbine, the moon, night, and serenades, but in contexts far removed from their usual surroundings. A translation of one of the poems will suggest the prevailing mood:

*See page 28.

Nocturnal, deathly-sick moon,
There on the dark pillow of the sky,
Your look, so full of madness,
Enchants me as a strange melody.

You die of unappeasable sorrow,
Of longing, deep within,
You nocturnal, deathly-sick moon,
There on the dark pillow of the sky.

The lover, who in his intoxication
    impulsively goes to his love,
Enjoys the play of your beams,
Your pale, tormented blood,
You nocturnal, deathly-sick moon!*

The most novel feature of the work is the fact that the poems are recited above the instrumental accompaniment rather than sung. The recitation, moreover, is not in a natural tone of voice, but is highly stylized with extreme variety of pitch and rigidly controlled rhythm. The part is indicated in the score in regular notation, but the composer gives directions that it is not to be sung, but to be intoned in *Sprechstimme* (speaking voice), which is neither conventional singing nor recitation. The effect, in performance, is eerie and disturbing, particularly for Americans, who as a rule have little experience with stylized recitation or acting.

The instrumental music is as strange in its way as is the manner of reciting the verse. James Huneker wrote this description of a performance in Berlin in 1912:

> What did I hear? At first the sound of delicate china shivering into a thousand luminous fragments. In the welter of tonalties that bruised each other as they passed and repassed, in the preliminary grip of enharmonics that almost made the ears bleed, the eyes water, the scalp to freeze, I could not get a central grip on myself. . . . What kind of music is this, without melody, in the ordinary sense; without themes; yet every acorn of a phrase contrapuntally developed by an adept; without a harmony that does not smite the ears, lacerate, figuratively speaking, the ear-drums; keys forced into hateful marriages that are miles asunder or else too closely related for aural matrimony . . . .[10]

*Translated by Charles Hamm.

While *Pierrot Lunaire* no longer calls forth such purple prose, it still impresses the listener with its originality. The small group of instruments that varies with every number sounds more bizarre than the large orchestra of *Erwartung*. The musical characteristics are much the same—an atonal idiom with a preponderance of dissonant intervals both melodic and harmonic, chords in fourths, and unusual timbres. There is a great deal of imitation between the instrumental lines, and even with the voice line where the pitches are indefinite.

Several of the pieces have a complex contrapuntal structure. For instance "Night," no. 8, is a strict passacaglia. "Parody," no. 17, is even more contrived and the viola is imitated by the spoken voice (in direction and rhythm only). Later there is a crab-canon between the speaker and the piccolo and at the same time there is another crab-canon progressing between the clarinet and viola. Perhaps the most complicated structural plan is found in "Moonspot," no. 18, where from the middle of the tenth bar the whole piece reverses itself, achieving the symmetry of an ink blot. While all this is going on, the piano has a three-part fugue, the subject of which is an augmentation of the canon's theme in the clarinet and piccolo. This use of contrapuntal devices as a means of organization foreshadowed the music Schoenberg was to write after World War I.

Stravinsky heard a performance of *Pierrot Lunaire* in 1912. His reactions as reported in his *Autobiography* are revealing:

> I was not at all enthusiastic over the estheticism of the work which seemed to me a reversion to the superannuated cult of Beardsley. But as an instrumental achievement, the score of *Pierrot Lunaire* is unquestionably a success.[11]

After hearing *Pierrot*, both Stravinsky in *Three Japanese Poems* and Ravel in *Chansons madécasses* wrote compositions for voice and an unusual combination of instruments. This was Schoenberg's last composition before the outbreak of World War I. When he returned to Vienna after being released from the army, he entered his third and most important style period. This will be discussed in Chapter X.

OTHER COMPOSERS

Closely associated with Schoenberg at this time were two student-colleagues, Alban Berg and Anton Webern. While they studied composition with the older man, theirs was more than a teacher-and-pupils relationship, for all three explored the new idioms together. For the rest of their lives the three composers held each other in the warmest personal affection and respect.

After the war, Berg and Webern achieved their own personal styles and wrote compositions that are among the most important of the twentieth century. These later works will be discussed in Chapter XI. At this point, however, the prewar compositions will be mentioned to show their close relationship to those of Schoenberg.

Berg started to study with Schoenberg in 1904. Never a prolific composer, he wrote six works before 1914. His Piano Sonata (op. 1, 1908) as well as the String Quartet (op. 3, 1910) are good examples of his youthful style: they are intensely chromatic and close to *Tristan* and *Verklaerte Nacht*. He followed Schoenberg in the atonal aphoristic style in his *Four Pieces for Clarinet* (op. 5, 1913) and the Three *Pieces for Orchestra* (op. 6, 1914).

Webern wrote eleven compositions before the war. They are similar in idiom and type to Schoenberg's and Berg's, consisting of: songs; brief atonal pieces for violin and piano, cello and piano, and string quartet (*Five Movements for String Quartet,* 1909, and *Six Bagatelles,* 1913); and pointillistic short pieces for orchestra (*Six Pieces for Orchestra,* 1909; *Five Pieces for Orchestra,* 1913). They are works of great originality, startling in the audacity of musical ideas, in their brevity and sonority. Schoenberg described Webern's short pieces as "a whole novel condensed in a single sigh."

Webern's *Six Pieces for Orchestra,* op. 6, is dedicated to "Arnold Schoenberg, my teacher and friend, with utmost love." In dimension, they are similar to Schoenberg's Opus 19 piano pieces, for the whole set takes less than ten minutes to perform. In spite of this, a large orchestra is called for (quadruple brasses and an augmented percussion section) although the instruments are never used together. As in *Pierrot Lunaire,* each piece has its own instrumentation.

The opening of the first piece can serve as an example of Webern's pointillism. The melodic line, divided among several instruments, changes from one fleeting, ravishing timbre to another as it progresses. Since each instrument plays but a few notes, the changes succeed each other rapidly, and many listeners are at first baffled and then fascinated by the effect. Here are the first few notes:

EXAMPLE 38*

Webern uses some of his favorite timbres in these few measures—muted trumpet, flute in the low register, and celesta—sounds associated with French impressionistic music of the time. Through the unusual timbres and the original musical ideas, each of the remaining pieces evokes an immediate mood.

The emotional climate of the whole opus seems to be highly neurotic. This is particularly true of the fourth piece which is accompanied throughout by pendulumlike strokes on the bass drum, tam-tam, and a bell of undetermined pitch. It builds to a shattering climax, and although the piece is but forty measures long, its expression of the "shriek of the soul" is both masterful and complete. It would be a fitting "accompaniment" to Munch's painting, *The Shriek.*

STYLE CHARACTERISTICS

As indicated by the foregoing, there is too much variety in the prewar compositions of Schoenberg and his colleagues to make possible valid generalizations concerning their style. Starting as late-romantic Wagnerian composers, around 1908 they gradually turned to an atonal, highly dissonant idiom. Not having solved the problem of writing extended independent compositions without the structure provided by tonality, these composers wrote works that achieved their form through association with words, or they avoided the problem of form by writing one-sentence statements. They increasingly resorted to contrapuntal devices to provide structural frameworks.

All three were extremely sensitive to unusual, subtle tone color. Avoiding the mass effects of the late romantic orchestra, they sought sounds at the top and bottom of instrumental ranges and were fascinated by flutter tonguing and mutes for the brass instruments, as well as harmonics and glissandos for the strings. Instruments such as the celesta and xylophone were raised to positions of great importance.

This extreme sensitivity to tone color as well as the fragmentary quality of their melodies and the freedom with which they treated dissonances make for interesting points of contact with the music of Debussy. The French composer is objective and cool, while these composers are subjective and burning, but the sound worlds they inhabit are not totally disassociated. Most of the composers of the time were faced with the problem of writing music without the structure provided by major-minor tonality. It is not surprising that their various solutions were similar at times.

SUGGESTED READINGS

The bibliography of Schoenberg will be found at the end of Chapter X, and that of Berg and Webern in Chapter XI.

CHAPTER V

MUSIC
IN AMERICA

It's a complex fate, being an American, and one of the responsibilities it entails is fighting against a superstitious veneration of Europe. HENRY JAMES

What was happening to music in the United States in these rich years of the early twentieth century? Was anything produced comparable to *Le Sacre* or *Pierrot Lunaire?* The answer is an unqualified *no,* for the lack of a musical environment such as that enjoyed by Berlin, Paris, or Vienna, with their great opera houses, orchestras, and well-established conservatories, made the creation of musical masterpieces in the United States virtually impossible. If a genius had been born in our Midwest in the 1870's and if he had spent all of his formative years there, think what his musical experiences would have been in comparison with Debussy's or Schoenberg's! What would he have heard of Wagner or Moussorgsky? It is not surprising that the United States did not make strong contributions to music in these years, for great works of art do not appear spontaneously in a barren atmosphere.

This is not to say, however, that there was no musical activity at all. A few of our larger communities had orchestras, conservatories, and opera houses, but in most cases these were but pale copies of European organizations. Since

75

broadcasts and recordings had not yet appeared on the scene, "serious" musical experiences were limited to those living in one of not more than a dozen cities. When one considers the vastness of our country it is clear that most of the population lived without hearing concert music, whether old or new.

The music that was heard was in all probability written and performed by Europeans. Foreign virtuosos, conductors, opera singers, and orchestra musicians completely dominated the American musical world. Children took lessons from a German *Professor* while their parents applauded the *signore* and *signori* at the opera.

If an American aspired to enter the profession it was taken for granted that he would complete his studies in Europe, preferably in Germany. When one reads the biographies of prominent musicians of the day—such men as John Knowles Paine (1839-1906), Dudley Buck (1839-1909), George Chadwick (1854-1931), Horatio Parker (1863-1919), or Edward MacDowell (1861-1908)—the story is invariable. Each studied piano with a German-born piano teacher (or with someone who had studied in Germany). Some continued their studies at Harvard or Yale and all went to Germany for advanced study at the conservatories at Munich, Leipzig, or Berlin. Depending on where they studied, and under whose influence they came, they returned home conservative followers of Brahms or progressive followers of Liszt and Wagner. They wrote piano pieces, songs, tone poems, oratorios, and occasionally an opera. A few attempted to write "American" music by basing their compositions on Negro spirituals or on Indian themes.

It is not difficult to assess these compositions. They are sincere, honest, well written, but completely without the essential touch of genius that gives music lasting value. Nevertheless, these composers and their music were of genuine temporary value for they produced an environment in which stronger musical personalities could thrive. Without these American composers of the *fin de siècle* we would not be enjoying our present musical life, which differs so radically from that just described.

While these academic compositions and limited musical experience are characteristic of the musical life in the United States in the early years of the century, under the surface and in quiet isolation there was some indigenous musical activity which proved to have great significance and interest. During these years, American ragtime and jazz, soon to be heard around the world, was in its formative stage, and one American composer, Charles Ives, was writing compositions that were as audacious as anything being written on the continent.

IVES, 1874-1954

I feel strongly that the great fundamentals should be more discussed in all public meetings, and also in meetings of schools and colleges. Not only the students but also the faculty should get down to more thinking and action about the great problems which concern all countries and all people in the world today, and not let the politicians do it all and have the whole say.

I have often been told that it is not the function of music (or a concert) to concern itself with matters like these. But I do not by any means agree. I think that it is one of the things that music can do, if it happens to want to, if it comes naturally, and is not the result of superimposition—I have had some fights about this. CHARLES IVES*

The solitary Charles Ives is the grand exception to this genteel tradition; he is one of the most thorny of rugged individualists in all music history.

As the son of a band director in Danbury, Connecticut, he was intimately associated with music from his earliest youth. His father, by no means the usual town band master, had a remarkable interest in novel combinations of sounds and a flair for experiments. He tried to imitate the sound of church bells on the piano and contrived musical instruments that would play quarter tones. Dividing the members of his band into small groups, he had them play different pieces in an antiphonal and overlapping manner. He encouraged his son Charles to experiment with dissonances at the piano, and often had the family sing a familiar tune in one key while he accompanied in another.

*In a letter to Lehman Engel.

Charles attended Yale as a music student and received traditional instruction, but after graduation he went to New York, entered the insurance business, and composed music as a hobby until the mid-twenties while becoming a successful and wealthy business man.

Because Ives made little effort to have his work performed, it was virtually unknown until the 1930's when a small group of musicians became aware of this inspired amateur. Two movements of his Fourth Symphony were played in New York in 1927, and four years later an orchestral piece, *Holidays*, was played in Europe. In 1939 his *Concord Sonata* for piano was heard in New York. From that time the Ives legend has grown, for the imagination of the public was captured by the idea of a businessman-composer-recluse who wrote astonishingly complex and dissonant music.

In 1947 he was awarded a Pulitzer Prize for the Third Symphony he had written some twenty years previously, and in 1955, a year after his death, a full-scale biography and critical study of his works was published.

IVES' COMPOSITIONS

Ives' music includes four symphonies, four sonatas for violin and piano, two piano sonatas, two string quartets, over a hundred songs, and smaller pieces for orchestra and for piano. Since much of this was written before 1918, it belongs to the pre-World War I period which witnessed so many changes in music.

The *Concord Sonata* (1909-1915) is a good example of his work. At a first hearing of this huge work one is likely to be stunned, for it is long, loud, and thick with notes. There are surprising differences in style from page to page and it is entirely unpredictable. The best way to approach the piece is through the titles and the written introductions provided by the composer.

The first movement is a portrait of Emerson, one of Ives' heroes. The composer describes him as "America's deepest explorer of the spiritual immensities," and his style of writing as "based on the large unity of a series of particular aspects of a subject, rather than on the continuity of its expression. As thoughts surge to his mind, he fills the heavens with them, crowds them in if necessary, but seldom arranges them along the ground first."[1] This applies to Ives' sonata.

The movement starts with two lines of dissonant counterpoint in contrary motion. The notes in the left hand form a motive which is used throughout the whole sonata.

EXAMPLE 39

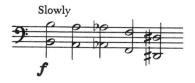

A moment later the signal theme of Beethoven's Fifth Symphony is heard, somewhat disguised. The latter theme also permeates the whole work. Ives tells us that it signifies:

> ... the spiritual message of Emerson's revelations—the Soul of humanity knocking at the door of Divine mysteries radiant in the faith that it *will* be opened—and that the human will become the Divine.

The piece progresses without barlines, meter (the omission being programmatic, in that the music relates to Emerson's prose as contrasted to his poetry), and without definite tonality. This is rambling, rhapsodic music with occasional references to the two main motives. It soon becomes violent in its dissonance and dynamics, one particularly astringent chord being explained as "but one of Emerson's sudden calls for a Transcendental Journey."

EXAMPLE 40

The structure in seconds is characteristic of the many tone clusters in the piece. A quieter section follows where the writing for several pages resembles Debussy's or Ravel's with a pedal established in the bass, and widely dispersed arpeggios in the left hand against a fragmentary melody in the right. Sections of "heaven-filling thoughts" alternate with pages of reflective music while the references to the Beethoven theme become more insistent. The end of the movement is pure impressionism, with its pedal built on a diminished fifth while intervals are sounded *pppp* above.

Another aspect of New England culture is expressed in the second movement, entitled "Hawthorne." Ives explained that he was not dwelling on the guilt-obsessed aspect of the author of *The Scarlet Letter* in this movement, but rather that he was "trying to suggest some of his [Hawthorne's] wilder, fantastical adventures into the half-childlike, half-fairylike phantasmal realms." This piece, a scherzo in mood, makes tremendous demands on the performer. The opening suggests the figuration of Ravel's "*Scarbo.*" Passages of wild syncopation, probably never notated before this time, alternate with passages to be played with a "board 14¾ inches long, and heavy enough to press the keys down without striking." In the middle of this vertiginous music there is suddenly a quotation from a simple old hymn with directions to play it "as a hymn is sometimes heard over a distant hill just after a heavy storm." A moment later a perky march-tune appears. These allusions to popular music are literal; that is, with their original chords and meter, and result in an almost surrealistic incongruity with the general climate of dissonance.

The slow third movement of the sonata is called "The Alcotts" and is an evocation of the simple, domestic life of the period. It is the most approachable movement and the allusions to additional gospel hymns, parlor songs, and "Here Comes the Bride," form a cohesive whole. The movement ends with a triumphant statement of the Beethoven theme in C major.

The last movement, "Thoreau," is a landscape with a figure. A detailed program concerned with a day in the life of the philosopher of Walden Pond accompanies the piece. The rhapsodic style of the first movement returns near the end, when a pedal figure starts, and above it are heard ever slower and more expressive versions of the basic melodic theme. At the very end, the Beethoven theme is referred to once again.

In this brief description of the *Concord Sonata,* the programmatic content has been stressed. Its musical originality has been mentioned, but the composition must be heard and the score studied to be believed. Written between 1909 and 1915, it is undoubtedly the most advanced, the most radical music written anywhere at that time. The *Concord Sonata* is unique and unprecedented in harmony, where chords in seconds and fourths vie with large clusters of notes; in rhythm, where a non-metrical, non-barred, free, prose style prevails; in tonality, where long stretches of music without tonal center are normal; and in form, where sections of the utmost difficulty alternate with references to banal, trite popular music of the nineteenth century. Other radical composers of the time were more modest and not courageous enough to assault all aspects of music at once. When Stravinsky exploited asymmetrical rhythmic patterns, for instance, he reduced the other elements (such as melody) to relative simplicity. When Schoenberg was writing his first pieces without a tonal center he made them very short. Ives took on all the difficulties at once.

For that reason, some of his shorter pieces and songs are more successful than the extended compositions. For instance, "The Housatonic at Stockbridge" from *A New England Symphony* (1903-1914) is a beautiful piece of impressionistic music with a shimmering, hazy atmosphere. Fragmentary melodies in the oboe, English horn, and French horn (typical impressionist timbres) are in the foreground, while the background is provided by the violins in quite another key. The early date of this piece makes it one of the first polytonal compositions. Another unqualified success is the *Unanswered Question* (1908) written for trumpet, four flutes, and string orchestra. Here the strings play simple diatonic chords in the background while the solo trumpet enters from time to time with a cryptic, wide-interval melody in a different key. At unexpected intervals the four flutes play flourishes in still another key. All of this is programmatic. According to the composer's directions,

> The strings play *ppp* throughout with no change in tempo. They are to represent "The Silence of the Druids—Who Know, See, and Hear Nothing." The trumpet intones "The Perennial Question of Existence," and states it in the same tone of voice each time. But the hunt for "The Invisible Answer" undertaken by the flutes and other human beings (sic), becomes gradually more active, faster and louder. . . .[2]

This composition stands the test of good program music. It is deeply expressive to the listener who has no knowledge of its program or even that a program exists. It is complete in its evocative sound.

The collection, *114 Songs*, privately printed by the composer, contains an essay in which he writes, "Some have written a book for money; I have not. Some for fame; I have not. Some for love; I have not. . . . In fact, gentle borrower, I have not written a book at all—I have merely cleaned house." Later he writes, "Some of the songs in this book, particularly among the later ones, cannot be sung."[3]

Such candor on the part of a composer prevents any criticism, but the volume does show further examples of Ives' untiring imagination and range of styles. Songs burlesquing popular songs of the nineties, with all of the naïveté of the time, are printed next to songs in the advanced idiom of the *Concord Sonata,* including fourteen-note tone-clusters and unbarred measures. A few songs avoid such extremes and can be judged highly successful and worthy of performance.

STYLE CHARACTERISTICS

Some of the outstanding characteristics of Ives' writing have been mentioned in the description of the *Concord Sonata.* His style is difficult to describe because of its great originality and apparent lack of system or order.

The idioms of the composers already discussed can be talked about with reference to their musical heredity and environment. For example, we saw that there was something of Massenet in Debussy and more than a little of Wagner in Schoenberg. In creating their own languages and syntax, these composers extended and developed the aspects of music they knew best. Although Ives had a powerful connection with his musical past, it is a relationship different from those we have just seen. When he uses his heritage—American popular music, both sacred and secular—he does so blatantly in literal quotations. Such quotations, however, usually interrupt music which is startingly new in syntax and vocabulary.

Because he was completely emancipated from the normal musical practices of the day he had no qualms about using any type of complexity. His dissonant counterpoint, for instance, proceeds with no regard for the ensuing clashes.

His chords are chosen from a range of possibilities not limited by any preconceived notion of what a chord must be. Cluster combinations of seconds, played with the help of a piece of wood cut to a specified length, vary with accumulations of thirds, fourths, or wide, dissonant intervals.

Rhythms are often so complicated that they challenge the ingenuity and experience of highly trained performers and conductors. A decade before *The Rite of Spring* Ives wrote irregular meters commonly associated with Stravinsky, such as 5/8, 11/8, 7/4, and in orchestral works he sometimes writes as many as ten different simultaneous patterns that do not coincide until the end.

Ives' formal structures are also without precedent. In his symphonies and sonatas there is little if any adherence to the conventions of sonata structure beyond the fact that they contain several contrasting movements. Within the movements there is more variety than unity as highly contrasting sections succeed each other. An over-all unity is achieved more through programmatic or external concepts than through strictly musical means.

The complexity of Ives' music has several bases. First in importance is the experimental attitude he inherited from his father. Most of the composers of his generation growing up in the musical centers of Europe only gradually found musical emancipation from their immediate backgrounds; but paradoxically, Ives, growing up in a small town in New England, became familiar with dissonances that were undreamed of in other parts of the world.

Ives' freedom from such practical considerations as finding publishers or performers for his music meant that he could give full play to his original ideas. He wrote to please only himself and he chose a career in business rather than in music so that he could continue to do so. He never reorchestrated a piece as even the unyielding Schoenberg did "to make it more practical for performance," nor did he ever write music on commission with attached conditions as Stravinsky often did, nor did he write a set of piano pieces of graded difficulty as Bartók did. Ives' music was uninfluenced by external considerations.

The difficulty of Ives' music also had a philosophical origin. As a follower of the New England transcendentalists, he believed life's important matters were so complex and difficult that any attempt to simplify or reduce them to easily understood statements would be weak and dishonest. He had deep scorn for what he termed "pretty" or "nice" music. Ives knew that his music was complex and he wanted it to be that way.

It is as difficult to summarize the position and importance of Ives in twentieth-century music as it is to describe his compositions. There is no question that he is a genuinely American composer rooted in his own landscape. There is no question about his Yankee integrity and humor nor about his originality.

In spite of this, his influence on later music has been only a moderately strong one, and the question of whether Ives' music achieves "greatness" or not is a debatable one. Still, there is much to be admired. He is somewhat like a dedicated genius who, in the privacy of his attic, invents fantastic, sometimes unbelievably complicated and impressive machines without caring if they work or not.

RAGTIME AND JAZZ

Unquestionably, the most significant contribution made to music by the United States in the period under discussion lay in the field of popular music. Although this is not the place for a thorough investigation of the development of jazz, its most important characteristics should be known by students of twentieth-century music because it strongly influenced European music of the between-the-wars period.

Of the first importance in ragtime and jazz is the prevalence of syncopation. Winthrop Sargeant has pointed out that this is of two types: the obvious off-beat accent, and a type of polyrhythm that superimposes a melodic unit of three notes over a rhythmic background of four units:[4]

It has already been pointed out that Stravinsky and Schoenberg wrote similar rhythms before 1914, and countless other composers employed the device in the following decades.

A second characteristic is the use of certain modifications of the major scale through the so-called blue notes. This flatting of the 3rd and 7th tones of the scale, used mainly in *Blues,* was of interest to European composers in the period when new scale patterns were sought.

A third characteristic of jazz which was to influence twentieth-century music was its timbre. Although the instrumentation of the original bands most often included cornet, piano, tuba, trombone, and banjo, it was not standardized and it varied from group to group. A raucous, nonblending combination, its blatant quality was particularly attractive to certain composers in the 1920's when there was a reaction against the lush sounds of the impressionist orchestra.

A fourth element of great importance, although perhaps not so influential to "serious" music, was the improvisatory, unplanned character of the performances. The fact that in true jazz each player is a soloist who plays his version of the piece presented the opportunity for musical invention and ornamentation. This was an aspect of performance that had been ignored for a long time; for many people, it was the most attractive aspect of jazz.

JAZZ ELEMENTS IN "SERIOUS" MUSIC

American popular music was first introduced to Europe by the minstrel shows that toured the continent after the Civil War, later by jazz bands immediately following World War I, and eventually through phonograph recordings. From the beginning, many European composers were fascinated by the fresh rhythms and timbres of American popular music and they incorporated some of the elements in their work. Among the first European compositions showing the influence of this music were Debussy's *Golliwog's Cakewalk* (1908) and *Minstrels* (1910). After World War I the popularity of ragtime is shown in Satie's "Ragtime du Paquebot" from *Parade* (1917) and in Stravinsky's *L'Histoire du Soldat* (1918) and *Ragtime for Eleven Instruments* (1918). During the 1920's—the "jazz age"— the use of jazz idioms became more frequent. Examples are Milhaud's *La Création du Monde* (1923), Hindemith's *1922 Suite* for piano, and the jazz operas, *Jonny spielt auf* (1925-26) by Krenek, and *Mahagony* (1927) by Kurt Weil. George Gershwin's career presents the opposite side of the coin. A gifted composer of popular music, he had the ambition to combine the idioms he knew so well in the more intricate forms of "serious" music. His *Rhapsody in Blue* (1924), Piano Concerto (1925), and the opera *Porgy and Bess* (1935) have had lasting, world-wide popularity. Among American composers Aaron Copland made considerable use of jazz in his early compositions such as his Piano Concerto (1926) and *Music for the Theatre* (1925). Stravinsky's *Ebony Concerto* (1945), Liebermann's *Concerto for Jazzband and Orchestra* (1954), and Lucas Foss' *Concerto for Improvising Solo Instruments and Orchestra* (1960) are later examples of the infiltration of jazz elements into concert music.

SUGGESTED READINGS

The most complete study of Ives' music is *Charles Ives and His Music*, Henry and Sidney Cowell (New York, 1955).

Two books that cover the whole field of American music are *Our American Music*, John Tasker Howard (New York, 1946, 3rd ed.), and *America's Music*, Gilbert Chase (New York, 1955).

There are many surveys of jazz. Among the more recent are: *They All Played Together*, Rudi Blesh and Harriet Janis (New York, 1950); *A Pictorial History of Jazz*, Keepnews and Grauer (New York, 1955); *Modern Jazz, A Survey of Developments Since 1939*, Morgan and Horricks (London, 1957); *The Story of Jazz*, Marshall Stearns (New York, 1956); and *A Handbook of Jazz*, Barry Ulanov (New York, 1957). *Jazz, Hot and Hybrid*, Winthrop Sargeant (New York, 1946; 2nd ed.) is of particular value because of the careful analysis it contains of the musical elements.

CHAPTER VI

EXPERIMENTS IN MUSIC

Kill the nineteenth century dead! GERTRUDE STEIN

Each of the composers already discussed believed, to some extent, that the musical resources of the past were exhausted and that the twentieth century must find a new vocabulary and syntax. The compositions of Debussy and Stravinsky, and of Ives and Schoenberg, suggested some of the directions in which music might progress.

These recommendations were modest, however, compared to the plan of some composers who had a simple and drastic suggestion—to scrap all of the music of the past and start again with a new medium for sound—noise. This truly radical group argued that the time had come when the familiar and traditional material of music—"musical" tones produced by the human voice and instruments—was no longer capable of expressing man's feelings and emotions. "We are living in a new world," they said, "Let us develop a musical style that is equally new." Their contemporaries dismissed them as being publicity-seeking lunatics, but curiously enough, time has proved that there was merit in some of their ideas. Avant-garde music of the second half of the century is once again exploring these areas. These experiments will be discussed under noise music or microtonal music. While the latter developed mainly after 1914, germinal ideas appeared before then.

87

NOISE MUSIC

The impulse to increase the material of music by including noises originated in Milan, Italy. It was part of the program of the futurists, a group of poets, painters, and musicians who felt that all art needed a new aesthetic if it were to express the modern world. The painters of the group decided that speed and motion expressed the essence of their times. Consequently they painted objects as if they were in motion, by superimposing images, much like the photographs taken by a stroboscopic camera (which had not been invented at the time). The best-known picture of this school was painted somewhat later by the French artist Duchamp, the famous *Nude Descending a Staircase*.

In a manifesto written in 1913 by Russolo, the case for futurist music is made. He says, "Life in ancient times was silent. In the nineteenth century, with the invention of machines, Noise was born." He then goes on to trace the course of contemporary music and the ways in which it reflects the complexity of modern life. However, even the most extreme modern music is too limited in expression, he feels.

> We must break out of this narrow circle of pure musical sounds, and conquer the infinite variety of noise-sounds. . . . Let us wander through a great modern city with our ears more attentive than our eyes, and distinguish the sounds of water, air, or gas in metal pipes, the purring of motors (which breathe and pulsate with an indubitable animalism) the throbbing of valves, the pounding of pistons, the screeching of gears, the clatter of streetcars on their rails, the cracking of whips, the flapping of awnings and flags. We shall amuse ourselves by orchestrating in our minds the noise of the tall shutters of store windows, the slamming of doors, the bustle and shuffle of crowds, the multitudinous uproar of railroad stations, forges, mills, printing presses, power stations, and underground railways.[1]

Finally he suggests the instrumentation of a futurist orchestra and recommends six families of noises, to be produced mechanically:

1	2	3	4	5	6
Booms	Whistles	Whispers	Screams	Noises obtained by percussion on metals, wood, stone, terra cotta, etc.	Voices of animals and men:
Thunderclaps	Hisses	Murmurs	Screeches		
Explosions	Snorts	Mutterings	Rustlings		Shouts

1	2	3	4	5	6
Crashes		Bustling noises	Buzzes		Shrieks
Slashes		Gurgles	Crackling sounds obtained		Groans
Roars			by friction		Howls
					Laughs
					Wheezes
					Sobs*

Not much came of these concepts before World War I because the manifesto was only one in a time when manifestos were everyday occurrences. However, in the twenties the works of the Franco-American composer Varèse moved in this direction, and after World War II the composers of *musique concrète* in France employed the sound medium that Russolo, the futurist, had recommended in 1913.

MICROTONAL MUSIC

Another group of experimenters felt that the solution to the problem lay in scales consisting of more than twelve semitones to the octave. Of these *microtone scales,* the one that has received most attention is that involving quarter tones, but there have also been experiments with sixth tones, eighth tones, and even smaller divisions of the octave. Although they were not numerous, proponents of this program could be found throughout the world, for experimenters in Germany, Italy, Russia, Mexico, and the United States worked on the idea.

Busoni, the celebrated pianist and composer, suggested in his book *New Musical Aesthetics* that sixth tones be used in music of the future, and his ideas were followed by the Czech composer Alois Hába who wrote many compositions including the opera *Die Mutter,* using microtones. There was sufficient interest to warrant his appointment as a professor of microtone music at the Prague Conservatory.

Although the use of microtones appeared to be reasonable (because the natural overtone series, the basis of traditional Western music, contains intervals smaller than semitones in the higher par-

*Music Since 1900 (1949, 3rd ed.); reproduced by permission of the publishers.

tials) there was no immediate wide acceptance of the idiom. The fact that the usual instruments (except strings) are incapable of playing such music created an impasse, and furthermore, because a new system of notation is necessary other problems have arisen. The most serious deterrent to microtonal music lies in the limitations of the human ear. Although it might be possible to train musicians to produce small divisions of the whole step, and although listeners could conceivably learn to discriminate among these divisions, we have not reached this point yet. Until we have, these small intervals simply will sound "out of tune."

LATER DEVELOPMENTS

After World War II, with the development of the tape recorder and electronically produced tone, all of the mechanical difficulties met by the pioneers of noise music and microtonal music disappeared, and since 1950 great interest has been shown in these areas. These later developments will be described in Chapter XVII.

DEBUSSY AND STRAVINSKY, 1911

SCHOENBERG, PAINTING BY OSCAR KOKOSCHKA IN EXPRESSIONIST STYLE

STRAVINSKY, DRAWING BY PICASSO IN NEOCLASSIC STYLE

CHARLES IVES

SATIE, DRAWING BY PICASSO

LES SIX ON THE EIFFEL TOWER, c. 1920 (TAILLEFERRE, POULENC, HONEGGER, MILHAUD, COCTEAU, AURIC)

STRAVINSKY IN 1960

LES SIX AND COCTEAU, 1951 (MILHAUD, AURIC, HONEGGER, TAILLEFERRE, POULENC, DUREY. COCTEAU AT THE PIANO.)

SCHOENBERG TEACHING AT U.C.L.A., c. 1940

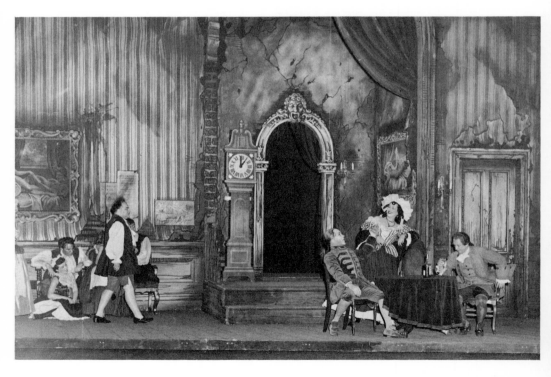

"THE RAKE'S PROGRESS," Act I, Scene 2

	France	Germany & Austria	Other Countries	Other Arts, Events
1900	Debussy: *Nocturnes for Orchestra*		Puccini: *La Tosca*	Freud: *The Meaning of Dreams*; Exposition Universelle in Paris
1901	Ravel: *Jeux d'eau*; Debussy: *Pour le Piano*	Mahler: Symphony #4		Picasso: Blue Period
1902	Debussy: *Pelléas et Mélisande*		Sibelius: Symphony #2; Ives: Symphony #2	Kandinsky opens art school in Munich
1903	Satie: *3 Morceaux en forme de Poire*; Debussy: *Estampes*	Strauss: *Sinfonia Domestica*	Ives: Symphony #3	Strindberg: *A Dream Play*
1904		Schoenberg: Quartet #1; Mahler: *Kindertotenlieder*	Puccini: *Madame Butterfly*; Scriabin: Sonata #4	

	France	Germany & Austria	Other Countries	Other Arts, Events
1905	Ravel: *Miroirs* Debussy: *La Mer* Ravel: *Sonatine*	Strauss: *Salome* Mahler: Symphony #5	Falla: *La Vida Breve* Scriabin: *Divine Poem* Sibelius: Violin Concerto	Picasso: Circus Period Founding of *Die Brücke* Fauves exhibit (Rouault, Matisse, Derain, Dufy, Braque) Einstein: *Theory of Relativity*
1906		Mahler: Symphony #6 Schoenberg: *Kammersymphonie*		Picasso: Negro period Wedekind: *Frühlings Erwachsen*
1907	Ravel: *L'Heure Espagnole*			Picasso: *Les Demoiselles D'Avignon* Kokoschka: *Mörder, Hoffnung, der Frauen* (drama) Bergson: *Creative Evolution*
1908	Debussy: *Ibéria*	Mahler: *Das Lied von der Erde* Schoenberg: Three Pieces for Piano Webern: Passacaglia	Bartók: Quartet #1 Prokofiev: *Suggestion Diabolique* Ives: *The Unanswered Question* Ives: Sonata #1, Violin-piano	Brancusi: *The Kiss* Cubism: name coined Gertrude Stein: *Three Lives*
1909		Schoenberg: *Erwartung* Strauss: *Elektra* Schoenberg: Five Pieces for Orchestra Webern: Six Pieces for Orchestra	Rachmaninoff: Piano Concerto #3	First season of Diaghilev's Ballet Russe in Paris Marinetti: *Futurist Manifesto*

Year	France	Germany & Austria	Other Countries	Other Arts, Events
1910	Debussy: *Préludes,* BK.I.	Strauss: *Der Rosenkavalier*; Berg: String Quartet; Mahler: Symphony #9	Ives: Sonata #2, Violin-piano; Puccini: *Girl of the Golden West*; Stravinsky: *The Firebird*; Vaughan Williams: Symphony #1	Exhibition of Post-Impressionist art in London
1911	Ravel: *Valses nobles et sentimentales*	Schoenberg: *Gurre-Lieder* (completed)	Sibelius: Symphony #4; Stravinsky: *Petrouchka*; Bartók: *Duke Bluebeard's Castle*; Bartók: *Allegro barbaro*; Irving Berlin: *Alexander's Ragtime Band*	Marc: *Red Horses*; First exhibit: *Der Blaue Reiter*; Lehmbruck: *Kneeling Woman*
1912	Milhaud: Quartet #1; Ravel: *Daphnis et Chloé*	Schoenberg: *Pierrot Lunaire*	Cowell: First performance of tone-clusters; Prokofiev: *Toccata*	Duchamp: *Nude Descending a Staircase*; Kandinsky: *Art of Spiritual Harmony*; Picasso: Collages; Mann: *Death in Venice*
1913	Debussy: *Préludes,* BK.II.; Milhaud: *Agamemnon*; Ravel: *Trois Poèmes de Mallarmé*; Satie: *Descriptions automatiques*	Schoenberg: *Die Glückliche Hand*; Berg: Four pieces for clarinet and piano	Stravinsky: *Le Sacre du Printemps*; Scriabin: *Prometheus*	Proust: *Swann's Way*; Malevitch: Suprematism; New York: Armory Show
1914	Ravel: Trio; Satie: *Sports et Divertissements*		Ives: *Three Places in New England*; Prokofiev: *Scythian Suite*; Vaughan Williams: *London Symphony*; Handy: *St. Louis Blues*	Milan: Concert of Noise Music; Gertrude Stein: *Tender Buttons*; Robert Frost: *Home Burial*

PART TWO

1914-1945

CHAPTER VII

PARIS AFTER WORLD WAR I

Musicians ought to cure music of its convolutions, its dodges and its tricks, and force it as far as possible to keep in front of the listener.   JEAN COCTEAU

Except in terms of the calendar, the twentieth century was not born until after the 1918 victory of the Allies, for only then was it apparent that many of the basic premises of nineteenth-century life had disappeared. Before the war much of Europe had been ruled by kings and aristocrats, but after 1918 most of the monarchs were deposed and sent into exile. The founding of democratic systems of government was not easily accomplished, and the transition period was difficult. The most drastic of these social upheavals took place in Russia; but Germany, Austria, Italy, and many of the central European countries, once a part of the Austro-Hungarian empire, were faced with the problem of learning to govern themselves. It was a time of confusion, but there was general optimism too, for everyone felt the war had not been fought in vain and the world had been saved for democracy.

France, having escaped the necessity of changing her form of government, recovered rather rapidly. Paris quickly regained its importance as an international art center, and for some years this position was uncontested while Germany and Austria were struggling to re-establish their economic lives. Darius Milhaud, twenty-seven years old at the time, has described Bastille Day, 1919:

> On the night preceding July 14th, the scene in the streets was unforgettable. There was dancing at every street corner, to the strains of little Bal Musette orchestras. On the 14th at dawn, Honegger, Vaurabourg, Durey, Fauconnet and I made our way towards the Étoile. We managed to clamber up on a seat from which we had a view over the heads of the crowd. There were people everywhere; every tree, every roof, every balcony had its cluster of human faces, and from all sides the crowd continued to arrive in an uninterrupted stream. . . .
> The march-past began at eight o'clock. Now at last the Victory that had been paid for so dearly was felt to be something tangible, visible, making our hearts swell with boundless hope. All the great Allied leaders, whom we only knew by their photographs or the newsreels in the cinemas were now before us in flesh and blood: Marshal Foch, Marshal Joffre, Field Marshal Lord Haig, and General Pershing preceded the French regiments each with the flag they had covered in glory, ... Everything at that time seemed to us to be big with promise for the new era of peace.[1]

The painters and sculptors of prewar Paris reopened their studios. Gertrude Stein's home became the meeting place of young writers such as Ernest Hemingway and Sinclair Lewis. James Joyce managed to find a publisher for *Ulysses,* and chapters of *Finnegans Wake* started to appear in *transition,* the publication of the avant-garde. Stravinsky became a French citizen, and Nadia Boulanger, that amazing teacher, spread the doctrine of neoclassicism among the first of hundreds of students who were to study with her. Paris was a magnet, attracting artistic young people from all over the world to sit at the feet of the great—or beside the great in the Café du Monde.

COCTEAU, 1891-

A key figure of this exciting time was a man difficult to classify. He was the originator and propagandist of many of the new ideas in the arts, and the friend and adviser of the most important creators. A poet, an artist, a playwright, he also directed and produced some of the most advanced films of the century. This was Jean Cocteau who was to be an unpredictable and stimulating figure in the art world for the next fifty years.

In 1918 he published a little book called *Coq et Arlequin*, consisting of a number of aphorisms that succinctly expressed a new aesthetic creed for composers. This creed repudiated romanticism as an ideal, whether of the Wagnerian *Gesamtkunstwerke* variety or its French counterpart, impressionism. Its fighting words were *precision, clarity,* and *order.* Here are a few of the aphorisms from the book. The economy with which Cocteau expresses his ideas is characteristic, for by principle he avoided anything long-winded.

> With us, there is a house, a lamp, a plate of soup, a fire, wine and pipes at the back of every important work of art.
>
> A young man must not invest in safe securities.
>
> The Nightingale sings badly.
>
> Beethoven is irksome in his developments, but not Bach, because Beethoven develops the form and Bach the idea. Beethoven says, "This penholder contains a new pen; there is a new pen in this penholder; the pen in this penholder is new." Bach says: "This penholder contains a new pen in order that I may dip it in the ink and write, etc." There is a difference.
>
> A poet always has too many words in his vocabulary, a painter too many colors on his palette, and a musician too many notes on his keyboard.
>
> A dreamer is always a bad poet.
>
> Wagner's works are long works which are long, and long drawn out, because this old sorcerer looked upon boredom as a useful drug for the stupefaction of the faithful.
>
> Debussy missed his way because he fell from the German frying pan into the Russian fire. Once again the pedal blurs rhythm and creates a kind of fluid atmosphere congenial to *short sighted ears.* Satie remains intact. Hear his "Gymnopédies," so clear in their form and melancholy feeling. Debussy orchestrates them, confuses them, and wraps their exquisite architecture in a cloud. Debussy moves further and further away from Satie's starting point and makes everybody follow in his steps. The thick lightning-pierced fog of Bayreuth becomes a thick snowy mist flecked with impressionist sunshine. Satie speaks of Ingres; Debussy transposes Monet "à la Russe." Satie teaches what, in our age, is the greatest audacity, simplicity. Enough of hammocks, garlands and

gondolas; I want some one to build me music I can live in, like a house. Enough of clouds, waves, aquariums, water-sprites, and nocturnal scents; what we need is a music of the earth, everyday music. We may soon hope for an orchestra where there will be no caressing strings. Only a rich choir of wood, brass and percussion.[2]

It was inevitable that Diaghilev, returning to Paris shortly after the war to re-establish his ballet (now the Ballet Russe de Monte Carlo), would immediately call upon the talents of Cocteau for his new creations. The two created some of the most novel ballets of the era, always staying one step ahead of the public. Diaghilev had no desire to continue producing the grand ballets of prewar days. His aim now was to shock, to startle, to amuse, and to amaze. *Pulcinella,* a ballet score based on fragments by Pergolesi, brought together Cocteau, Picasso, and Stravinsky, and the excursion into the eighteenth century by these completely modern artists set the pattern for many other forays into a pre-nineteenth-century past.*

SATIE, 1866-1925

While Beethoven, Wagner, and Debussy are frequently taken to task in *Coq et Arlequin,* one composer is praised—Erik Satie. Chronologically, this strange man belongs to an earlier generation of composers, the period of Debussy. However, since he was always ahead of his time in his musical style, and since it was not until the 1920's that he was widely recognized, it is proper to discuss his works here.

He was born in Honfleur on the Normandy coast, but his family moved to Paris a few years later. Because he showed musical talent he was sent to the Conservatoire, but his real interest lay in the cafés of Montmartre where he played the piano and for which he composed sentimental ballads. Even from the beginning he showed a flair for novel musical ideas, and his first serious compositions reveal this originality. The *Gymnopédies* published in 1897 avoid all of the clichés of the time and strike a note of chasteness quite differ-

*According to Nicolas Slonimsky, "Pulcinella contains virtually no themes by Pergolesi (though they are attributed to Pergolesi in Stravinsky's sources)." See the Preface to *Baker's Biographical Dictionary of Musicians,* 5th Ed.

ent from the feverish music of the day. His *Three Sarabandes* for piano of the same year include some very interesting parallel ninth chords which were later to become an important feature of the styles of Debussy and Ravel. In some of his compositions of the next few years he used Gregorian modes as well as chords built in fourths, again anticipating musical idioms that would be extensively developed in the next twenty-five years.

In 1898 Satie "retired" to Arcueil, a suburb of Paris, and for the next twenty-seven years he earned a well-deserved reputation for eccentricity. He lived quietly, spending much of his time in cafés. He was known by a small group of musicians including Debussy, whose home he visited. Because he was unusually sensitive and erratic, friendship with him was precarious and often ended abruptly with some imagined affront.

During these years he wrote a number of piano pieces and gave them ridiculous titles, perhaps parodying the elaborately evocative titles Debussy sometimes gave to his compositions. Debussy called one of his preludes *La terrace des audiences au clair de lune*, while Satie used titles such as *Three Pieces in the Shape of a Pear* written after someone had criticized his music for having no "form," *Three Flabby Preludes for a Dog*, and *Dessicated Embryos*.

On the scores the performer is bombarded by directions far different from those used by other composers: "Play like a nightingale with a toothache"; "with astonishment"; "sheepishly"; "from the top of the teeth." Other jokes are found in the scores, such as a perfectly simple passage written in an extremely complicated notation, or popular tunes that are suddenly quoted. His fantastic sense of humor is also shown in the words which accompany some of these pieces. These are not meant to be recited during the playing of the piece—they are simply there. For example:

> This vast portion of the globe has only one inhabitant—a negro. He is so bored he is ready to die of laughter. The shade of the thousand-year-old trees shows it is 9:17 A.M. The toads are calling each other by their family names. In order to think better the negro holds his cerebellum with his right hand, with the fingers spread out. From a distance he resembles a distinguished physiologist. Four anonymous snakes fascinate him, hanging to the skirts of his uniform, which is rendered shapeless by sorrow and solitude combined. By the edge of the river an old mangrove tree

slowly bathes its roots, which are revoltingly dirty. This is not the hour propitious to lovers.[3]

Paradoxically, the real joke comes from the music, for it is often serious in tone. *Three Pieces in the Shape of a Pear*, for instance, are ingratiating, straightforward, and unpretentious. They suggest a mood of gentle melancholy and contain some unusual harmonic progressions. Strikingly absent are any of the usual characteristics of the time—rich Debussyan or Franckian harmonies, or sweetly sentimental tunes.

Satie would have been an interesting subject for psychoanalysis, for he was undeniably maladjusted. Perhaps his humor and his ridiculous titles were defenses for himself and his music, similar to the actions of a sensitive person who plays the clown in social situations to hide his insecurities.

This tendency to underplay the importance of his compositions reached its climax in the music he wrote in 1920 for the opening of an art gallery. Rollo Myers has described the occasion:

> The music was played by a little band of instruments consisting of a piano, three clarinets, and a trombone and was introduced . . . in the following terms: "We present for the first time, under the supervision of MM. Erik Satie and Darius Milhaud and directed by M. Delgrange, furnishing music to be played during the entr'actes. We beg you to take no notice of it and to behave during the entr'actes as if the music did not exist. This music . . . claims to make its contribution to life in the same way as a private conversation, a picture, or the chair on which you may or may not be seated. . . ."[4]

Unfortunately the audience disregarded these instructions and kept silent while the music was being played. This greatly annoyed Satie who went around urging people to talk and make a noise, since the music, which consisted of fragments of popular refrains from *Mignon* and the *Danse Macabre* and isolated phrases repeated over and over again, like the pattern of wallpaper, was meant to be nothing more than a background and was not intended to attract attention in any way.

This is a complete reversal of values when one considers the reverence with which many people listen to music. The contrast between this attitude and that of Wagner, for example, who didn't want to have his music performed except in a specially constructed temple, throws into relief the sharp differences between the nineteenth- and this early twentieth-century aesthetic. Cocteau in another of his aphorisms scorned the traditional point of view:

> *Pelléas* is another example of music to be listened to with one's hands. All music which has to be listened to through the hands is suspect. Wagner's is typically music which is listened to through the hands.[5]

Whether we like it or not, we must accept the fact that music that is "simply there," like wallpaper, is a part of the modern world. Today, in fact, we encounter such music at every turn—in supermarkets, department stores, restaurants, and factories—and millions of people "listen" to their radios while reading, doing housework, or driving. The role such music plays in modern life is not being defended here; it is merely being recognized as an unfortunate reality.

Most of Satie's pieces are short, but after World War I he wrote four extended compositions. By this time he had been "discovered" by the younger composers and he came to the attention of Diaghilev. The result of this meeting was the ballet *Parade.* It brought together four outstanding talents of the day: Cocteau, who provided the subject; Picasso, who designed the curtain, stage settings, and costumes; Massine, who created the choreography; and Satie. This was an important work in the history of the theater and ballet for it brought cubism to the stage for the first time. The costumes and settings of Picasso were like pieces of animated sculpture in which human traits were no more evident than they were in the pictures he was painting then. The large, angular costumes made it necessary to find a whole new vocabulary of the dance. Cocteau has given a synopsis of the "action":

> The Chinaman pulls out an egg from his pigtail, eats and digests it, finds it again in the toe of his shoe, spits fire, burns himself, stamps to put out the sparks, etc.

> The little girl mounts a race-horse, rides a bicycle, quivers like pictures on the screen, imitates Charlie Chaplin, chases a thief with a revolver, boxes, dances a rag-time, goes to sleep, is shipwrecked, rolls on the grass on an April morning, buys a Kodak, etc.

What of the music for *Parade?* Again we quote Cocteau:

> Satie's orchestra abjures the vague and the indistinct. It yields all their grace, without pedals. It is like an inspired village band.

It will open a door to those young composers who are a little wary of fine impressionist polyphonies. "I composed," said Satie modestly, "a background of certain noises which Cocteau considers indispensable in order to fix the atmosphere of his characters."

Satie wanted to employ a battery of noise makers, including compressed air, a dynamo, Morse apparatus, sirens, express train, airplane and propeller, and typewriters; but he settled for a conventional dance band.[6]

There is a great deal of the "wallpaper" quality in this music, evidenced by an inordinate repetition of the simplest figures. The music accompanying the first Manager (one of the leading roles in the ballet) consists of repetitions of this figure in rhythmic variants:

EXAMPLE 41[*]

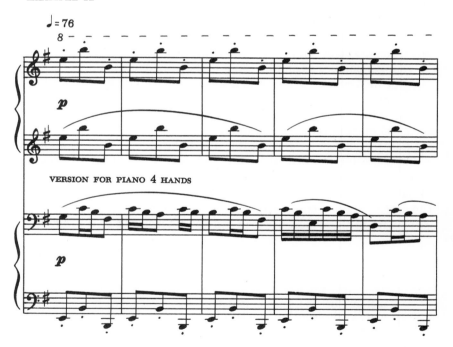

VERSION FOR PIANO 4 HANDS

*Permission for reprint granted by Rouart, Lerolle et Cie., Paris.

Later sections consist of pseudo-Chinese music, a "rag-time of the steamboat," and music-hall waltzes to accompany the acrobats.

Two later works, *Mercure* (1924) and *Relâche* (1924), again with the collaboration of Picasso and Massine, anticipate surrealism with their noticeable lack of connection between the action on the stage and the mood of the music. A surrealist movie, which is part of the ballet, is accompanied by music that alternates these two "themes," shown in Examples 42a and 42b.

In 1918 Satie wrote *Socrate*, a "symphonic drama," which many critics consider his most important work. A setting to music of fragments of three Platonic dialogues, the *Symposium, Phaedrus,* and *Phaedo* (the last having to do with the death of Socrates), it shows an unsuspected serious side of the composer. Four solo sopranos sing the words, accompanied by a small chamber orchestra consisting of

EXAMPLE 42a

EXAMPLE 42b

Pas trop vite

flute, oboe, English horn, clarinet, horn, trumpet, harp, kettle drums, and strings. The work is distinguished by its atmosphere of calm and gentle repose. The words are set exclusively to eighth and quarter notes in a kind of rhythmic recitative which avoids regularity and tunefulness.

Socrate is completely nondramatic in concept, for the words of Socrates are sung by one of the sopranos. The role of the orchestra is merely to accompany; it rarely takes part in the melodic line. A few characteristically neutral figures are shown in Examples 43a and 43b.

Socrate, according to Collaer in *La Musique Moderne* is the "masterpiece of its composer, and one of the capital works of contemporary music."[7] Other critics have been equally enthusiastic, but some listeners find an undeniable monotony in the work. The unvarying rhythms, the extreme continuity of the vocal line, the unrelieved vocal timbre, the repetitiousness of the accompaniment, the absence of high and low moments—all of these elements make it less

Example 43a

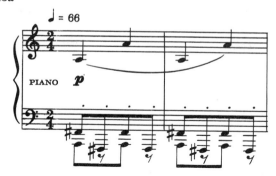

Example 43b

than a complete success. Of course one cannot argue with Satie for having written *Socrate* in this manner, for he wanted it to be pale, undramatic, and neutral. One can say, however, that these are qualities that are more successfully projected in shorter compositions.

The historical, as contrasted with the artistic, importance of the work is undeniable. *Socrate* is an extreme example of music dedicated to ideals that are totally different from Wagnerian-impressionist-romantic ideals. This is a work of cool objectivity and deliberate modesty in its means and effects—the values that Cocteau had encouraged. These values were to be increasingly important in the music written in the next decade.

LES SIX

Henri Collet, a French critic, published an article in 1920 entitled *The Russian Five and the French Six and Erik Satie.* In it he called

*Copyright 1920, renewed 1947 by Editions Max Eschig, Paris.

Paris After World War I / 117

attention to the music of a group of young composers who had joined together to present concerts of their compositions. The six were Darius Milhaud (b. 1892), Arthur Honegger (b. 1892), Francis Poulenc (b. 1899), Georges Auric (b. 1899), Louis Durey (b. 1888), and a young woman, Germaine Tailleferre (b. 1892). Even though they had been friends from their school days, they were not united by any group "program" or even by a similarity of style. Cocteau was their spokesman; and perhaps the only platform they shared was a negative one—to purge French music of nineteenth-century grandiloquence and impressionist fog. But each had his own idea as to how this should be done, and one rugged individualist, Arthur Honegger, was not sure that it should be done at all.

The general public, however, likes labels, and "Les Six" caught its fancy. No matter how different the composers were to become, they were never allowed to forget this youthful association, sometimes to their annoyance. Milhaud, many years later, described the creation of Les Six:

> Quite arbitrarily he (Collet) had chosen six names: Auric, Durey, Poulenc, Tailleferre, Honegger, and my own, merely because we knew one another, were good friends, and had figured on the same programmes; quite irrespective of our different temperaments and wholly dissimilar characters. Auric and Poulenc were partisans of Cocteau's ideas, Honegger derived from the German Romantics, and I from Mediterranean lyricism. I fundamentally disapproved of joint declarations of aesthetic doctrines, and felt them to be a drag, an unreasonable limitation on the artist's imagination, who must for each new work find different, often contradictory, means of expression. But it was useless to protest. Collet's article excited such world-wide interest that the "Group of Six" was launched and willy-nilly I formed part of it.[8]

For a short time the group was young and gay together and even collaborated on a joint work written on a libretto of Jean Cocteau called *Les Mariés de la Tour Eiffel*. Auric wrote the Overture, Milhaud the "Wedding March," Tailleferre the "Quadrille" and "Waltz of the Telegrams," Poulenc the music for a bathing-beauty scene, and Honegger the "Funeral March," the bass of which was the "Waltz" from *Faust*. The atmosphere of the ballet can be caught from this opening dialogue, all of which is spoken by two actors representing phonographs, who explain the accompanying pantomime:

PHONO 1	You are on the first platform of the Eiffel Tower.
PHONO 2	Look! An ostrich. She crosses the stage. She goes off. And here's the hunter. He's tracking the ostrich. He looks up. He sees something. He raises his gun. He fires.
PHONO 1	Heavens! A telegram! (A large blue telegram falls from above.)
PHONO 2	The shot wakes up the Manager of the Eiffel Tower. He appears.
PHONO 1	Hey mister: where do you think you are—hunting?
PHONO 2	I was trailing an ostrich. I thought I saw it on the cables of the Eiffel Tower.
PHONO 1	And so you kill me a telegram!
PHONO 2	I didn't mean to do it.
PHONO 1	End of the dialogue.
PHONO 2	Here comes the Photographer of the Eiffel Tower. He speaks. What is he saying?
PHONO 1	You haven't seen an ostrich around here anywhere, have you?
PHONO 2	I most certainly have! I'm trailing it right now!
PHONO 1	Well, it's like this: My camera's out of order. Usually when I say "Steady now, watch for the little bird"—a little bird comes out. This morning I said to a lady, "Watch for the little bird"—and out came an ostrich. So now I am looking for the ostrich in order to make it get back into the camera.[9]

SOME TYPICAL COMPOSITIONS

At the time of this common enterprise each of Les Six except Honegger went through a Cocteau-Satie phase. A few characteristic compositions will now be examined. Poulenc's *Mouvements perpétuels* is a good example. These are three unpretentious, amusing pieces for piano. The first starts with an innocent, almost folklike melody over a recurring bass. In the third bar the "shock" occurs. The right hand starts playing a melody involving an unexpected E natural. The important tritone relationship is involved and the effect is like seeing a nice little girl, dressed in her Sunday best, suddenly giving a large and sophisticated wink to her audience. All is not so innocent as appeared at first. Later these dissonances occur over the recurring bass:

EXAMPLE 44*

This use of dissonance is characteristic of Les Six, for the ninths are used not as a point of climax of emotion, but quietly, as an added color. This is, of course, a continuation of Debussy's attitude toward dissonance.

The second and third pieces of the set continue in the same mood of sophisticated play. The second is marked *indifférent* and the third has a music-hall flavor so popular at the time.

Milhaud's song cycle, *Catalogue de Fleurs*, is also a typical Les Six conception. These are musical settings of words that might have come out of a seed catalog. For instance, the words to the second song read, "Begonia Aurora, double blossom, apricot mixed with coral, very pretty, rare and unusual." There is something impertinent about setting words like these to music when one remembers the hundreds of "flower" poems set by the romantic composers, such as *"Du bist wie eine Blume"* ("Thou art like a flower"). The romantic was always personal, but the young composers in question did their best to stay away from personal involvement in their music.

Milhaud's and Cocteau's ballet, *Le Boeuf sur le Toit, (The Ox on the Roof)* perfectly embodies the spirit of the twenties. It was an immediate success and it "typed" the composer more than any other of his works, a fact that he regrets to this day. In his autobiography, he summarizes the action of the ballet:

> The setting is in a bar in America during Prohibition. The various characters were highly typical: A Boxer, a Negro Dwarf, a Lady of Fashion, a Red-headed Woman dressed as a man, a Bookmaker, a Gentleman in evening clothes. The barman, with a face like

*Permission for reprint granted by J. W. Chester, London.

Antinous, offers everyone cocktails. After a few incidents and various dances, a Policeman enters, whereupon the scene is immediately transformed into a milk-bar. The clients play a rustic scene and dance a pastorale as they sip glasses of milk. The Barman switches on a big fan which decapitates the Policeman. The Redheaded Woman executes a dance with the Policeman's head, ending up standing on her hands like the Salome in Rouen Cathedral. One by one the customers drift away, and the Barman presents an enormous bill to the resuscitated Policeman.[10]

As might be expected, the music of Milhaud is anything but "appropriate" to this outrageous libretto, for it consists exclusively of South American popular music he had learned to like in Brazil: tangos, rhumbas, sambas, street marches, and fados. The trite tonal melodies are usually accompanied by instruments playing in other keys, but these sounds do not give the impression of a complex chord, for the ear separates the planes of the harmony. The effect is as if one's hearing were out of focus, for it is impossible to form a single, clear sound image (see Example 45). Here the top voice is in E-flat, the second, doubling the melody, in G, with the accompaniment also in these two keys.

EXAMPLE 45*

Animé

*Copyright 1950 by Editions Max Eschig, Paris.

VERSION FOR VIOLIN AND PIANO

Le Boeuf sur le Toit fully embodies Cocteau's recommendations. It is full of fun and irreverence and is close to the music of cafés, music halls, and the streets.

SUGGESTED READINGS

There are many interesting memoirs that give insights into the artistic world of Paris during the twenties. Recommended to all students of the period are: *The Autobiography of Alice B. Toklas,* Gertrude Stein

(New York, 1933); *Passport to Paris,* Vernon Duke (Boston, 1955); and *Bad Boy of Music,* George Antheil (Garden City, N.Y., 1945).

    Erik Satie by Rollo Myers (London, 1948) is the best treatment of the composer's life and music in English. *The Banquet Years* by Roger Shattuck (New York, 1958) contains an illuminating chapter on Satie. *Jean Cocteau* by Margaret Crossland (New York, 1956) surveys the life and works of this versatile artist.

CHAPTER VIII

LES TROIS

Half artist and half anchorite, part siren and part Socrates

PERCY MACKAY: *France*

No greater mistake could be made than to believe that Cocteau's ideals dominated Les Six throughout their creative lives. We have already said that Honegger did not enter this Cocteau-Satie phase at all, and for the others it was merely a passing one. Thus it would be erroneous to think of Milhaud or Poulenc as an eternal *enfant terrible.*

The group had no formal or dramatic break-up, for it was too informal an association for that. In the following years the young composers followed their individual destinies and developed their personal styles of composition, reassembling occasionally for reasons of sentiment or publicity. Durey retired to the country and from music; Mlle. Tailleferre wrote little of lasting importance; Auric became one of the most successful composers of music for motion pictures and eventually achieved international fame with his waltz, *Moulin Rouge.*

The remaining three, Milhaud, Honegger, and Poulenc, became France's leading composers of the second quarter of the century. Although their music was by no means similar—Milhaud's description of their essential characteristics (cited in the previous chapter) makes this clear—they carried forward the ideals of order, clarity, and charm always associated with their country. Their careers and music will be the subject of this chapter.

125

MILHAUD, 1892-

Down with Wagner!   DARIUS MILHAUD

"I am a Frenchman from Provence and of the Jewish faith." This is the opening sentence of Milhaud's autobiography *Notes Without Music*. Its directness and straightforward quality reflect the man and his music.

He was born in Aix-en-Provence, a charming old city in the south of France. His boyhood as reported in the autobiography seems to have been idyllic, for his parents were cultured, well off, and solicitous of his education and well being.

He began to study the violin at the age of seven, but it was not until he was seventeen and had completed his general education that he went to Paris to enter the Conservatory. Paris in 1909 was an exciting place for a student from the provinces. Milhaud immersed himself in the musical world, attending the ballet and opera and becoming acquainted with the new works of Debussy, Ravel, and Stravinsky. He lost no time in making allegiances. He was attracted to the music of Chabrier, Satie, and Roussel, and was repelled by Brahms and Wagner.

By 1912 he had given up the idea of becoming a violinist in order to concentrate on composition. His teachers were Widor and Gédalge, excellent disciplinarians, who sensed that they were working with an unusually gifted student. At the outbreak of World War I in 1914, Milhaud, whose health had never been robust, was not called to serve. Instead, he went to Brazil as the secretary of the French ambassador, Paul Claudel, an extraordinary diplomat, poet, dramatist, and man of letters. The association with Claudel was to result in some of Milhaud's most significant compositions. However, the most important musical experience of this stay in South America was his exposure to the popular music there, which made a lasting impression on him.

Returning to Paris after the war by way of the United States, he discovered jazz, which was also to influence his music. Milhaud has written of his pleasure in going to night clubs in Harlem:

> The music I heard was absolutely different from anything I had ever heard before, and was a revelation to me. Against the beat of the drums the melodic lines criss-crossed in a breathless pat-

tern of broken and twisted rhythms.... Its effect on me was so overwhelming that I could not tear myself away.[1]

The jazz records he purchased in Harlem were his most precious travel souvenirs.

The role Milhaud played in the twenties as a member of Les Six has already been described. The following years were full of excitement and growing achievement. Although increasingly handicapped by arthritis, he made extensive tours of Europe and the United States to conduct his works. He usually spent summers at his home in Provence where he continued his indefatigable composing.

World War II changed the pattern of his life. Escaping the German occupation of France, he came to the United States with his wife and son and spent the war years teaching at Mills College in Oakland, California. As soon as the war was over, however, the travelling resumed; this included teaching at Mills College and the Paris Conservatory during alternate years, and teaching at the Aspen Music School in Colorado during summers.

MILHAUD'S COMPOSITIONS

Milhaud is one of the most prolific contemporary composers. In 1952, at the age of sixty, he completed his Opus 300 and during the next four years he added fifty additional titles—an average of one composition a month. By this time he had written thirteen operas, thirteen ballets, incidental music to thirty-five plays and twenty films, twenty-eight choral works, thirty works for orchestra (symphonies, suites, etc.), twenty-four concertos for various instruments (including one for marimba and one for vibraphone), ten works for voice and orchestra, eighteen string quartets and many sonatas for piano and various instruments, a setting of the Sacred Service for synagogues, about two hundred songs with piano, and vocal duets and quartets.

This stream of music shows great diversity in dimension and quality and therefore a comprehensive impression of it is difficult to obtain, not only because of its sheer quantity, but also because some of the larger compositions are rarely performed while some of the less important have become popular through recordings and frequent performances.

Most of Milhaud's compositions have been commissioned and the various functions they fulfill account for their dimensions and characteristics. When large, serious operas were called for he wrote *Christophe Colomb* (1928), *Maximilien* (1930), and *Bolivar* (1943). When asked to write a work commemorating the 3,000th anniversary of the founding of Jerusalem, he wrote the pageant-opera *David* (1954). The popularity of ballet in Paris during the twenties brought forth *Le Boeuf sur le Toit* already discussed, and three other jaunty, irreverent scores, *Le Train Bleu* (1923), *La Création du Monde* (1923), and *Salade* (1924). Among the compositions written for theatrical production are *Protée* (1913), a mythological farce; *Les Euménides* (1922), an adaptation of the classical Greek tragedy; *L'Annonce faite à Marie* (1932) a devout Catholic play, and incidental music for a fireworks spectacle. Many of the absolute works are the result of requests from soloists, chamber music ensembles, orchestras, or institutions that desired a commemorative piece. These multifarious works elude style-period classification, for Milhaud is not the type of composer who follows a steady line of evolution. Three contrasting compositions will now be discussed.

Les Choëphores (1915) is the incidental music written for Paul Claudel's translation of Aeschylus' play. Although written during the First World War when the composer was still in his early twenties, it must be counted among his important large-scale works. The first section, the "Funereal Vociferation," starts as shown in Example 46. This is a clear-cut use of two keys simultaneously, and such *bitonality*, or *polytonality* as it is called when several keys are involved, became one of Milhaud's favorite modes of expression.

The two sections "Présages" and "Exhortation" are very exciting. Here Milhaud dispenses with musical sounds and writes rhythmic word-settings for the chorus accompanied by a large battery of percussion instruments. In the preface to the score he tells why he abandoned singing at this point:

> Two scenes are to be found which create a difficult problem for the composer: they are savage, cannibal, as it were. The lyrical element in these scenes is not musical. How was I to set to music this hurricane? I finally decided to make use of a measured speech, divided into bars, and conducted as if it were sung.[2]

The result is as striking and startling as a savage chant.

EXAMPLE 46*

La Création du Monde (1923), like *The Rite of Spring,* was based on primitive legends, but the differences in conception and production between the two ballets clearly show how the postwar aesthetic differed from that of prewar days. In order to express the savagery and mystery of the primeval forest Stravinsky wrote a score of tremendous difficulty that called for an orchestra of more than one

*Permission for reprint granted by Heugel & Cie., Paris.

hundred players. Milhaud, writing ten years later, used a seventeen-piece jazz band. In his autobiography he writes:

> At last I had the opportunity I had been waiting for to use those elements of jazz to which I had devoted so much study. I adopted the same orchestra as used in Harlem, seventeen solo instruments, and I made wholesale use of the jazz style to convey a purely classical feeling.[3]

The settings and costumes for Stravinsky's ballet were semirealistic and aimed at giving an illusion of primitive times. Léger's colorful and childlike settings and costumes for *La Création du Monde* made no more attempt to depict the African forest realistically than Milhaud's music did to sound authentically or evocatively primitive. The earlier ballet was for the theatre of illusion, the later for the theatre of stylization—another way of describing the difference between late romantic and early twentieth-century art.

The introduction starts with a neutral Satie-like figure in the piano and strings, playing an accompaniment to a mournful melody played on the E-flat saxophone. There are quiet, syncopated "breaks" by the trumpets and other instruments. The harmonic planes are often rich in contrast when various groups of instruments enter in keys other than that of the melody. The polytonality in this piece is always of this nature, for one hears a principal key against which other keys appear. There is no feeling of equality among them; the effect is of an enrichment of one basic key. The basic key is D minor, frequently colored with the major third, F-sharp.

The first dance is fuguelike with this jazz theme as subject:

EXAMPLE 47*

DOUBLE BASS

*Copyright 1929, renewed 1957 by Editions Max Eschig, Paris.

This shows how well Milhaud had listened to jazz in Harlem. The piano is treated as a rhythm instrument.

The second dance starts with a slow chorale, followed by a section that bears a startling resemblance to a Gershwin melody:

EXAMPLE 48

The third features a three-note figure against a background of four:

EXAMPLE 49

The "Gershwin" melody returns in strings.

The last section is very close to jazz, for the solo instruments play improvised-like flourishes over a barbershop chord progression (F#, G#⁷, C#⁷, F#⁷) played by the rhythm section. The atmosphere becomes frenetic as the piece moves with convulsive rhythms. Themes from earlier sections are recalled and the work ends with a quiet coda in which Example 48 is played by the oboe with an obbligato in the horn. The final cadence is appropriate (see Example 50). This use of jazz was not unnoticed by the critics. Milhaud summarizes their reaction:

> The critics decreed that my music was frivolous and more suitable for a restaurant or a dance hall than for the concert hall. Ten

EXAMPLE 50

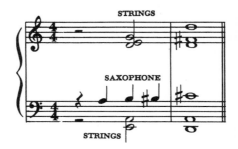

years later the self-same critics were discussing the philosophy of jazz and learnedly demonstrating that *La Création du Monde* was the best of my works.[4]

Milhaud's Symphony #1 was started in 1939 when the composer was forty-seven. When it is compared with his early works, however, one finds little difference in style, for it contains the elements that have always characterized his works—exuberance; folk-like dance rhythms; noisy, polytonal processional sections; quiet pastorals; and sweetness and charm.

The order of the movements is not the usual one for symphonies, for it opens with a pastorale, featuring the flutes. The rhythmic "strumming" in the strings suggests a country dance. The movement is relaxed and amiable, with gracefully flowing melodic lines.

The second movement is loud and brassy with jagged melodic lines and dissonant polytonal chords. In the middle there is a *fugato*.

The third movement starts with a chorale played by wind instruments, but soon a style reminiscent of the "blues" section in *La Création du Monde* is established. Two contrasting themes, a noisy and energetic polytonal march and a rhythmic folk dance, are contrasted in the last movement.

Although this symphony was written during the darkest days of World War II, it does not in any way reflect the anguish he felt on leaving France or the problems he faced in adjusting to life in a new country. Regardless of where he might be or his frame of mind, Milhaud's music usually reflects Mediterranean lyricism and exuberance.

STYLE CHARACTERISTICS

While most of the older composers of twentieth-century music (Debussy, Schoenberg, and Stravinsky) gradually worked their way free
from nineteenth-century music in a process that can be traced from
work to work, Milhaud began to compose at a time when the new
resources were at hand. His earliest compositions are as dissonant as
his latest, and because he has never been an adherent of any particular *ism* (expressionism, primitivism, neoclassicism), he has moved
freely from one idiom to another.

Polytonality is the style characteristic most commonly associated with Milhaud. He was not the first to write music progressing in
two or more keys simultaneously, for Bartók, Stravinsky, Szymanow-
ski (the Polish composer), and others had also used this idiom. Milhaud, however, made systematic studies of the effects of combining
keys and made this device an important feature of his compositions.
Examples have already been cited in the works discussed but none
is as striking as that found in the fourth of his five short symphonies
written during the 1920's. These are not symphonies in the usual
sense, for they are one-movement pieces for various chamber-music
combinations. The Fourth Symphony is for ten solo strings, and the
last movement is a ten-voice canon with two subjects. Each part enters in one of five different keys.

The concept of a musical texture consisting of several planes
of harmony underlies much of Milhaud's music. This manner of writing is often polytonal, for the planes may be differentiated by key, but
there are many other possibilities. For instance, in *Les Euménides*
Milhaud combines four *ostinatos* (each note thickened with a dissonant chord) of different overlapping lengths, with rhythmic figures
and a melodic line.

The combination of so many different factors makes for an
extraordinary complexity and thickness of texture, usually alleviated
by clear orchestration. Such passages have tremendous vitality, but
occasionally, when the individual parts cannot be differentiated, tur-
gidity results. An example of the latter situation is the joint performance of his fourteenth and fifteenth quartets. They were written to be
played separately or together, and played separately they sound all
right. Together they affect most listeners as being a jumble.

Milhaud does not always use such a complex style. His many compositions inspired by folk or popular music are simple and direct. Among his best-known pieces of this type are the *Suite Provençale* (1936) and the *Suite Française* (1944), two compositions for orchestra. He did not limit himself to French folk music, as some of the following titles indicate: *Saudades do Brazil* (1920), *Le Bal Martiniquais* (1944), *Carnival at New Orleans* (1947), and *Kentuckiana* (1948). In these compositions he retains the folk melodies, adding a pungent harmonization and a loud, brassy orchestration.

His rhythms are usually regular but marked with strong syncopations. One of his favorite rhythmic devices is to group a series of eighth notes in irregular patterns.

EXAMPLE 51

Milhaud is a composer with an excellent technique and a practical attitude toward his art. He is neither an introspective poet waiting for inspiration to move him to write profound works nor a philosopher-theorist concerned with aesthetic problems. He is like a versatile architect who designs a factory or an embassy, a church or a stadium, according to the wishes of his clients. Such an architect keeps abreast of his times, employing appropriate new materials and methods of construction. His creative personality is apparent in everything he does, not through the exploitation of personal idiosyncracies, but through the good taste, restraint, and efficiency that mark all of his works.

HONEGGER, 1892-1955

My desire and my endeavor have always been to write music which would be noticed by the large masses of listeners and which would, at the same time, be sufficiently devoid of banalities to interest music lovers.

ARTHUR HONEGGER

Honegger should never have been included with Les Six for he had little in common with the other composers of the group. He was not even French (although born in Le Havre where his Swiss father was a coffee importer), and he received his early musical training in Zurich where the training was Germanic. When he enrolled at the Paris Conservatory in 1913 his musical gods were Bach, Wagner, Strauss, and Reger—scarcely the idols of his friend Darius Milhaud, whose battle cry was "Down with Wagner!"

Honegger's experiences as a composer were different from those of his young friends in that his compositions met with approval instead of the hisses and riots that greeted Milhaud's premieres. He continued to write program music at a time when the other members of Les Six felt that tone poems were hopelessly out of date. For example, his piece for orchestra called *Pacific 231* (1923), is a vivid description of a train starting, accelerating, and stopping. Although the subject comes from the mechanized twentieth century (as the futurists recommended) and a very dissonant style is employed, it is still in the tradition of descriptive music. Because the piece had a firm structure, being a series of figurations over a chorale-like set of chords, it could also be easily enjoyed by the "large masses as well as by music lovers."

By the mid-twenties Honegger was recognized as one of the foremost composers of his generation. He settled in Paris and lived the life of a twentieth-century composer, writing free and commissioned works for movies, plays, and radio productions, teaching composition, conducting his own works, and writing criticism and essays on music.

In this last role he wrote a very interesting book, *Je Suis Compositeur* (1951), in which he not only states his creed as a composer but also expresses his outlook for the future of music. He clearly states the differences between his attitude and that of some of his colleagues, particularly those who followed Satie and renounced the resources of romantic music in favor of a more austere language. As for himself:

> I am neither a polytonalist, atonalist, nor dodecaphonist. My great model is J. S. Bach. I do not attempt, as do certain anti-impressionists, to return to simple harmony.[5]

Honegger disapproves of composers who feel that they must adopt a different style in each new work, and remain in a state of constant revolution.

He is frankly bitter about the lack of interest in new music at the mid-century:

The profession of composer has the peculiarity of being an activity and preoccupation of a man who strives to make a product which no one wishes.[6]

He believes that while more concerts are given now than ever before, less music is heard because only the same few classics are repeated continually. Furthermore, he accuses the audience of being more interested in virtuoso soloists and conductors than in the music:

The most important attribute of a composer is that he be dead.

Honegger goes even further in writing:

I sincerely believe that, in a few years, the art of music such as we know it will no longer exist. It will disappear along with the other arts, but no doubt more rapidly. Finally, I believe that we are living in the last moments of our civilization; inevitably these last moments are miserable. They will become more so.[7]

It is not often we hear such gloomy views from a widely respected, honored, and successful man. Perhaps Honegger's experiences during the war (he remained in Paris) and declining health account for them. Perhaps he came to doubt the possibility of writing for the masses as well as the connoisseur. In any event, for some reason his book reflects a pessimistic attitude rarely expressed openly, even if felt by many in this age of anxiety.

HONEGGER'S COMPOSITIONS

Honegger wrote approximately two hundred works in a great variety of forms and media. Perhaps the best known are his "big machines," written for narrator, chorus, soloists, and orchestra: *King David* (1921), *Jeanne d'Arc au Bûcher* (1935), and *La Danse des Morts* (1938). There is an austere opera on Cocteau's version of *Antigone* (1927). He wrote five symphonies between 1930 and 1951 and symphonic poems such as *Pastorale d'Été* (1920), *Horace Victorieux* (1920), and *Pacific 231* (1923). The charming Concertino for piano and orchestra (1924) pays its tribute to jazz. In addition, he wrote a great deal of piano music, chamber music, many songs, and background music for films and plays.

King David was Honegger's first important work and its success did much to establish his reputation as a composer. He wrote it originally as incidental music for a Biblical drama produced in Switzerland in 1921, and a few years later it was recast so that it could be performed as an oratorio, with a narrator taking the place of the actors. In this form it has been very popular and continues to be performed widely.

As given now, the work is divided into three parts. The first part is concerned with David as a young shepherd, his battle with Goliath, and his conflict with Saul. It consists of fourteen musical numbers each separated by the words of the narrator. This makes for a rather fragmentary style since many of the music sections are short. Furthermore, there is a surprising change of musical style from number to number.

King David begins with an orchestral introduction in which the Jewish-Oriental setting is suggested by an oboe melody rich in augmented seconds. Immediately some of the style traits of the composer are evident, such as the dissonant pedals, chords in fourths, and the clear differentiation between the orchestral choirs. The second piece, David's shepherd song, is in folksong style, with dissonant counterpart in the violins. The third section, a psalm sung by the chorus in unison is unmistakably in Bach style, with its clear diatonicism, strong rhythms, and bright trumpets.

Simple, lyrical solos alternate with theatrical, polytonal fanfares in the following sections. Battle scenes of strong dissonance flank Jewish songs of mourning. One of the most effective numbers of the first part is the "Incantation of the Witch of Endor." "The March of the Phillistines" that follows shows Honegger's talent for original orchestral timbres.

The second part consists of but two extended numbers, a festive song and the "Dance before the Ark," celebrating the crowning of David as king of the Jews. The contrary motion of the outer voices in the opening chorus is characteristic of the composer. This section is a huge canvas that Honegger skillfully fills with large musical gestures, such as the unison passages between the orchestra and chorus, simple, four-square rhythmic patterns, figures rising chromatically to points of climax, and responsorial singing between men and women. The middle section, in triple meter, is the dance of King David, which reaches a strong climax through repetitions of rhythmic figures. A soprano solo, the voice of an angel, predicts the birth of Solomon.

The section closes with an alleluia, one of Honegger's happiest inspirations.

EXAMPLE 52*

This chorus is somewhat Bach-like, but moves freely from one key to another.

Part III is concerned with events of David's maturity and death; here one finds more large numbers alternating with quiet solos. Particularly striking are the songs of penitence (Numbers 19 and 20), the instrumental march of the Israelites, and the psalm (Number 25) in which the violence of the orchestra reminds one of *Le Sacre*. The work ends on a note of great amplitude and spaciousness. The magnificent alleluia that closed Part II reappears, this time in combination with a chorale melody. Even if the Protestant melody is anachronistic in this scene of Jewish splendor, the effect is undeniably powerful.

Honegger has written with disarming frankness about *King David*, admitting that there are too many short pieces in the first part. He comments on hearing a performance:

> I find myself getting bored at Number 6, and I start thinking about Number 8 because I am curious to see if it is going to be played much too fast again this time. At the *Chorus of the Prophets* and at the *Camp of the Israelites* I doze off. I awake at the words, "The Eternal is my light." The *Dance before the Arc*, in spite of certain details, gives me a sort of satisfaction for the development contains a good progression. In the third part, my preference goes to the *Chorus of Penitence*. Naïvely and with pride, I must confess that the combination of the *Chorale* with the *Alleluia* at the end seems to me to realize something of what I hoped.[8]

Honegger's Symphony #5 is an example of his mature, serious style. It was written after World War II and received its first performance in 1952 by the Boston Symphony Orchestra. This work is subtitled *di tre re* (of three D's), referring to the note *d* on which each movement ends.

The first movement opens immediately with a statement of the main theme played by the whole orchestra, except for the horns, moving in solemn, thickly dissonant chords. Because the passage is characteristic of the composer, it is worthy of investigation in some detail. It consists of two melodic lines in contrary motion:

EXAMPLE 53*

The relation of the two voices is a further example of Honegger's penchant for contrary motion. Each note of this two-voice theme is harmonized with a triad, built down from the upper note serving as the fifth of the chord, and up from the bass serving as a root, resulting in a double series of parallel polychords.

After this presentation in the full orchestra, the same material is heard in trumpets and trombones until a second, contrasting theme enters stealthily in the bass clarinet.

*Permission for reprint granted by Editions Salabert, Paris.

EXAMPLE 54

BASS CLARINET

The new theme is treated contrapuntally and rises throughout the
orchestra until the first theme recurs fortissimo. This time a new
element is added to the polychords—shrill, protesting figures in the
trumpets.

　　After a climax, the first theme complex returns in the strings,
but pianissimo against gentle figuration in the woodwinds. The movement ends somberly with an occasional reference to the second theme.
It ends on the note *d*, low in the strings.

　　The second movement, an allegretto, contrasts with the first in
mood and tempo. It, too, has a two-voiced theme presented by the
violins and clarinets.

EXAMPLE 55

CLARINET

VIOLINS

The nine-measure structure of the phrase is noteworthy, for it is
maintained for some time, each succeeding nine bars consisting of a
contrapuntal derivative of the violin theme. Thus, in Bars 10-19 the
retrograde inversion is heard in the bassoon; in Bars 20-29 the inversion is heard in the flutes, and in Bars 30-39 the retrograde version is
given to the oboes and English horn. This material is interrupted by
woodwind passages punctuated with chords in the strings at irregular

intervals, but fragments of the main theme in its various forms are seldom absent.

A short and serious adagio interrupts the scherzo. When the allegretto resumes, the clarinet and violas present the first theme and its inversion in one-measure fragments. The adagio returns, but this time the allegretto theme appears simultaneously. A climax in volume and excitement occurs with material resembling that of the first movement, treated with the triad harmonization and in contrary motion. The movement ends quietly on a low *d* after further contrapuntal developments.

The third movement is bustling and busy, suggesting the energy and mechanization of the modern world. It is a type of piece not uncommon in the music of Honegger and his contemporaries. Stravinsky and Prokofiev also are fond of writing similar passages of reiterated eighth notes with unexpected and unpredictable accents.

The most prominent theme of this movement is:

EXAMPLE 56

HORNS, BASSOONS

Note the augmented fourth; it still makes its effect.

In moments of climax, polychords reminiscent of the first movement are heard. Various fragments of the basic theme appear and a tremendous amount of energy is created by the perpetual motion of the strings. Suddenly a diatonic theme is heard in dialogue between two horns. Later it appears in canon between the strings and horn, recalling the last movement of the Franck Sonata for violin and piano.

But the movement does not end in this positive mood. The equivocal, tonally ambiguous main theme of the movement returns, the motion slackens, and the basses sink to low *d* for the final notes.

This is a far cry from the "victory after difficulty" pattern that Beethoven established and so many composers of the romantic era followed. The Symphony *di tre re* is a statement that parallels the disillusioned, pessimistic views expressed in the composer's book.

STYLE CHARACTERISTICS

Honegger was not a revolutionary composer who ruthlessly cast aside the ideals and vocabulary of late nineteenth-century music. Neither was he a composer who exploited any single facet of the newer developments. His credo, cited earlier, defines his position. When it served his expressive purpose Honegger used polytonality, chords in fourths, dissonant counterpoint, and complex rhythms. At the other times he wrote with great simplicity.

However, there are several characteristics that are often found in his music. One is his habit of changing the order of the first- and second-theme groups in the recapitulation of sonata-form movements, producing an "arch" structure:

DEVELOPMENT

SECOND THEME   SECOND THEME

FIRST THEME   FIRST THEME

He is also fond of writing outer voices in contrary motion—a characteristic found so often that it is almost a mannerism; examples have been cited from *King David* and the Symphony *di tre re*. Along with other composers of the time, Honegger makes frequent use of ostinato figures that are in dissonant relationship to the rest of the material. This is one of his favorite ways of building a climax. Examples can be found in the opening and the "Porcus" chorus of *Jeanne d'Arc au Bûcher;* and in the "Procession," "Dance before the Arc," the end of "Alleluia," and "Psalm of Mourning" from *King David*. In purely instrumental works, stirring pedal passages occur in the coda of the first movement of the First String Quartet, and in the first, second, and fourth pieces of *Sept Pièces Brèves* for piano.

Many of Honegger's scores are characterized by the expression of powerful, driving energy. *Pacific 231, Rugby*, and *Horace Victorieux* are examples of this aspect of his style. The effect is often gained by using constantly repeated eighth notes in bustling, clashing counterpoint.

Many twentieth-century composers avoid large gestures and big, stirring effects. Not Honegger. He has written some of the most rousing compositions of the time.

POULENC, 1899-

I would by far prefer to write something mediocre with full consciousness and lucidity, than to give birth to a masterpiece among masterpieces in a state of trance and agitation. PAUL VALÉRY

Francis Poulenc is the member of Les Six who has been most faithful to the ideals of Cocteau and Satie. To amuse, to charm, to be gauche in a well-mannered way, to please—these seem to be his aims.

He is thoroughly Parisian, having been born in Paris just before the turn of the century to a family that was artistic, musical, and affluent. His mother was a fine pianist and Francis began lessons at the age of five. Eventually he became an excellent pianist after working with Ricardo Viñes, a friend of Debussy and Ravel who first performed much of their piano music. While still in his teens Poulenc met Satie, who left a permanent mark on his musical ideals. When he was eighteen he wrote *Rapsodie nègre* for baritone, string quartet, flute and clarinet. Its light-hearted irreverence and music-hall atmosphere established his right to be a charter member of Les Six when the group was named a few years later.

Poulenc has spent most of his life in Paris, except for concert tours that included several trips to the United States after World War II. Although he served briefly in both world wars, active duty was ruled out in World War I because of his youth, and in World War II because of his age. The humor and uncomplicated, direct expression of his music reflect a life that seems to have been singularly untroubled. As a result, there is little difference in style between Poulenc's early and later works, or between his religious and secular compositions.

POULENC'S COMPOSITIONS

Poulenc's musical interests are primarily lyric, and of his compositions those for voice are certainly his most important. These include almost 150 songs with piano accompaniment, and many choral works both with and without accompaniment. Among the choral works are a setting of the Mass (1937), a Stabat Mater (1950), and secular works. He has written over twenty compositions for piano as well as a sonata for two pianos, one for violin and piano, concertos for piano, for organ, and for two pianos. Poulenc has written no large formal works for orchestra, but the music he wrote for a Diaghilev-inspired ballet, *Les Biches* (1923), was very successful. Two operas, *Les Mamelles de Tirésias* (1944) and *Dialogues des Carmélites* (1957), are among his larger works.

The early set of songs, *Cocardes* (1919) written to poems by Cocteau, perfectly embodies the poet's aphorisms. These are songs that suggest Paris streets—the accompaniment, consisting of cornet, violin, bass drum, and trombone, resembles the little street bands that still play there. There is no old-fashioned sentiment here. On the contrary the words follow each other in free association in the manner of Gertrude Stein, while the music proceeds with childish simplicity, with an occasional, planned *gaucherie*. However, not all of Poulenc's songs are in this vein. The cycle *Tel Jour, telle Nuit* (1937) written to poems of Paul Éluard, celebrates the quiet pleasures of life with sincerity and directness. The melody of the first song, *Bonne Journée*, moves in a calm and beautiful line over the simplest of accompaniment figures, reaching its climax only at the end. There are no dissonances, but there are unprepared modulations. The other songs in the cycle continue this mood of quiet simplicity. Not all twentieth-century music is difficult!

Poulenc's two operas differ strikingly from each other. *Les Mamelles de Tirésias* (1944) is a surrealistic farce. The mood is gay, and uproarious people changing from one sex to the other, babies being born in incubators, duels, and fortune telling are all reflected in the music. The approach is satirical with innumerable allusions to well-known composers and to old-fashioned popular music. It is a witty and clever opera with the style of the music perfectly matched to the libretto.

Les Dialogues des Carmélites is another matter. Here the drama is intensely serious without relief. The story is set in eighteenth-century France, during the revolution. It is concerned with the spiritual development of Blanche, daughter of an aristocrat, who becomes a Carmelite nun and chooses death by the guillotine with her sister nuns rather than return to the world.

The opera is divided into three acts, each consisting of four scenes. Most of the action takes place inside the convent with each scene showing Blanche in some phase of her vocation. There is little dramatic conflict, and only in the final scene in which the nuns are guillotined before the mob at the Place de la Victoire is there any opportunity for scenic display.

Musically, each scene is an entity in itself, although a few motives recur throughout the work. As in most French operas, the words of the libretto are treated with great respect. They are set simply and directly without the rhythmic distortion sometimes found in Italian opera, and the orchestra never threatens their intelligibility as is frequently the case in German opera. Except for a few religious choruses for the nuns, logically introduced as part of the story, the opera progresses in solo passages which vary from a recitative to an arioso style.

The lack of dramatic impetus and the monotony that results from a predominantly female cast prevents *Dialogues des Carmélites* from being a complete success. Poulenc's gifts are eminently better suited to surrealistic farce than to psychological drama. Perhaps his place in twentieth-century music will be comparable to that held by Raoul Dufy, who avoided all complications of execution in his breezy paintings and presented absolutely no difficulties to his viewers. The ebullient charm of his pictures added a welcome element of playfulness to a world beset with problems—a contribution one thinks of as being typically French.

SUGGESTED READINGS

Milhaud's autobiography *Notes Without Music* (London, 1952) is highly recommended for the insights it gives into the musical world up to World War II. The useful *Catalogue of the Works of Milhaud* by Georges Beck was published in 1949 with a supplement in 1956 by Heugel in Paris. Humphrey Searle (*op. cit.*) devotes a chapter to "Milhaud and polytonality" in *Twentieth Century Counterpoint* (New York, 1954).

Honegger's book of essays *Je suis Compositeur* (Paris, 1951) has not been translated. There is no full-scale study in English. Landowski's *Honegger* (Paris, n.d.) contains many interesting photographs.

An authoritative biography of Poulenc is Henri Hell's *Francis Poulenc* (London, 1959).

	France	Germany & Austria	Other Countries	Other Arts, Events
1915	Milhaud: *Les Choëphores* Debussy: *Etudes*		Falla: *El Amor brujo* Prokofiev: *Chout* Ives: *Concord Sonata*	T. S. Eliot: *The Love Song of J. Alfred Prufrock* Kafka: *Metamorphosis* Picasso: Classic Period Einstein: General Theory of Relativity
1916	Debussy: Sonate for Flute, Viola, Harp		Bloch: *Schelomo* Ives: Symphony #4 Prokofiev: *Scythian Suite* Holst: *The Planets*	Kaiser: *From Morn Til Midnight* Joyce: *A Portrait of an Artist as a Young Man* Dadaism invented
1917	Satie: *Parade* Stravinsky: *Renard* Ravel: *Le Tombeau de Couperin* Debussy: Sonata for Violin and Piano Poulenc: *Rapsodie nègre* Honegger: String Quartet #1		Prokofiev: *Classical Symphony*	Apollinaire: *Les Mamelles de Tirésias* Word surrealism invented Term expressionism defined Kokoschka: *Self Portrait* Bolshevik revolution in Russia U.S. enters World War I
1918	Stravinsky: *L'Histoire du Soldat* Poulenc: *Mouvements Perpétuelles* Stravinsky: *Ragtime*			Zurich: Dada Manifesto Cocteau: *Coq et Harlequin* Spengler: *The Decline of the West*
1919	Stravinsky: *Pulcinella* Milhaud: *Le Boeuf sur le toit* Milhaud: *Protée* Poulenc: *Cocardes* Satie: *Socrate*	Strauss: *Die Frau ohne Schatten*	Bartók: *The Miraculous Mandarin* Prokofiev: *The Love for Three Oranges* Falla: *The Three Cornered Hat*	Gide: *La Symphonie Pastorale* Kafka: *In the Penal Colony* Bauhaus founded Treaty of Versailles

	France	Germany & Austria	Other Countries	Other Arts, Events
1920	Ravel: *La Valse* Honegger: *Pastorale d'été* Les Six named			Picasso: neo-classic period T. S. Eliot: *Gerontion* First commercial radio broadcast Lewis: *Main Street*
1921	Honegger: *King David* Milhaud: *Saudades do Brazil*	Berg: *Wozzeck* Hindemith: *Mörder, Hoffnung der Frauen*	Bartók: Sonata for Violin and Piano #1 Prokofiev: Concerto for Piano #3	Picasso: *Three Musicians* Pirandello: *Six Characters in Search of an Author*
1922	Stravinsky: *Mavra*	Hindemith: *Die Junge Magd*	Vaughan Williams: *Folk Song Symphony* Shostakovich: *Three Fantastic Dances*	Gertrude Stein: *Geography and Plays* Joyce: *Ulysses* T. S. Eliot: *The Wasteland* Klee: *Twittering Machine*
1923	Honegger: *Pacific 231* Stravinsky: *Octet* Milhaud: *La Création du Monde* Poulenc: *Les biches*	Hindemith: *Das Marienleben* Schoenberg: Five Piano Pieces Schoenberg: *Serenade* (first 12 tone)	Sibelius: Symphony #6 Walton: *Façade* Prokofiev: Piano Sonata #5	von Stroheim: *Greed*
1924	Satie: *Mercure* Stravinsky: Concerto for Piano Stravinsky: Sonata for Piano Varèse: *Hyperprisme* Milhaud: *Les Malheurs d'Orphée*		Sibelius: Symphony #7 Gershwin: *Rhapsody in Blue* Puccini: *Turandot* Prokofiev: *Le Pas d'acier*	Breton: *Manifesto of Surrealism* Mann: *The Magic Mountain*

	France	Germany & Austria	Other Countries	Other Arts, Events
1925	Stravinsky: *Serenade for Piano* Ravel: *L'Enfant et les Sortilèges*	Berg: *Wozzeck* (1st performance) Berg: *Chamber Concerto* Hindemith: *Kammermusik* Webern: Three songs	Shostakovich: *Symphony #1* Varèse: *Intégrales*	Kafka: *The Trial* Gide: *The Counterfeiters* Fitzgerald: *The Great Gatsby* T. S. Eliot: *The Hollow Men*
1926	Ravel: *Chansons Madécasses* Milhaud: *Le Pauvre Matelot* Roussel: *Suite en Fa*	Berg: *Lyric Suite* Hindemith: *Cardillac* Schoenberg: *String Quartet #3*	Bartók: Piano Sonata	Hemingway: *The Sun Also Rises*
1927	Ravel: *Boléro* Honegger: *Antigone* Stravinsky: *Oedipus Rex*	Hindemith: *Hin und Zurück*	Prokofiev: *The Flaming Angel* Bartók: *Quartet #3*	
1928	Stravinsky: *Le Baiser de la Fée* Milhaud: *Christophe Colomb* Honegger: *Rugby*	Schoenberg: *Variations for Orchestra* Webern: *Symphony* Weill: *The Three-penny Opera*	V. Thomson: *Four Saints In Three Acts* Bartók Quartet #4 Prokofiev: *L'Enfant Prodigue*	Huxley: *Point Counter Point* D. H. Lawrence: *Lady Chatterley's Lover*
1929	Stravinsky: *Capriccio*	Hindemith: *Neues vom Tage* Schoenberg: *Von Heute auf Morgen*	Walton: *Viola Concerto*	Faulkner: *The Sound and the Fury* New York Museum of Modern Art founded

CHAPTER IX

STRAVINSKY

For I consider that music is, by its very nature, essentially powerless to express anything at all, whether a feeling, an attitude of mind, a psychological mood, a phenomenon of nature, etc. . . . Expression has never been an inherent property of music. That is by no means the purpose of its existence. If, as is nearly always the case, music appears to express something, this is only an illusion and not a reality. It is simply an additional attribute which, by tacit and inveterate agreement, we have lent it, thrust upon it, as a label, a convention—in short, an aspect which unconsciously or by force of habit, we have come to confuse with its essential being. IGOR STRAVINSKY

At the outbreak of World War I in 1914, Stravinsky moved to neutral Switzerland, where he lived for the next five years. The war made great changes in his life, heretofore singularly free from two problems that often plague young composers—lack of money and lack of recognition. Now, the revolution in Russia cut off his income and the disbanding of the ballet meant that his music was no longer performed. He lived quietly, recovered from a serious illness, and worked on compositions that had little in common with the prewar ballets that had brought him such quick fame.

After the armistice, he returned to France and lived

for a time in several cities on the Riviera until 1925, when he settled in Paris. Several years later he became a French citizen. Paris was the right setting for Stravinsky, for he represented in music the ideal of neo-classicism which Picasso, Gide, and Valéry—also Parisians at the time—were expressing in paintings, novels, and poetry. This doctrine will be discussed later in the chapter.

Stravinsky did not restrict his activities to Paris, for he started the world tours as a conductor and pianist which continued for the rest of his life. His autobiography tells about his musical journeys, giving an excellent picture of the musical world in the twenties.

In 1939 Stravinsky came to the United States to give a series of lectures at Harvard University (since published as *The Poetics of Music*). When the outbreak of World War II made his return to Europe impossible, he settled in Hollywood and in 1945 became an American citizen. The change of locale and nationality did not alter the pattern of his life, for he continued composing and conducting his new works in all parts of the world. While his succeeding premieres did not cause riots, each was awaited with interest and followed by controversies. He has never been a neglected composer.

For almost five decades Stravinsky has been an acknowledged leader of twentieth-century music and the chief representative of an attitude toward life and the arts which underlies much of the aesthetic activity of the era. Since an understanding of this point of view is necessary in order to enjoy contemporary art, it will be described here.

STRAVINSKY'S POSITION

It has long been recognized that there are two ideals or poles of art. Various pairs of words have been used to describe them: such words as classic and romantic; Apollonian and Dionysian; objective and subjective; of-the-head and of-the-heart. These antonyms indicate that although works of art express the feelings and emotions of their creators (romantic attitude), they are also man-made constructions created by the artist's sensitivity to the materials he uses (classic attitude). While the supreme works of art embody both attitudes, there seems to be a demonstrable shift of emphasis from one ideal to the other in different style periods. Many historians of culture have noted these shifts, but Curt Sachs has perhaps documented them most fully in his book *The Commonwealth of the Arts*.

There is no doubt where Stravinsky stands in this matter. Since World War I he has been the embodiment of the classical, the objective, the Apollonian ideal. This does not mean, of course, that his music is inexpressive, for sounds and rhythms by their very nature are expressive. It simply means that when Stravinsky writes a composition he is not concerned (as Schoenberg was) about "writing from the heart" but in constructing a logical and controlled structure in sound. He has explained his position in these words:

> What is important for the clear ordering of the work, for its crystallization, is that all the Dionysiac elements which set the imagination of the creator in motion and cause the life sap to rise should be properly subjugated and finally subjected to the rule of law before they intoxicate us: for this Apollo demands.[1]

If Stravinsky, then, writes music not to "express himself" (compare the statement of Schoenberg quoted at the beginning of Chapter IV) what are his motivating forces? Tansman has described his attitude in this manner:

> Each work presents for Stravinsky a certain particular problem to resolve, a problem of order for the intelligence, an obstacle to conquer, and if he doesn't have one, he creates one in order to conquer it.[2]

The chapter "The Composition of Music" in his *Poetics* further explains his attitude toward creation. As might be expected, Stravinsky gives inspiration only a small role in the process. Instead, he speaks of an "appetite" to compose:

> This appetite that is aroused in me at the mere thought of putting in order musical elements that have attracted my attention is not at all a fortuitous thing like inspiration, but as habitual and periodic, if not as constant as a natural need.[3]

The actual composition, the writing down of notes, the making of a musical construction, is the activity that delights Stravinsky.

> The idea of work to be done is for me so closely bound up with the idea of the arranging of materials and of the pleasure that the actual doing of the work affords us, that, should the impossible happen and my work suddenly be given to me in a perfectly completed form I should be embarrassed and nonplussed by it, as by a hoax.[4]

At the end of the chapter the most pertinent remarks are made. "The more art is controlled, limited, worked over, the more it is free," he writes. He speaks of his terror in the limitless possibilities he faces when starting a new composition:

> What delivers me from the anguish into which an unrestricted freedom plunges me is the fact that I am always able to turn immediately to the concrete things that are here in question. . . . My freedom thus consists in my moving about within the narrow frame that I have assigned myself for each one of my undertakings. . . . The more constraint one imposes, the more one frees one's self of the chains that shackle the spirit.[5]

Stravinsky then, is a controlled, anti-Bohemian, orderly man of the twentieth century. Everything about his daily life is on a regular schedule, from setting-up exercises in the morning, through hours of composition, to a relaxing game of Chinese checkers. His workroom has been described by Ramuz, a friend of the Switzerland years:

> Stravinsky's writing table resembles the instrument stand of a surgeon . . . the bottles of different colored inks set out according to rank. Each has its little role in the grand affirmation of a superior order. They were ranged together with rubber erasers of various kinds and sizes, all sorts of shining steel objects, rulers, eradicators, penknives, drawing pens, not to mention a kind of instrument with wheels Stravinsky had invented for drawing staves . . . . Here was an order which did enlighten, by its reflection of an inner clarity. This clarity revealed itself too in all those large pages covered with writing made more complex, persuasive, and demanding by means of various inks, blue, green, red, black—two kinds of black, ordinary and Chinese—each having its own place, meaning, and special utility. One ink was for notes, another for the first text, a third for the second, still others for titles, and a special one for the various written indications that go into a score. The bars were drawn with a ruler and errors carefully removed with a steel eraser.[6]

THE PROBLEM OF STYLE CHANGES

One of the results of this attitude led to much confusion and misunderstanding in the world of music. This was Stravinsky's penchant for stylistic changes and for composing "in the manner of" other composers. In the nineteenth century, an original musical language and manner of composing was assumed to be of prime importance; most composers strove to achieve a highly personal style. Stravinsky, on the other hand, seemed now to abandon deliberately the style that had brought him such quick success and, instead, to flit irresponsibly from one manner of composition to another.

It was pointed out earlier that *Le Sacre* was a landmark of violently expressive music. The effects of its dissonances and irregular rhythmic patterns and the brutal sound of the orchestra have already been described. When Stravinsky resumed his composition after the war, his admirers and detractors alike were confused and disappointed because his new compositions seemed completely different from earlier works. *Pulcinella,* for instance, the first postwar ballet, was based on melodies of Pergolesi, and its charm and lack of pretension baffled an audience expecting musical violence.

But this was just the beginning. Next came pieces more or less in the style of Bach or other baroque composers. Then a series of austere ballets and oratorios appeared, bathed in the atmosphere of classical Greece. Following these came compositions based on composers as different as Rossini, Tchaikovsky, and Grieg. These posed even greater problems, for everyone knew that Stravinsky was anti-romantic. "What could he be doing?" "Was he serious?" the public asked. Some critics accused him of being a "time-traveler," looking over the whole past history of musical styles and choosing now this composer and now that one—whichever would be the most unlikely and startling—to serve as a model.

After World War II Stravinsky found a new love, the music of Webern and the other two composers of the second Viennese school, Schoenberg and Berg, and started to use the twelve-tone technique. This was embarrassing, for critics and scholars had pointed out that the differences between his music and Schoenberg's were utterly irreconcilable and that the two styles formed, as a matter of fact, diametrically opposed poles of twentieth-century music.

What was not commonly understood was that Stravinsky, no matter what the inspiration for a particular piece, was always true to himself and his conception of music. If a composition is primarily a construction, something made, and is not the expression of a composer's inner life, then it is immaterial if the initial impetus is something original or something given. The composition itself is the important matter and not its revelation of the composer's unique feelings.

Stravinsky's mind and musical imagination are far-reaching and his curiosity and appetite insatiable. His problem-solving attitude has already been described, and one can see that all styles, past and present, interest and inspire him as points of departure. His public has gradually learned that every bar he writes is imbued with his own musical personality, no matter what the particular idiom happens to be.

The public has also learned that no composer, not even Stravinsky, writes an unbroken series of masterpieces. Living composers do not share the advantage that time bestows on those long dead in separating their great from their lesser works. We do not often hear the weak compositions of Beethoven or Bach, and our opinion of these masters is formed through knowledge of their masterpieces. When the total output of Stravinsky is sifted, some of the derived as well as some of the nonderived works will disappear, and in both categories a few will undoubtedly be counted among the masterpieces of his time.

RELATION TO PICASSO

It was pointed out that Stravinsky has not been alone in his attitude toward creativity. Picasso's career and works, for instance, offer many parallels. He too has been the best-known creator in his field whose every work has been awaited with interest and greeted with acclaim or angry confusion because of his frequent changes in style. No sooner has the public recovered from the shock of one kind of intellectual, problem-solving painting than Picasso has started painting according to a whole new "set of rules." Thus, he too has had his famous periods —rose, blue, cubist, neoclassic, and others—which varied from extremes of abstraction, to realistic portraits, to wildly expressionist, highly charged paintings—a bewildering variety of styles and media.

At an age when many artists would be repeating themselves, both Picasso and Stravinsky continue their tireless experimentation. They reflect the artistic atmosphere of the first half of the twentieth century, a time of searching and probing, of asking questions rather than finding answers.

STRAVINSKY'S COMPOSITIONS

Stravinsky's first style period came to an end with *Le Sacre*. Because of his constancy of purpose on the one hand and his variability from piece to piece on the other, his compositions after that elude stylistic classification. For convenience, they will be discussed here in three groups: those written during the early twenties, the compositions of the thirties and forties, and finally, the later works.

Period 2: c.1914-c.1925

The main compositions of this period are:

STAGE WORKS

Le Rossignol (lyric tale; 1909-14)
L'Histoire du Soldat (pantomime with narrator; 1918)
Pulcinella (ballet; 1919)
Mavra (comic opera; 1922)
Les Noces (ballet with songs; 1923)

ORCHESTRAL AND CHAMBER WORKS

Ragtime (for 11 instruments; 1918)
Symphonies of wind instruments (1920)
Octet for Wind Instruments (1923)
Piano Concerto (1924)

PIANO

Sonata (1924)
Serenade (1925)

L'Histoire du Soldat is a stage work written for two dancer-pantomimists and a narrator. It immediately proclaims the "new" Stravinsky. Postwar Europe could no longer afford Diaghilev's sumptuous ballets, so the composer collaborated with the poet C. F. Ramuz to create a little theatrical piece that could be presented with a minimum of expense. Limitations of this kind did not hinder Stravinsky— they simply provided him with a new "set of rules" to compose by. Instead of writing for a full ensemble he called for a skeleton orchestra of one violin and a double bass, a clarinet and a bassoon, a cornet and a trombone, and a large number of percussion instruments. This strident group, somewhat resembling a dance band, accompanies the stage action in a series of harshly dissonant, satirical pieces. There are tangos, paso dobles, marches, ragtime pieces, and chorales. The violinist has an important part, as does the tympanist who concludes the work in a cadenza of the greatest rhythmic complexity.

In 1919 Diaghilev resumed his activities. Sensing that postwar Europe would no longer be interested in fairy-tale or folk ballets, he turned to the eighteenth century for inspiration. This neoclassic trend was antiromantic in effect, for instead of large, emotionally charged works he now projected modest but highly "chic" productions.

Pulcinella, one of the first of the postwar ballets, was the product of Diaghilev, Picasso, Massine, and Stravinsky. The impressario presented the composer with some melodies purportedly by Pergolesi (1710-1736) and Stravinsky based his score on them. It is his first composition based on another composer's music, and he has described his frame of mind in approaching it:

> Before attempting a task so arduous, I had to find an answer to a question of the greatest importance by which I found myself faced. Should my line of action with regard to Pergolesi be dominated by my love or by my respect for his music? Is it love or respect that urges us to possess a woman? Is it not by love alone that we succeed in penetrating to the very essence of a being? But, then, does love diminish respect? Respect alone remains barren, and can never serve as a productive or creative factor. In order to create there must be a dynamic force, and what force is more potent than love? To me it seems that to ask the question is to answer it.[7]

What is the result of this love? *Pulcinella* resembles both mother and father. Some sections seem to be little more than Stravinsky's strongly personal orchestration of Pergolesi's melodies. The dry, staccato bassoons, the bright treble reeds, the boisterous flourishes of the trombones, and the grotesque double bass solos all proclaim Stravinsky. As Example 57 indicates, the harmonizations are also his. Polychords and dissonant pedals add a touch of salt to the bland melodies. Occasionally the regularity of Pergolesi's melodies is disturbed by contracting or elongating the measures.

This novel mixture of old and new was confusing and disturbing, and the composer did not help the situation when he complained:

EXAMPLE 57*

Allegro moderato

PIANO PART OF VERSION FOR VIOLIN AND PIANO

What am I to do? Some say they want me to write music that is shocking and provoking like my earlier works; others say that only now do I write proper music. They think I write like Verdi—such nonsense! They don't listen right. These people always want to nail me down. But I won't let them! On the next occasion I do something different and that bewilders them.[8]

In the Octet for Wind Instruments the instruments called for are flute and clarinet, two bassoons, two trumpets, and two trombones. This combination is further evidence of Stravinsky's reaction against the large, prewar orchestra, and his avoidance of lush string quality. He now consciously limits his palette of sound, just as the early cubists restricted themselves to browns and grays, reacting against the exuberant color of the impressionists.

Stravinsky has explained why he chose this group of instruments:

*Copyright 1926 by Edition Russe de Musique.

I began to write this music without knowing what its sound medium would be—that is to say, what instrumental form it would take. I only decided that point after finishing the first part, when I saw clearly what ensemble was demanded by the contrapuntal material, the character, the structure of what I had composed . . . I remember what an effort it cost me to establish an ensemble of eight wind instruments, for they could not strike the listener's ear with a great display of tone. In order that this music should reach the ear of the public it was necessary to emphasize the entries of the several instruments, to introduce breathing spaces between the phrases (rests), to pay particular care to the intonation, the instrumental prosody, the accentuation—in short, to establish order and discipline in the purely sonorous scheme to which I always give precedence over elements of an emotional character.[9]

The first movement starts with an introduction called "Sinfonia," a title used by baroque composers designating an introductory movement. It has the characteristic dotted rhythms of the French overture. The neutral melody is given rhythmic interest as the meter changes from 2/8 to 3/16 to 3/8 to 2/4. This section closes on a complex chord that turns into a dominant seventh.

The movement proper starts with this theme:

EXAMPLE 58

Note the leap of a seventh and the "extra" eighth in the sixth measure which throws the beat off from where it is expected. This theme, the basis of much of the movement, is developed and given bustling counterpoints. Later, the trumpet has a second, contrasting theme:

EXAMPLE 59*

The constant displacement of accents, the syncopations and the somewhat banal character of this theme show Stravinsky's awareness of jazz. There is a healthy, vigorous optimism about the piece.

The second movement is a set of variations on this theme:

EXAMPLE 60

The first half is given to the flute and clarinet. While the two woodwinds sing the melody, the rest of the instruments accompany in short after-beat chords. After eight measures the melody passes to one of the trumpets and then to one of the trombones. The pace is comfortable, and the mood is one of quiet melancholy.

The first variation presents the theme without the graceful turn of the second measure. The theme is first played by the trombone, while the other instruments provide sweeping flourishes from low to high register. The second half of the theme is heard from the flute, oboes, and trumpet in after-beat fragments. This variation, along with the trombone scale at the end is repeated several times in the course of the movement.

In the second variation, resembling a march, the trumpet is prominent. The mood is gay and the dotted-eighth figure recalls *Funiculi-Funicula*. In the second half, the woodwinds have a more delicate version but the trumpet reappears at the end.

Material from the first variation is repeated as an interlude to the third which, in its pastoral coloring and innocent, hesitating rhythms, is a marked contrast to the preceding variation. Few changes of meter occur in this section, which has the feeling of a slow waltz.

This idyll is interrupted by another "busy" variation introduced by the bassoons playing a staccato figure. The melody appears in its original form against figures in the other instruments which are as gay as ballet music of Offenbach. Once again the long scales of the first variation are heard as an introduction to the last variation, which is a *fugato*.

An unaccompanied flute solo serves as a transition to the last movement, which starts with:

Example 61

The atmosphere is unmistakably Bach's. A little later, a jazz-inspired melody by the trumpet is heard and the rest of the movement is concerned with the development of these two themes. The ending is particularly striking as it dissolves into rhythmic fragments. As in the concluding measures of *L'Histoire du Soldat*, melody and harmony disappear and only rhythm remains.

The Octet was one of the first neoclassic compositions by Stravinsky. It would be more accurate to call such pieces neobaroque since they contain certain features that bring them close to the spirit of Bach and Vivaldi: the contrapuntal texture, the use of instruments and forms suggesting the concerto grosso, and the avoidance of chromatic harmonies and romantic shadings in dynamics.

Period 3: c.1925-c.1950

There is no break in style between the pieces of Period 2 and those of Period 3. Several of the latter are neoclassic in a strict sense, in that they are inspired by subjects of ancient Greece. Others pay homage to various composers, while still others show no external models. The principal works are:

STAGE WORKS

        Oedipus Rex (opera-oratorio; 1927)
        Apollon Musagète (ballet; 1928)
        Le Baiser de la Fée (ballet; 1928)
        Perséphone (for speaker, tenor, chorus; 1934)
        Jeu de Cartes (ballet; 1936)
        Orpheus (ballet; 1948)
        The Rake's Progress (opera; 1951)

CHORAL WORKS

        Symphony of Psalms (1930)
        Mass (for mixed chorus and double wind quintet; 1948)

ORCHESTRAL, CHAMBER AND SOLO WORKS

        Capriccio (for piano and orchestra; 1929)
        Violin Concerto (1931)
        Concerto for Two Pianos (1935)
        Dumbarton Oaks (concerto for 16 strings; 1938)
        Symphony in C major (1940)
        Danses concertantes (for chamber orchestra; 1942)
        Sonata for Two Pianos (1944)
        Ebony Concerto (for Woody Herman; 1945)
        Symphony in Three Movements (1945)

In his *Autobiography,* Stravinsky tells of the "rules" he set up in composing his *Symphony of Psalms.* He was invited to write a symphony for the Boston Symphony Orchestra and accepted even though he had no intention of writing a conventional symphony, "the latter being simply a succession of pieces varying in character." Deciding to write a work with "great contrapuntal development" he chose a choral and instrumental ensemble in which "the two elements should be on an equal footing." After this, he decided to set verses from the Psalms. This sequence of calculations (so different from the motivations of a romantic composer who would probably have started with an urge to write religious music, then found an appropriate text, and then chosen his medium) is characteristic of his objectivity.

Stravinsky often gives individuality to a composition by employing a unique, *ad hoc* combination of instruments chosen for their appropriateness to the work in question. The *Symphony of Psalms* has no violins or violas, and the score leans heavily on the woodwinds, a fact which adds to the stark, ancient, biblical flavor of the work. The text of the opening section is taken from Psalm 39, verses 12-13. In the King James Version it is as follows:

> Hear my prayer, O Lord, and give ear unto my cry; hold not Thy peace at my tears: for I am a stranger with Thee, and sojourner, as all my fathers were. O spare me, that I may recover strength, before I go hence, and be no more.

It starts with a sharp E-minor chord spaced and orchestrated in such a manner that it sounds entirely new, both in timbre and in effect. It is an example of what Walter Piston reported from a conversation with the composer about another piece. "How happy I was when I discovered that chord," said the composer. Piston comments:

> It was an ordinary D-major chord but he meant this particular setting, spacing, and dynamics . . . . When we realize that such precision marks Stravinsky's approach to every technical and esthetic problem connected with musical composition, we begin to see why his influence has been inescapable, why his music has been so great a stimulation to other composers.[10]

If the first chord alone has such precision and effect, it is not surprising to find that every detail of the movement is as carefully planned. After the opening chord, oboes and bassoons play a broken chord figure consisting of major and minor thirds. This juxtaposition of thirds gives unity to the entire movement; there is scarcely a measure in which they do not appear. When the chorus enters with its supplication

EXAMPLE 62

the accompanying thirds appear in this form:

EXAMPLE 63*

CELLOS AND DOUBLE BASSES

The second movement is a large double fugue. A translation of the text follows:

> I waited patiently for the Lord: and he inclined to me, and heard my cry. He brought me up also out of an horrible pit, out of the miry clay, and set my feet upon a rock, and established my goings. And He hath put a new song in my mouth, even praise unto our God: and many shall see it, and fear, and shall trust in the Lord.

The first subject starts in the orchestra, stated by the oboe in a high register. Although it outlines a major 7th, the relationship to the basic theme of the whole work is obvious:

EXAMPLE 64

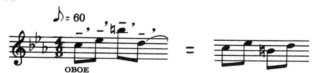

OBOE

Here is an example of a favorite device of the composer, that of transferring a note an octave away from its original position. In this case the octave displacement results in a seventh rather than a third.

The chorus enters with the second subject of the fugue, while the orchestra continues with the first. There is a short section for the chorus *a cappella* including a *stretto*. It ends with a beautifully quiet cadence reminding one of sixteenth-century voice leading. The ending is particularly lovely in its seraphic calm. The chorus sings E-flats spread over two octaves while the basses continue the basic theme.

Simultaneously, the theme is played by the soprano trumpet and by the flutes as a cluster.

The third and longest movement is a setting of Psalm 150, a song of praise and thanksgiving, a translation of which follows:

> Praise ye the Lord. Praise God in His Sanctuary: praise Him in the firmament of His power. Praise Him for His mighty acts: praise Him according to His excellent Greatness. Praise Him with the sound of the trumpet: praise Him with the psaltery and the harp. Praise Him with the timbrel and dance: praise Him with stringed instruments and organs. Praise Him upon the loud cymbals: praise Him upon the high sounding cymbals. Let everyone that hath breath, praise the Lord. Praise ye the Lord.

This is one of Stravinsky's noblest achievements. It begins with the words *alleluia, laudate,* set with the simplicity and directness of truly great statements; even on first hearing these measures are memorable:

EXAMPLE 65

The two ideas shown above recur in the middle and at the end of the movement. After this solemn opening an orchestral interlude introduces the main body of the movement. Here again is the familiar Stravinsky atmosphere of strong, irregular rhythms, reiterated chords in the horns and bassoons, brilliant flashes of sound, and strong dissonances. Throughout the section prominent use is made of the basic interlocking third motive. The chorus enters into this new milieu giving words to the horn's repeated-note motive:

EXAMPLE 66

The mood of almost barbaric exultation is interrupted by another statement of the alleluia phrase, and then much of the early material reappears in a free recapitulation. The coda starts with a diatonic D-major canon of great simplicity leading into a section in E-flat
of the utmost calm. One is reminded of tolling bells by the constant
reiteration of E-flat, D, C, D over an ostinato moving in fourths. The
alleluia laudate is heard for the last time and the work ends on a seraphic C major chord. The *Symphony of Psalms* is one of Stravinsky's
masterworks and it may well enter into the small group of twentieth-
century masterpieces.

The opera *The Rake's Progress* (1951) is another of Stravinsky's major compositions. Its first performance in Venice followed by
the production at the Metropolitan Opera in New York aroused great
interest.

Given his predilections, it is not surprising that Stravinsky wrote
The Rake's Progress on an eighteenth-century, Mozartian model, with
the result that it is a "number" opera consisting of arias, duets, and
occasional choruses. The numbers are separated by *recitativo secco*,
accompanied on a harpsichord. It is a singer's (as opposed to a singing actor's) opera, with high notes at the expected places and opportunities for bravura display. The orchestra part, although rich in
unusual instrumental effects, does not compete with the vocal line.

Written by W. H. Auden and Chester Kallman, the libretto is a
dramatization of Hogarth's series of well-known engravings depicting
realistic scenes in the "progress" of a dissipated young man who finds
corruption and death in eighteenth-century London. As is usual in

earlier operas, the story is developed during the recitatives while the resulting emotional states are expressed in the arias.

The third scene of Act I is typical. It is sung entirely by Ann, the sweetheart whom Tom has abandoned when he goes to London with the evil Nick Shadow. After expressing her concern over Tom's safety in a recitative, she sings a beautiful aria invoking the night and the moon to watch over him. It starts:

Example 67*

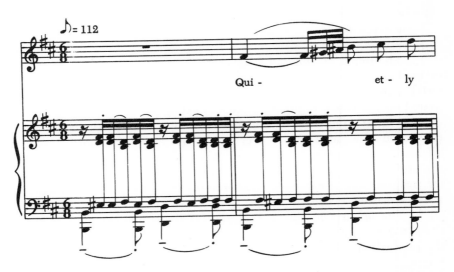

The throbbing accompaniment figure is used throughout. Note the characteristic "blurring" of the otherwise consonant harmony.

In the short recitative that follows, Ann decides to leave her father and go to London to find Tom. The succeeding brilliant C-major *cabaletta* in which she expresses her joy and excitement is an aria as demanding as Mozart's *Martern aller arten*, and ends, as might be expected, on a sustained high *c*.

There is great variety in the opera, from scenes of ribald humor to scenes of pathos. One of the latter is the moving scene in Bedlam, where Tom is confined after he loses his sanity. It is interesting to

*Copyright 1949, 1950, 1951 by Boosey & Hawkes, Inc.

compare this scene with the close of *Erwartung*, which is also concerned with insanity. Schoenberg expresses madness through the accumulation of atonal dissonance and wide leaps in the melody. The music itself, in other words, is irrational. On the other hand, Stravinsky expresses the pathos of Tom's madness, instead of the madness itself, in a quiet song in A major.

The Rake's Progress, like *Don Giovanni,* concludes with an epilogue in which a homely moral is brought home to the audience. This conventional ending underlines Stravinsky's intentions. He never thought of his characters as real people whose fate would move his audience to tears. They are simply characters in a fable providing the excuse for a series of beautifully written, contrasting songs.

Period 4: 1950-

During the time that Stravinsky was writing his eighteenth-century opera he was exploring in other musical fields and becoming interested in the music of the Renaissance, particularly that of Isaac (c.1450-1517) and the earlier contrapuntists. This new interest is evident in his Mass (1948). During the 1950's his ever-active curiosity roved in other directions. The music of Webern now attracted him and his principal works since then have been written within the framework of the twelve-tone or serial idiom. They are:

> Cantata (on old English texts; 1952)
> Septet (for violin, viola, cello, clarinet, horn, bassoon, and piano; 1953)
> 3 *Songs from William Shakespeare* (for mezzo-soprano, flute, clarinet, and viola; 1953)
> *In Memoriam Dylan Thomas* (for tenor, string quartet, and four trombones; 1954)
> *Canticum sacrum* (1956)
> *Agon* (ballet; 1957)
> *Threni* (a setting of the Lamentations of Jeremiah; 1958)
> Movements for Piano and Orchestra (1959)

In choosing to write music organized according to the principles of serial composition, Stravinsky has once again chosen a new "set of rules," but as in the past, this has not taken away from his individuality as a composer.*

Agon is a ballet of about twenty minutes' duration for twelve dancers. It is completely abstract, having neither a story nor personifications, and unlike the earlier ballets *Orpheus* or *Apollon Musagète,* it is performed in rehearsal attire. *Agon* is simply a series of seventeenth-century dances written for various combinations of the four male and eight female dancers.

The orchestra consists of three flutes, two oboes, English horn, two clarinets and bass clarinet, two bassoons and contrabassoon, four horns, four trumpets, two tenor trombones and bass trombone, harp, mandolin, piano, percussion, and strings. Although it is a large group, Stravinsky never uses it in tuttis. Each dance calls for a different chamber group, and the composer's imagination for new combinations is unflagging. Thus, a male solo dance is accompanied by a solo violin, xylophone, and tenor and bass trombones. The *Gaillarde* for two female dancers is for strings (without violins), harp, mandolin, and three flutes. The ever-different timbres are one of the fascinations of the piece. Much of *Agon* is based on three tone-rows:

EXAMPLE 68

*The principles of serial music are discussed in Chapters X and XI. If the student is unacquainted with this type of music it might be well to postpone study of this phase of Stravinsky's career until later.

The prevalence of seconds should be noted, for their presence makes it possible for Stravinsky to write melodies of typically narrow range:

EXAMPLE 69*

Stravinsky's attraction to the music of Webern is clearly shown in certain sections of the score where the aerated, one-note-to-an-instrument style is employed. An example is the adagio *Pas de Deux with Variations.*

But even when Stravinsky writes in what seems to be a pure Viennese manner his music is always his own. His melodies, dry timbres, and above all, his sinewy rhythms give an individual profile to a style that can be amorphous and merely sound "like Webern" when used by composers of less personality. *Agon* is lithe, athletic, and healthy—qualities that we almost always associate with Stravinsky's music, whether it be an early ballet, a neoclassic sonata, a piece for jazz band, or a setting of the Mass.

STYLE CHARACTERISTICS

Stravinsky's melodies are often built on short fragments of diatonic scales. They frequently have a narrow range and a sing-song quality as they revolve around a central axis and turn back on themselves, gaining directional power from the interplay of the irregular rhythmic patterns. Sometimes this conjunct motion is interrupted by octave transposition, resulting in a jagged line.

Another type of melody frequently found is based on the notes of a broken chord. One of many examples can be found at the opening of the third movement of the *Danses concertantes*. Stravinsky has been accused by some critics of being a poor melodist, and it is true that when one thinks of any of his compositions one usually recalls a complex of rhythm, harmony, and tone color rather than a melody. He will not be remembered as the great melodist of the age.

On the other hand, no one ever called Stravinsky's rhythms weak, for his loosening of the shackles of metrical consistency by his irregular groupings is possibly his greatest technical contribution to music. Attention has been called to specific examples in the compositions already discussed. Almost any passage chosen at random from any of his works reveals striking rhythmic devices—from the polyrhythms of *Petrouchka* to the Webern-inspired silences of *Agon*. Throughout his scores the rests take on great importance, giving an effect like the drop into an unexpected airpocket when one is flying in an airplane. One loses one's breath, equilibrium is momentarily lost, and then one proceeds smoothly until the next jolt. Stravinsky's rhythmic devices are compelling and exhilarating.

Stravinsky uses a wide variety of chords. He likes to add or substitute major or minor seconds to ordinary triads, giving the blurred, out-of-focus effect mentioned earlier. It has also been called the "wrong-note" technique—an inaccurate term, since there is nothing accidental in any of his writing. It must be admitted, however, that the chorales of *L'Histoire du Soldat* sound as though they were willfully harmonized with wrong notes.

If Stravinsky can be said to have a favorite chord, it would be that which contains both a major and a minor third. Examples can be found at the beginning of the second movement of the Symphony in Three Movements, the postlude to Tom's aria, "Vary the song," opening the second act of *The Rake's Progress,* the "Devil's Dance" from *L'Histoire du Soldat,* and the "Rondoletto" movement of the Serenade in A.

Frequently a complex structure can be analyzed as a polychord, the combination of two different chords. The unforgettable tom-tom chord of the "Auguries of Spring" in *Le Sacre* is an example (see Example 28). Another famous polychord is that found in *Petrouchka,* already mentioned. Stravinsky's polychords are not always complex. He often simply combines tonic and dominant. Other dissonant combinations result from polytonal writing or from the combination of two or more planes of harmony.

In spite of his extensive and freely treated dissonance, Stravinsky (up to the serial works) is essentially a tonal composer in that a basic tonality underlies all of his pieces. The term *pandiatonic* has been used to describe his harmonic practice; this is a useful, if somewhat loose, concept implying the use of the diatonic scale without functional harmony. Such music, of course, eludes analysis with Roman numerals, for the chords are not limited to structures built in thirds nor is there any predictable sequence of root progressions, except that the piece will ultimately end on the tonic.

Another of Stravinsky's major contributions is his revelation of a whole gamut of new sound potential in the conventional instruments. His musical ideas demanded an effect frequently described as "dry," obtained through precise articulation and the exploitation of ranges and combinations of instruments usually avoided. The bassoon solo at the beginning of *Le Sacre,* the spiky, percussive writing for the piano in the Concerto, the scratchy, multiple stops in the violin part of *L'Histoire du Soldat,* and innumerable other examples show the unusual demands he makes on the instrumentalists. The instrumental combinations are equally novel and tend to be different for each composition. It is seldom that Stravinsky writes for the conventional symphony orchestra.

Stravinsky's interest in precise articulation is revealed in one of his published *Conversations:*

> For fifty years I have endeavored to teach musicians to play
> ♪𝄾𝄾𝄾 instead of 𝄽 in certain cases, depending on the
> style. I have also labored to teach them to accent syncopated notes and to phrase before them in order to do so.

A wide variety of textures is found in Stravinsky's works, with a trend toward pure counterpoint becoming more and more apparent. While the earlier compositions were often conceived in planes, the lowest of which was an ostinato figure, more recent works show a greater interest in linear texture.

SUGGESTED READINGS

Stravinsky's own books are of prime importance. An English translation of Stravinsky's autobiography, *Chronique de ma Vie* was published in London in 1936 as *Chronicle of my Life* and in New York as *Stravinsky, an Autobiography*. The lectures given at Harvard in 1939 which formulate his aesthetic of music are published as *The Poetics of Music* (New York, 1956). *Conversations with Stravinsky* edited by Robert Craft (Garden City, N. Y., 1959) gives invaluable insights into the composer and man, as the conversations range over a wide variety of subjects. A second volume of conversations with Robert Craft, called *Memories and Commentaries* (Garden City, N. Y., 1960), contains more reminiscences and many photographs from all periods of his life. A useful *Complete Catalogue of the Published Works of Stravinsky* was published by Boosey and Hawkes in 1957.

Among numerous biographies and studies of his works, Tansman's *Igor Stravinsky, The Man and His Music* (New York, 1949) containing a lengthy analysis of his style elements, Eric White's *Stravinsky* (London, 1947) and Roman Vlad's *Stravinsky,* (New York, 1960), are recommended. *Stravinsky in the Theater* edited by Minna Lederman (New York, 1949) and *Stravinsky* edited by Edwin Corle (New York, 1949) contain essays written by a wide variety of critics and acquaintances as well as photographs of the composer and his friends, ballet sets, etc. Nicholas Nabakov's *Old Friends and New Music* (Boston, 1951) contains an interesting account of a visit to Stravinsky's home.

CHAPTER X

SCHOENBERG

Composition in twelve tones has no other aim than comprehensibility. ARNOLD SCHOENBERG

When Schoenberg returned to civilian life in 1917, he found Austria impoverished, demoralized, and dismembered. Vienna, once the proud capital of a far-reaching empire, ornamented with opera houses, theaters, and universities, was now reduced to the shabby center of a small, unimportant country. Run-away inflation that completely wiped out savings and inheritances contributed to the confusion and desperation of the people.

In spite of this, Schoenberg entered what were probably the happiest years of his life. He received no official appointment, the musical taste of Vienna being far too conservative for that, but he resumed the roles he had played before the war—those of composer, teacher, and theorist. A group of enthusiastic and brilliant young musicians gathered around him, among them Alban Berg and Anton von Webern, who had been with him before the war. There were also younger men such as Paul Pisk and Egon Wellesz, pianists Rudolph Serkin and Edward Steuerman, violinist Rudolf Kolisch, and others.

Schoenberg's disciples regarded him with awe and devotion usually reserved for religious leaders. As he developed a new "gospel" of music, they became convinced he was revealing the path they must follow; they were fanatical in their devotion and firm in the belief that here

175

they had found musical salvation. Some of them wrote commentaries on his compositions, while others busied themselves performing them. Some were to spend the rest of their lives in this service—even after Schoenberg left Europe, and even after his death when a new generation of disciples, commentators and, finally, apostates appeared.

This parallel with the career of a religious leader is not suggested satirically. There was really something about the man and his ideas which inspired devotion and enthusiasm. His complete earnestness and dedication; his courage in persisting in spite of official neglect; the apparent chasm that separated his musical doctrine from that of the past (although one of the disciples' favorite occupations was to "prove" that the chasm did not exist*); and the tremendous difficulty and complexity of his music—all of these elements were conducive to forming a cult. The laudatory commemorative volumes published in 1924 and 1934 on the occasion of Schoenberg's fiftieth and sixtieth birthdays are important documents of the group. This statement of von Webern is typical:

> For truly, it is more than rules for art that you learn under Schoenberg. Whoever has an open heart is here shown the path of good.[1]

In 1925 Schoenberg accepted an invitation to become professor of composition at the Prussian Academy of Fine Arts in Berlin. Germany's recovery from defeat and inflation had been quicker than Austria's, and the years of the Weimar Republic (1919-33) witnessed tremendous activity in all of the arts. It is not surprising then, that Schoenberg, the most radical German-speaking composer, was invited to teach at the State music school. This long overdue public recognition and financial security came to an abrupt end in 1933, however, with the election of Hitler as Chancellor. Immediately thereafter, all advanced art was branded "bolshevik" and banned, and Jews were removed from civil-service positions. This was, of course, the mildest act perpetrated against persons of Jewish faith, but it was the beginning of the great exodus of European Jews to other parts of the world. One result of this purely political action was the profound enrichment of the cultural and scientific atmosphere of the United States where so many distinguished artists, scholars, and musicians emigrated.

*See, for example, the translation of a speech given by Alban Berg in 1930 on the Vienna radio entitled "What is Atonality" in Slonimsky's *Music Since 1900*.

Schoenberg left Europe, never to return again, and fled to the United States. En route, stopping in Paris, he re-embraced Judaism, having become a Catholic earlier in his life. He arrived in New York on October 31, 1933, at the age of fifty-nine, and started to build a new life. He spent a year in Boston, teaching at the Malkin Conservatory, but the effects of the severe winter convinced him he should live in the more temperate climate of Los Angeles. He arrived there in 1934, where he lived until his death at the age of seventy-seven in 1951.

As a person, he did not mellow or become the benign old master. Aware of the contributions he had made to the art of music, he was bitter that his compositions were not played. He was sarcastic and extremely critical of other living composers and depressed at the horrible fate of fellow Jews in Hitler's Europe. His greatest satisfaction was his family—the youngest son was born when Schoenberg was sixty-seven—and his home was a hospitable center for Americans as well as for fellow refugees.

If anyone had predicted in the 1920's that the two great European composers, the cosmopolite Stravinsky and the Austrian Schoenberg, would one day be neighbors in Southern California, the notion would have been dismissed as being too fantastic to consider. Nevertheless, the vagaries of the twentieth century brought this to pass. In spite of their proximity, however, the two composers did not associate with each other. Their totally different personalities, their diametrically opposed ideas as to the nature and function of music, the world-wide fame of the one and the relative obscurity of the other—all this made contact and communication impossible between them.

TWELVE-TONE MUSIC

It will be recalled that before World War I Schoenberg had already progressed through several style periods, from the chromatic idiom of the early works to the expressionist atonality of *Erwartung* and *Pierrot Lunaire*. It was after he returned to Vienna, following the war, that he developed an idiom that was to be among the most provocative and disturbing steps ever taken in the long history of music. This idiom, embodied in less than thirty compositions that are seldom performed, has nevertheless opened up musical horizons and musical space of staggering and bewildering proportions.

It is perhaps not too farfetched to make an analogy with developments in exploring outer space. There the problem is to become free and to exist outside of earth's gravity and atmosphere. In music, Schoenberg's problem was to learn how to exist outside the "gravitational" pull of tonality. His early solutions to the problem have already been described. Between 1915 and 1923 he worked on another:

> After many unsuccessful attempts during a period of approximately twelve years, I laid the foundations for a new procedure in musical construction which seemed fitted to replace those structural differentiations provided formerly by tonal harmonies. I call this procedure *Method of Composing with Twelve tones which are related only with one another.*[2]

In everyday language, various abbreviations or substitute expressions are employed. Some of these are *twelve-tone music, dodecaphonic music,* and *serial music.*

It is important to remember that twelve-tone music resulted from the search for a "new procedure in musical construction . . . to replace those structural differentiations provided formerly by tonal harmonies." The *row* and its manipulation was the solution to musical composition without tonality in the conventional sense.

A twelve-tone composition is based on a series of notes chosen from the twelve tones of the chromatic scale. Such a series, or row as it is called, functions in some ways as a scale does in tonal music in that it serves as the raw material out of which the composition is made. There are, on the other hand, many differences between a row and a scale. There is no hierarchy in a row—no tonic, leading tone, nor any functional tendencies. True democracy reigns; every tone is the equal of each of the others. Furthermore, the row is not simply the chromatic scale. It is a series of eleven intervals forming a melody with its own unique profile and character. For example, these are tone-rows on which compositions have been based:

EXAMPLE 70a, VARIATIONS FOR ORCHESTRA, OP. 31

Mathematicians have calculated that there are 479,001,600 different tone-rows available.

Where does a row come from? Schoenberg assures us that it is as much a product of inspiration as the tonal themes of other composers. He admits that a row is sometimes edited and revised in the same manner that Beethoven and other composers reworked their themes until suitable for use in a composition.

A distinction must be made between the basic row (grund-reihe) and the basic shape (grundgestalt). The row is simply a succession of tones without rhythmic differentiation. It is never used this way. It becomes a theme or shape only when the tones acquire rhythmic relationships. For example, the theme derived from the basic row of the *Variations for Orchestra* quoted above is as follows:

Example 71*

HOW THE ROW IS USED

The principles of twelve-tone composition developed gradually from composition to composition. Schoenberg did not write a textbook of procedures nor did he teach his students to compose in this manner, but in recent years several of his followers have attempted to describe his method of composition. Josef Rufer, one of the students, has provided one of the most thorough descriptions of the style in his book

---

*Copyright 1929 by Universal Edition A. G., Vienna; renewed 1952 by Mrs. Gertrud Schoenberg.

Composition with Twelve Tones. He gives a number of "rules" which will be paraphrased here and illustrated with examples from the *Variations for Orchestra,* which will be analyzed later in greater detail.

1. The row consists of the twelve different tones found in the chromatic scale, their order determined by the basic "shape." Once a tone is sounded it is not repeated until the series has been completed. (To repeat a tone would give it more prominence than another tone.) However, under certain conditions tones are repeated for reasons of sonority or rhythm (to sustain or articulate a tone), when used as a pedal point, or in trill or tremolo figures.
2. The row is used in four forms: Original (O), Retrograde (R), Inverted (I), and Inverted Retrograde (RI).

Example 72

3. The series can be used both horizontally and vertically, as melody tones, as melody and accompaniment, or as chords.
4. The series may be used in any transposition, i.e. starting on any tone as long as the sequence of intervals is retained. (This means that with the four forms of the row there are forty-eight different series potentially available.)
5. Any tone of the row can be sounded in any octave. Endless variants of the basic row forms are possible because of this important principle.
6. Sometimes the row is subdivided into subgroups; for example, two groups of six tones each, or three of four tones, or four of three. This more complex concept, often exploited by Schoen-

berg, will be illustrated later in the discussion of the Piano Concerto.

From this summary of some of the basic procedures of twelve-tone music it must be apparent that instead of being a restricting, limiting procedure, it offers a tremendous number of possibilities to the composer. As Schoenberg has written, "the introduction of my method of composing with twelve tones does not facilitate composing; on the contrary, it makes it more difficult." In order to show how plastically a row may be treated, here are the beginnings of the movements making up the Suite, op. 25. In each case the row is the same, yet the profile and character of the pieces are entirely different:

EXAMPLE 73a, BASIC ROW

EXAMPLE 73b*

EXAMPLE 73c

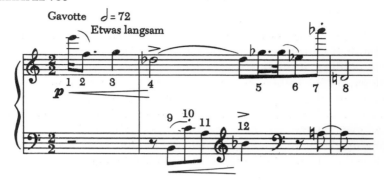

EXAMPLE 73d

EXAMPLE 73e

EXAMPLE 73f

EXAMPLE 73g

EXAMPLE 73h

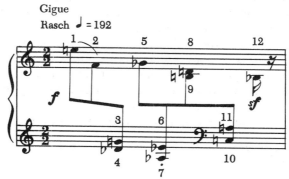

SCHOENBERG'S COMPOSITIONS

The mature works of Schoenberg may be divided into two groups (Periods 3 and 4): those written before and those written after his immigration to the United States. The "method" was developed while he was writing the former group of compositions, while the latter group shows modifications and relaxations of the doctrine; sometimes even a partial return to tonal principles.

Period 3: Twelve-Tone Compositions

It was not until 1923 that the *Five Piano Pieces* (op. 23) were written.* The last piece in the set is his first twelve-tone composition. Other works are:

Op. 24 *Serenade* (for clarinet, bass clarinet, mandolin, guitar, violin, viola, cello and bass voice; 1923)
Op. 25 Suite for Piano (1924)
Op. 26 Wind Quintet (1924)
Op. 27-28 Works for mixed chorus (1925)
Op. 29 Suite (for 2 clarinets, bass clarinet, violin, viola, cello, and piano; 1926)
Op. 30 String Quartet #3 (1926)
Op. 31 *Variations for Orchestra* (1927-28)
Op. 32 *Von Heute auf Morgen* (one-act opera; 1929)
Op. 33a,b *Two Piano Pieces* (1927, 1932)

Several general observations can be made about these compositions, all key examples of twelve-tone writing. Schoenberg's preferences for piano music and chamber music may be noted. The only composition for orchestra is the *Variations* and in his entire output there are few works for orchestra alone. In the works listed above Schoenberg returns to conventional forms; Opus 25 and Opus 29 are organized as baroque suites while the String Quartet and the Wind Quintet are sonatas. These works are no longer gloomy and heavy as were the prewar expressionist compositions. Instead, they are sprightly and precise, delicate in sound, and mercurial in expression.

*Many of Schoenberg's opus numbers parallel or approximate the years in which works were written.

The *Variations for Orchestra*, op. 31, is probably the most important work of the period. In it the twelve-tone principles of construction are employed with such richness of invention that it has become a source book of the manifold possibilities the idiom affords. But the *Variations* are much more than a textbook of procedures. A work of great expressiveness reflecting a wide gamut of contrasting emotions, beautifully sensuous sounds, and intense organization, it is one of the most significant compositions of the between-the-wars period.

Furthermore, it is important as the first twelve-tone work to be written for full orchestra. The idiom evokes a new manner of writing for orchestra because classic doublings and purely sonorous effects are foreign to the style. The orchestra used is the large, romantic assemblage woodwinds by fours in this case, a large percussion section, harp, celesta, the usual strings, and a mandolin. However, as in the early orchestral pieces, Schoenberg uses mass sounds sparingly and the large orchestra is used for color and clarity of line rather than for volume.

The *Variations* are based on the row quoted in Example 71.

Introduction: The work starts pianissimo; harp harmonics over violin tremolos establish the nebulous atmosphere before woodwinds start a triplet vacillation between B-flat and E (the tritone), the first two tones of the row. The wide-ranging violin melodies, unusual flute flutter-tonguings, frequent meter changes, and polyrhythms are elements that build to an exciting climax.

When the music becomes quiet again, the solo flute plays a graceful passage, under which appears the first statement of the B-A-C-H (B-flat, A, C, B-natural) theme which becomes very important in the "Finale." The opening oscillating figure returns and a pizzicato chord completes the introduction; a surprisingly conventional device, it reminds one of the similar spot in the overture to *Der Freischutz.* The introduction is based on the row (as is the whole composition), but up to this point the row has not been heard *melodically* in a single voice.

Theme: The theme is presented by the cellos, the first twelve tones corresponding to the basic row. The next twelve are the Retrograde of the Inversion (RI) in the tenth transposition (nine semitones higher than the original pitch level). The next twelve tones are the

Retrograde of the Original series (R), while the last twelve (in the violins) are the Inversion (I) of the tenth transposition. The theme, then, uses the row in all four versions:

EXAMPLE 74

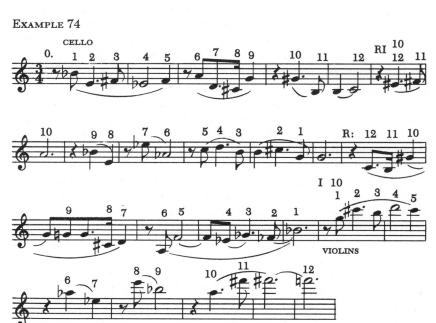

The rhythm of the theme, in contrast to that of the introduction, is regular and waltzlike even though the phrases are asymmetrical. The orchestral accompaniment is thinly scored so that the theme may be easily heard. Leibowitz points out that a subtle relationship exists between the number of tones in these chords and the number of tones in the melodic phrases.[3] Thus the first phrase, consisting of five tones, is accompanied by a chord of five tones; the second phrase, consisting of four tones, is accompanied by a chord of four; and the third phrase of three tones, by a triad. Further, the chords are derived from a version of the row that is in a planned relationship with everything else in the section. For example, the first twelve tones under discussion are accompanied by chords derived from I^{10} (tenth transposition of the Inversion). Leibowitz shows the relationship in this chart:

Melody	(O) 1 2 3 4 5	6 7 8 9	10 11 12
Accompaniment	1	6	10
derived from			
the tenth	2	7	11
transposition			
of the	3	8	12
Inversion			
(I^{10})	4	9	
	5		

The relationship of melody to accompaniment of the whole theme is as follows:

	Phrase A	Phrase B	Phrase C	Phrase D
Melody	O	RI^{10}	R	I^{10}
Harmony	I^{10}	R	RI^{10}	I

Variation I, Moderato, 23 measures, piano, cantabile: The theme is begun by the bass clarinet, bassoon and contra bassoon in a straightforward version, but it soon passes to other instruments. Surrounding the theme, the other instruments play bright, nervous figures; the piccolo adds a shrill touch. There is continuous sixteenth-note motion gained through the superimposition of rhythm patterns. The sweet quality of this variation is achieved through the numerous doublings in thirds, sixths, and tenths (an unusual sound in this style of music) resulting from the simultaneous use of various transpositions.

Variation II, Langsam, 23 measures, pianissimo, dolce: In contrast to the first variation, Variation II is written for eighteen solo instruments. Muted violins present the theme followed by the first oboe in canon one beat later. There are other canons between various instruments, and the contrapuntal texture provides another contrast to Variation I. The solo instruments continue in fixed canonic relationships, but the remaining instruments (still in their serial order) enter from time to time to add color. Shortly before the end of the variation, the B-A-C-H theme is played by the trombone.

Variation III, Mässig, 23 measures, forte: This is a bustling, repeated-note variation, with continuous sixteenth-note motion. Superimposed over this busy figure is an energetic, jagged, rhythmic figure.

The theme, played by two of the four horns, is in the middle register and remains there throughout the variation. The four phrases of the theme are punctuated by rests during which the other instruments continue their energetic conversations.

Variation IV, Walzer tempo, 47 measures, piano, grazioso: The notion of the "austere" Schoenberg writing musical puzzles without regard to their sound is completely belied by this variation. Scored for twelve solo instruments (others are added later), it is truly "delicious-sounding," as it has been described. The theme, transposed and manipulated, is heard in shimmering harp harmonics, celeste, and mandolin—but as an accompaniment to new counterthemes played by the flute, bassoon, and muted solo viola.

Variation V, Bewegt, 23 measures, fortissimo: The magic-garden atmosphere of Variation IV is brutally interrupted by Variation V. Here high-soaring melodies of opposing rhythmic patterns struggle against each other. The theme appears in the double basses but is scarcely heard because of the complications sounding above.

Variation VI, Andante, 35 measures, molto piano, dolce: Once again there is a marked contrast between this variation and the preceding. Variation VI is quiet in character with the theme played unobtrusively by the solo cello. The flute, English horn, and bassoon have important melodies derived from a transposition of the inversion of the original series.

Variation VII, Langsam, 23 measures, ppp: Here is an essay of the softest, most delicate sounds, the dynamics ranging from *p* to *ppp*. The theme is unobtrusive again, appearing high in the piccolo and glockenspiel in single notes, and in the solo violin in a short figure. A florid melody in the bassoon's high register pervades this section.

Variation VIII, Sehr rasch, 23 measures, forte: Variation VIII is another active, strident variation with an ostinatolike eighth-note motion in the bass and above it, an aggressive rhythmic pattern:

Strings and higher woodwinds punctuate in irregular groupings. Near the end, the theme is heard from the flute, clarinet, and violin.

Variation IX, L'istesso tempo, 24 measures, piano: The theme is played by the piccolo at the beginning. It is in original form but with a new rhythmic design, entirely changing the mood. In the second half, the whole orchestra partakes in the treatment of the theme.

Finale: The Finale is an extended piece of 211 measures, divided into definite sections, and permeated with the B-A-C-H theme. The first section, starting with flutter-tonguing by the flute and tremolos by the violin recalls the beginning of the work. A *grazioso* central section follows. Next comes a breathless presto that is interrupted by a six-measure adagio. The presto resumes and the work comes to a close with a final statement of the B-A-C-H theme. The final chord contains all twelve tones.

Variations for Orchestra demonstrated that it was possible to compose an extended piece for full orchestra according to the rules of twelve-tone music. Previously Schoenberg and his followers had favored suitelike structures scored for small combinations of instruments, but the *Variations* showed that full-scale compositions were possible.

Period 4: American Works

These compositions were written after Schoenberg came to the United States. The principal works are:

Op. 36   Violin Concerto (1936)
Op. 37   String Quartet No. 4 (1936)
Op. 38   Chamber Symphony No. 2 (1939)
Op. 39   *Kol Nidre* (for speaker, chorus and orchestra; 1938)
Op. 40   *Variations on a Recitative* for organ (1940)
Op. 41b *Ode to Napoleon* (for speaker, string orchestra, and piano; 1943)
Op. 42   Piano Concerto (1942)
Op. 43a *Theme and Variations* (for band; 1944)
Op. 45   String Trio (1946)
Op. 46   *A Survivor from Warsaw* (speaker, men's chorus, and orchestra; 1947)
Op. 47   *Fantasia* for violin and piano (1949)
Op. 50b *Psalm CXXX* (for unaccompanied six-part chorus, sung and spoken in Hebrew; 1950)
         Moses und Aron (opera, started in 1930; incomplete)

Several of these works were the direct result of the composer's reactions to the Second World War. *The Ode to Napoleon* and *A Survivor from Warsaw* are examples. The texts reveal Schoenberg's hate for dictators and his deep concern for the fate of European Jews under Hitler.

The two concertos, string quartet, organ variations, string trio, and the *Fantasia* show a continuing interest in large-scale instrumental works. The Trio is of particular interest, because of its autobiographical elements. It was written after a serious illness during which the composer's heart actually stopped beating for a moment. Schoenberg almost never discussed his compositions, but in an uncharacteristic moment of candor he stated that the illness and convalescence are portrayed in the music, even the thrust of the hypodermic needle.

Characteristic of some of the last-period works is an apparent coming-to-terms between tonality and twelve-tone writing. *Ode to Napoleon* and *Variations for Band* are unequivocally tonal. Other late compositions combine tonal and twelve-tonal practices resulting in a relaxed, autumnal mood quite different from the tenseness found earlier. The Piano Concerto is perhaps the best example of this phase of the composer's works.

The Piano Concerto, op. 42, is in four movements played without pause. The first, organized in sonata form, begins in an atmosphere of gentle melancholy with the following row-theme:

EXAMPLE 75*

The balanced regularity of the four-measure phrases and the lilt of a slow waltz give the movement an almost old-fashioned flavor.

At first the orchestra is subservient to the piano, but soon it takes over the main theme in a counterexposition. The fact that the violins start this section on a note a fifth higher than the opening sug-

*Copyright 1944 by G. Schirmer, Inc., New York, international copyright secured.

gests the tonic-dominant relationship of tonal music. Many similar relationships occur in this composition, since transpositions of the row and modulations from one to another are regular occurrences.

The development section starts with a trill-like passage in the middle register of the piano while the orchestra plays segments of the row. The piano is silent during the next section of the development, in which the basic rhythm patterns of the whole composition are fragmented and heard in shorter and faster versions. The piano re-enters with a cadenza leading to the recapitulation.

The main theme returns, starting on the same notes as in the exposition. The violins carry the soaring melody this time, while the piano adds figurations. The coda is marked by a *piu mosso* and contains raucous passages written for the trombones.

The second movement, based on transpositions of the basic row, is a scherzo in form and mood. There is a clear differentiation between the beginning section and the Trio which reverts to a slow triple meter. The outer sections of the movement exploit the xylophone, snare drum, and the flutter-tongue flute effect so attractive to the composer.

The third movement is cast in the form of a theme with variations. The poignant adagio theme, derived from a transposition of the row, is divided between the oboe and bassoon:

EXAMPLE 76

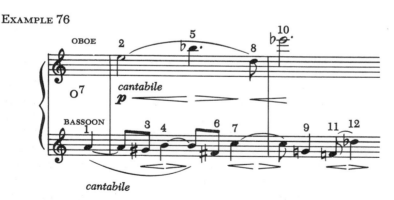

Five short variations and a coda follow. The latter is a cadenza for the piano, starting with a tremolo passage.

The last movement, a rondo, begins with an inverted version of the theme:

EXAMPLE 77

The form of the whole movement is A-B-A-C-A Transition D-A. The mood is that of the traditionally carefree last movement. There are occasional references to the original form of the theme. The work comes to an end after the original rows have been clearly established —another link with the practices of tonal music.

In this concerto Schoenberg makes extensive use of the sub-divided row, resulting in a great increase in the number of serial possibilities. For example, the basic row (Ex. 74) is so constructed that the first six tones of O can be combined with the first six tones of R without repetition of tones. Thus, a hybrid row is formed, utilizing all the tones but altering their order from any of the "pure" forms. An example follows:

	1	2	3	4	5	6	7	8	9	10	11	12
O:	Eb	Bb	D	F	E	C	F#	Ab	Db	A	B	G
R:	G	B	A	Db	Ab	F#	C	E	F	D	Bb	Eb

combining O(1-6) and R(1-6)

Eb	Bb	D	F	E	C	G	B	A	Db	Ab	F

The same relationships and combinations exist between I and RI and between O and R with I and RI when the latter two are transposed a perfect fourth higher. Thus another whole group of row combinations is made available, providing a much greater flexibility than when only the "pure" row forms are used. Furthermore, a process similar to modulation in tonal music ensues, in that hexachords common to two versions of the row (with the order of the notes changed) can function in the way tetrachords common to two keys do in tonal music.

The Piano Concerto is so expressive and its forms are so closely related to those of the classical concerto that the listener may have difficulty in realizing that it is completely built on a basic tone-row.

The technique of twelve-tone composition is synthesized with many conventions of the classic and romantic piano concerto and negates the view that Schoenberg was an eccentric composer, completely removed from the main stream of music history.

Another important work is the opera *Moses und Aron* started in the 1930's but left incomplete with Schoenberg's death in 1951. The composer did not lose interest in it; in the year of his death he still hoped to write the music for the third act but added that it could "simply be spoken, in case I cannot complete the composition." *Moses und Aron* was first heard in a concert performance in Hamburg in 1954 and was staged in Zurich three years later. Since then it has received occasional European performances, sometimes with, sometimes without the spoken third act. Actually, the last act is of little importance; it is very short and unessential to the plot.

This pageant-opera is concerned with the exodus of the Jews under Moses' guidance. As in *Boris Godounov*, the people, represented by the chorus, are the chief protagonists. They are on stage throughout most of the opera and express themselves through conventional singing, *Sprechstimme*, rhythmic speech, and various combinations of these techniques. The chief solo singing role is Aron's, a tenor. Moses speaks his lines except for one climactic sung phrase. The rest of the time he declaims, whispers, or uses *Sprechstimme*.

Most of the libretto is static dramatically and is given over to a theological discussion between Moses and Aron, but the long orgiastic scene before the Golden Calf is completely different. Here there is opportunity for spectacular and sensational staging.

If there is little dramatic unity in the opera there is a great deal of musical and textual unity. The whole of *Moses und Aron* is constructed on a single row, and the libretto, also written by the composer, is elaborately intricate. In addition to employing alliteration and onomatopeia, favorite devices of Wagner, Schoenberg organized each scene by using key words of opposite meaning but similar sound. Thus not only do the words tell a story but also their sounds, independent of meaning, are arranged in patterns at the same time. By associating such word sounds with versions of the musical row, a close connection between words and music is achieved.

The ultimate place of *Moses und Aron* in Schoenberg's lifework is difficult to determine at this time. If the opera survives, it will not be because of the complexity of its text and music, but for the same reason that other operas have survived—the power to interest and move audiences.

An intriguing hypothesis has been put forward that Schoenberg possibly identified himself with Moses. There are certain parallels in the two lives because, like the religious leader, the composer led his followers to a new realm of music. Like Moses, he experienced bitter betrayals and abandonment for what were to him false gods who were worshipped while the true leader was ignored.

STYLE CHARACTERISTICS

All the style traits of Schoenberg's mature works are determined by the twelve-tone idiom and many of the characteristics can be inferred from Rufer's codification of the practice, already summarized. There are problems in defining his style, for it is vastly different from one based on major-minor tonality, however modified and extended. Such concepts as modulation, dissonance, or chord have either no meaning or at least strikingly new connotations.

Because a tone in a row may be sounded in any octave, many of Schoenberg's melodies are characterized by wide leaps. He has a special fondness for sevenths, ninths, and compound intervals, as well as for diminished and augmented intervals. They are found in vocal lines as well as in instrumental, so that the distinction between vocal and instrumental style loses its former meaning.

Schoenberg rarely writes strongly accented rhythms, and any kind of literal repetition of melodic or rhythmic figures is generally avoided. As everything in his music is in a state of flux—of becoming —definite beginnings and endings are also avoided. The theme of the *Variations for Orchestra* is typical in that all of the phrases start after the beat (Example 74).

In keeping with his subjective and expressive attitude toward music, Schoenberg indicates a great many tempo modifications in his scores. In like manner, he is diametrically opposed to those composers of this century who write driving, machinelike rhythmic patterns.

When Schoenberg's harmonies are discussed, traditional terminology is strained, for we cannot talk about chords built in thirds or in fourths, or chord progressions, or even about consonance and dissonance. Vertical combinations are determined by the row of the piece, and may contain any number of tones, from two to twelve. As functional harmony is not used, there are no predictable root progressions. One can assess a chord as more complex than another, but in spite of Hindemith's theory (see Chapter XIII) such assessment is subjective.

The texture of his music is preponderantly contrapuntal, which is not to say that other textures are not employed. Schoenberg frequently writes melodies with accompaniment (for example, the beginning of the Piano Concerto) by extracting certain tones from the row for the melody and others for an accompaniment. Occasionally he writes a series of chords, as in the beginning of the first piano piece of Opus 33, where the twelve tones are presented in three four-note chords.

The twelve-tone idiom also has its effect on timbre, for many of the conventions of orchestration—sustained harmonies, repeated accompaniment figures, and a clear differentiation of function between the choirs of the orchestra—are foreign to this style.

Schoenberg has favorite instruments and instrumental effects which give his scores a personal sound. He is fond of the celesta, xylophone, and flutter-tonguing in the flute, and follows Mahler's lead in adding an unusual instrument to some of his most important works—the mandolin. Its nervous, tinkling sound often adds sheen to his music. When Schoenberg employs a large orchestra he almost never uses all of the instruments at once, for his style of writing is transparent and fragmentary, with constantly changing, fleeting sounds.

Schoenberg uses many of the forms of earlier music—sonatas, variations, and the stylized dances of the baroque suite. Regardless of the outer forms, the principle of developing variation underlies everything he wrote.

SUGGESTED READINGS

The most thorough exposition of the technical aspects of Schoenberg's music is found in *Composition with 12 Notes, Related Only to One*

Another, by Josef Rufer. (New York, 1954). Another basic book that gives an exposition of this method of composition as well as valuable analyses of compositions is René Leibowitz's *Schoenberg and His School* (New York, 1949). Richard Hill's article, "Schoenberg's Tone-rows and the Tonal System of the Future," *Musical Quarterly*, Vol. XXII, No. 1, January 1936, is still valuable. The collection of essays written by the composer called *Style and Idea* (New York, 1950) gives unique insights into his thinking and personality. "My Evolution," an autobiographical sketch published in the *Musical Quarterly*, Vol. XXXVIII, No. 4 (October 1952) tells of his early years. Walter Rubsamen's "Schoenberg in America," *Musical Quarterly*, Vol. XXXIX, No. 4 (October 1951) gives an account of Schoenberg's life in California. *Arnold Schoenberg* by H. H. Stuckenschmidt (New York, 1960) is the most complete study of the man and music.

Dika Newlin's *Bruckner, Mahler, Schoenberg* (New York, 1947) shows the continuity of the musical tradition in Vienna. Egon Wellesz' *Arnold Schoenberg* (London, 1925) is valuable for the early works. Among the analyses of particular works the accompanying booklet to the recording of *Moses und Aaron* (Columbia #K3L-241) by Milton Babbitt and Allen Forte and an article, "Schoenberg's Compositions for Piano" by T. Temple Tuttle, in *Music Review*, Vol. 18, 1957, are recommended. A fascinating book by Alma Mahler Werfel, *And the Bridge is Love* (New York, 1958), should be read by all students of the period. As the wife, successively, of Mahler, Gropius, and Werfel, the author was a leader of Vienna's cultural life.

CHAPTER XI

BERG
AND WEBERN

How I would like to be able to write happy music like that!
ALBAN BERG, IN CONVERSATION WITH PAUL COLLAER, AFTER
HEARING A COMPOSITION BY MILHAUD.

Of all the Schoenberg disciples Alban Berg and Anton Webern proved to be the most significant. Along with their teacher they have been called the second Viennese school—high praise indeed when one remembers that Haydn, Mozart, and Beethoven constitute the first.

As pointed out in Chapter IV, the young Berg and Webern adopted the style of their master and first wrote in a highly charged chromatic style; when he turned to atonality, they too abandoned the major-minor system and wrote short expressionist pieces for orchestra and chamber groups. When Schoenberg worked out the principles of twelve-tone composition they were at his side, but at this point the similarities in their music ceased and the younger men developed strongly personal styles. Although they remained lifelong friends, their later careers and music followed diverging paths. Stravinsky comments on the contrast in their personalities and appearances in one of his "Conversations."

I have a photograph on my wall of Berg and Webern together dating from about the time of the composition of the *Three Pieces for Orchestra.* Berg is tall, loose-set, almost too beautiful;

197

his look is outward. Webern is short, hard-set, myopic, down-looking. Berg reveals an image of himself in his flowing "artist's cravat; Webern wears peasant-type shoes, and they are muddy—which to me reveals something profound.[1]

We will now discuss the careers and mature works of these "two great musicians, two pure-in-spirit, *herrliche Menschen*, ... who made music by which our half century will be remembered," to quote Stravinsky again.[2]

BERG, 1885-1935

Outwardly Berg's life was uneventful—as uneventful as possible for a Central European living in the first half of the twentieth century. Born in Vienna in 1885 and raised in a family of comfortable means and strong artistic interests, he was well educated and had so much interest in literature that during one period of youthful enthusiasm he planned to become a poet.

Berg's interest in music became evident in 1899, but he made no commitment to the art at this time. His father died in 1900, and soon thereafter Berg suffered his first attack of asthma and severe illness. For the rest of his life he was a semi-invalid, never enjoying complete physical well-being. After failing a general humanistic studies examination in 1903, he attempted suicide.

In 1904 he began studying with Schoenberg and for the next ten years this strong personality brought stability and confidence to Berg. As the result of a small legacy, he was able to devote himself entirely to composition. Had it not been for his ill health, his life would have been unusually free from the vicissitudes that have plagued many twentieth-century artistic creators. His opera *Wozzeck* enjoyed popular success, receiving more than 166 performances between 1927 and 1936, a record for a full-length, serious twentieth-century opera. However, the success disturbed the composer, for he felt that if it found an audience so readily it must be weak and contain concessions to popular taste.

During World War I Berg was on limited duty in Vienna, and after the armistice he taught composition there, making occasional trips to European music centers in connection with performances of *Wozzeck,* and spending as much time as possible at his summer home in the Austrian Alps. He died in 1935 at the age of fifty, from blood poisoning induced by an insect bite. One wonders what other mature works Berg would have written had he lived.

BERG'S COMPOSITIONS

The list of Berg's compositions is very short. Before meeting Schoenberg he wrote a great many songs, most of which are unpublished *juvenilia.* The prewar works have already been mentioned—the songs, ultrachromatic Piano Sonata, and short atonal pieces.

The war interrupted his flow of composition (as it interrupted the work of all the composers under discussion). In 1921 *Wozzeck* was finished, followed by five other important works.

> *Chamber Concerto* (for violin, piano and thirteen instruments; 1923-25)
> *Lyric Suite* (for string quartet; 1925-26)
> *Le Vin* (a setting of a poem by Baudelaire, for soprano and orchestra; 1929)
> *Lulu* (opera, incomplete; 1928-35)
> Concerto for Violin (1935)

The reasons for the success of *Wozzeck* are not difficult to find. The music, although dissonant and at times apparently chaotic, expresses every nuance of a story that is human, timeless, and tragic. In performance its power to hold and move an audience is equalled by few operas, if any, old or new.

The libretto was put together from scenes of a play by George Büchner, a German writer of the early nineteenth century. The story is simple and sordid. Wozzeck is a poor soldier plagued by his superiors, poverty, the unfaithfulness of his common-law wife Marie, and his own unbalanced emotions. He lives in a world devoid of reason and order and filled with misery and oppression, fear and hopelessness.

There is little dramatic connection among the fifteen scenes grouped into the three acts that make up the opera. At the beginning Wozzeck is discovered shaving his captain. A realistic, but at the same time strange conversation follows, for the captain is completely erratic. Wozzeck stolidly accepts his taunts.

An orchestral interlude connects this scene with the second, which takes place in an open field. Wozzeck and another soldier are gathering wood, and at sunset when the sky is aflame, Wozzeck becomes hysterical with an irrational fear.

The next scene moves to the cottage in which Marie and her child live. A military band is playing and soldiers pass. Marie is attracted by a handsome drum major and flirts with him from the window until reminded by her friend Margret that she already has a husband and child. Marie closes the window, takes her son on her lap, and sings a lullaby. Wozzeck appears, still incoherent from his experience in the fields.

Scene 4 takes place in a doctor's office. Wozzeck, in order to supplement his wages, has become a subject for the doctor's dietary experiments. The doctor, a sadist, is delighted that the experiment is causing Wozzeck to have aberrations and urges him to cultivate them.

The last scene of the first act is between Marie and the drum major who is resplendent in black boots and red uniform and arrogantly aware of his appeal. It ends with the drum major sweeping Marie into his arms.

The five scenes in each of the two acts that follow carry the tragedy to its climax. Wozzeck becomes insanely jealous when he learns of Marie's unfaithfulness. He kills her and later goes mad and drowns himself. There are scenes in taverns, in the barracks filled with snoring soldiers, by a lake, and finally in a street before Marie's house where a group of children are playing. Among them is Marie's boy riding a hobbyhorse, unaware of the catastrophe. Some other children enter and announce that Marie's body has been found, but the child is too young to understand. He continues rocking and singing a nursery tune while the other children rush off, leaving him alone. After a few moments he too runs off, leaving the stage totally bare.

The problem of building extended musical structures without the foundation of major-minor tonality has already been discussed. How can a full-length atonal but not twelve-tone opera be written? Berg's solution was surprising, and surprisingly effective.

In order to give musical structure to the opera, Berg employs instrumental forms familiar through centuries of use. Thus, the five scenes of Act I are organized as follows: a *suite*, consisting of a prelude, sarabande, gigue, air, and gavotte; a *rhapsody* based on three chords; a *military march;* a *passacaglia* with twenty-one variations; and an *andante.* Act II is organized as a *sonata;* the first scene is in sonata-allegro form, the second is a slow movement, the third is a scherzo with three trios, the fourth and fifth, an introduction and a rondo. Each scene of Act III is an *invention;* based on a theme, a tone, a rhythm, a chord, or on a key, in the tonal sense.

The use of instrumental forms and devices to organize scenes of an opera is not so arbitrary and willful as it first appears. By using these Berg not only achieved organization but also added to the dramatic impact of the scenes by choosing for them the forms that had dramatic potentialities. For example, the murder scene in Act III is built on a note, *b,* used as a pedal throughout. It comes to a terrifying climax when Berg builds a gigantic crescendo by gradually bringing in the whole orchestra, instrument by instrument, on this note and its octaves. In this way, the brutality of murder is not only symbolized, but also bored into the consciousness of all who witness the scene.

The use of the structure of a passacaglia and a fugue in two different scenes gives the opportunity of stressing an important idea through repetition. The scenes organized on a march or dance rhythm have direct story connections. It is difficult to determine why the composer chose to accompany the opening scene between the irrational, cowardly officer and Wozzeck with the stylized niceties of the baroque suite. Perhaps this surprising juxtaposition ironically contrasts the meanness of the scene with the elegance suggested by the music.

There are many other musical riches in *Wozzeck* besides the forms the composer uses. The voices, for instance, are treated in several ways. In addition to the normal singing voice, *Sprechstimme* and the voice of everyday speech are used. The neurotic and very excitable quality of some of the characters is expressed through the use of falsetto.

The orchestra is treated in the plastic, timbre-rich manner of Schoenberg's *Erwartung* and the *Five Pieces for Orchestra,* and reflects everything that happens or is mentioned on the stage. The sound of the wind, the rippling of water, even the fall of the curtain at the end of the scene—all of this is heard in the orchestral music.

Orchestral interludes are played while the curtains are closed for changes of scenes. These interludes contribute a great deal to the opera, for not only do they make entire acts musically continuous, but also they allow the music to expand freely, in contrast to the tautness prevalent during the drama's progress. They also give the audience an opportunity to relax from the opera's almost unbearable tension without breaking its spell during an entr'act. The last interlude is particularly important for it synthesizes the main musical ideas of the opera.

Wozzeck is one of the richest creations of the twentieth century. It is an all-inclusive work drawing upon idioms and forms of earlier music, as well as employing tonal combinations and instrumentation of startling originality. Some scenes are definitely tonal while others are twelve-tonal. The orchestra is often reduced to chamber proportions but occasionally it roars in ear-splitting tuttis. It is a successful opera, for all these devices and idioms are dramatically valid and are used to further characterization and mirror the stage action.

It is similar in many respects to James Joyce's *Ulysses,* a contemporary work. *Ulysses* is a novel that can be approached on many levels, though essentially it is the story of one day in the life of a little man lost in our contemporary world. Told with the utmost artificiality of manner, Joyce draws upon the forms and idioms of past literature whenever such early styles are appropriate. Both *Ulysses* and *Wozzeck* are encyclopedic, complex, and contrived. Both are great works of art—not for these reasons, but because their elaborate forms successfully organize and project a deeply felt compassion for man.

It is interesting to compare *Wozzeck* with *The Rake's Progress.* They are so different in music, drama, and aesthetic basis, that it is difficult to believe that they were created in the same quarter of the century. They represent, respectively, two principal poles of twentieth-century art—expressionism and neoclassicism. Only time will tell which is the greater opera, but it seems safe to predict, however, that more people will be moved by the Berg than by the Stravinsky.

The *Lyric Suite* is Berg's first composition in the twelve-tone idiom. Although it was written and published at the same time as Schoenberg's first compositions in this style, it is in no sense derivative.

The title *Lyric Suite* helps to classify this unique work; it is not a sonata (it has six movements) nor is it a baroque suite. "Lyric" is the key word—meaning "expressive of the poet's feelings." The adjectives modifying the tempo indications of the various movements emphasize their emotional content. The movements are:

Allegretto giovale
Andante amoroso
Allegro misterioso—(trio estatico)
Adagio appassionato
Presto delirando—Tenebroso
Largo desolato

The unusual sequence of tempos should be noticed. Fast movements alternate with slow, the fast becoming faster and the slow becoming slower. The first movement is in baroque binary form as found in the Scarlatti sonatas and Bach suite movements. It is written on this row

EXAMPLE 78

in this rhythmic configuration:

EXAMPLE 79*

The difference between the two forms clearly shows the relationship between basic row and basic shape.

The second theme, divided between the second violin and the viola, is derived from RI. At the same time the cello has a rhythmically augmented version of O. The second half of the movement starts with O by the second violin.

EXAMPLE 80

*Copyright 1927, renewed 1954 by Universal Edition A. G., Vienna.

This is one of the most carefree of Berg's compositions. Lilting rhythms and long melodic lines recall the mood of Schoenberg's *Serenade*. While the movement is constructed according to twelve-tone practice, certain liberties are taken; for although every phrase is derived from the row so that there is continuous development, the sequence of tones in the row is not always slavishly followed.

The mood of the second movement is one of tender melancholy and nostalgia, much of it with a Viennese-waltz background. The frequent successions of chords that are almost, but not quite, parallel are surprising, as are the purely harmonic passages such as those which remind one of the pathetic parallel chords of Tchaikovsky's Sixth Symphony.

EXAMPLE 81

There is a reference to the first movement, establishing a pattern for the composition, as each movement is linked with the preceding.

The third movement is an amazing tour de force. The four instruments play the usual notes of the chromatic scale arranged in rows, but the effect is extremely bizarre since Berg exploits so many special effects. The performers are directed to play on the bridge and on the finger board, as well as in the customary place; to hit the strings with a bouncing bow, or play the strings with the wooden back of the bow instead of with the hair; and to play harmonics, pizzicato, and flautando as well as in the usual manner. The startingly original and unique effect is enhanced by continual use of mutes, pianissimo dynamics, and very rapid tempos. There is a contrasting middle section (Trio estatico) and then a condensed form of the first section is heard again, but this time backwards, or in mirror form.

The fourth movement is in some respects the heart of the entire piece. It is not in the twelve-tone idiom and is contrapuntal with prominent canons. Some of the principal themes of earlier movements appear, and the passionate intensity of the climaxes makes it one of the most eloquent of Berg's compositions.

The fifth movement rivals the third in fantastic, novel sounds. While the earlier scherzo was quiet in dynamics, this section sounds rude and shocking and is punctuated with glissandos. The twice-heard Trio, marked *tenebroso* (shadowy) is ghostlike in its scarcely heard, "breathy" chords, making the contrast of the return of the first section all the stronger.

The last movement is the slowest and most expressive. Wide-spanned, tension-filled melodies, typical of the period, are used. The chromatic texture prepares the way for the startling reference to the opening of the Prelude to *Tristan und Isolde*, which appears just before the end. The motive sneaks in, so to speak, divided among the four instruments so that no single performer can be held responsible for it (see Example 82).

This reference to Wagner's theme is perhaps the key to the whole work, for the *Lyric Suite* is best approached as music for an opera without singers or words, but still an opera in which love, mystery, ecstasy, passion, delirium, ghosts, and desolation—the words that Berg added to describe the movements—are the expressive content.

One by one the instruments stop playing. Finally only the viola remains, playing two notes in slow alternation, until they disappear into nothingness. This unusual ending (*Wozzeck* also ends in nothingness) seems to express the feeling of the concluding lines of T. S. Eliot's poem *The Hollow Men*, also written in 1926.

EXAMPLE 82

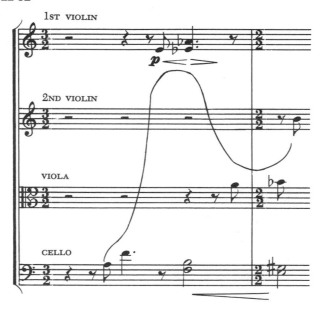

This is the way the world ends
This is the way the world ends
This is the way the world ends
Not with a bang but a whimper.[3]

Berg's last composition, the Violin Concerto, is also a work of synthesis, combining elements and forms of the past with twentieth-century procedures. In 1935 Louis Krasner, the American violinist, asked the composer to write a violin concerto. Berg accepted the commission and decided to make the concerto a memorial to a young friend who had just died. The piece is not only dedicated to Manon Gropius (the daughter of Mahler's widow and Walter Gropius, the architect) but it is also her portrait.

It is cast in two large movements, each in two parts. The first movement, a prelude and a scherzo, is a characterization of Manon in life. The second movement, a cadenza and an allegro, depicts her death and transfiguration. Such a program is typically romantic, and there is no doubt that this is a romantic work.

Musically, it consists of developments of three elements. The basic row:

EXAMPLE 83

This row is unique in that it consists entirely of thirds, except for the four seconds at the end. It will be apparent at once that chords constructed from this row will resemble conventional chord structures, and indeed much of the concerto has a strong tonal feeling.

The second element is an Austrian folk melody:

EXAMPLE 84

The sweetness and sentimentality of the tune aptly characterize the girl. Because of the prominence of the thirds, there are relationships with the basic row.

The third element is the chorale "*Es ist genug,*" the opening notes of which are implied in the last four notes of the row. It beautifully expresses the sorrow and resignation associated with death:

EXAMPLE 85

From these three elements Berg has created one of the most eloquent compositions of the century. As in *Wozzeck*, or as in Bach's music, intricacies of the structure completely serve the expressive content.

STYLE CHARACTERISTICS

Schoenberg's music was at all times the most important formative influence on Berg's style. To support this we need only consider the many similarities between the two composers. First of all, their melodies are similar; both wrote wide, jagged lines that made extensive use of sevenths and ninths as well as augmented and diminished intervals. In their vocal music both composers employed *Sprechstimme* to increase the intensity of the words they set. Their harmonies, too, are alike in the several steps of development from a highly chromatic idiom through an atonal to the twelve-tone idiom. Strikingly similar is the sound of their orchestras, for Berg also uses the fragmentary style of orchestration and the unusual instruments and instrumental effects of his teacher. Because of Wozzeck's popularity, Berg's music became widely known before Schoenberg's and its originality was at first overestimated. Recently, with recordings of such works as *Erwartung* and *Five Pieces for Orchestra*, Berg's debt to Schoenberg has become apparent.

There is no question of Berg's debt to Schoenberg, but what of his original contributions? These lie in his free use of materials, for he is never a "systematic" composer, limited by a doctrine or theory. In *Wozzeck* there are scenes written in major-minor tonality, others without tonality, still others organized according to a serial technique. Sometimes he writes in strict twelve-tone style, and in other pieces he varies the order of the notes in the row. In addition to jagged melodies, he writes melodies as simple as folksongs. At times his orchestra is an "instrument" of weird, new sounds; at others it has the richness of Strauss.

In writing of Berg's opera, Norman Demuth said, "The technique of *Wozzeck* defies categorization because it falls into every category."[4] This sentence is equally applicable to all of Berg's works. His achievement was his ability to combine new and old in a completely personal language.

WEBERN, 1883-1945

The relationship between Schoenberg and his principal disciples, Berg and Webern, has been described by René Leibowitz:

> While the genius of Berg always strove to establish a connection between the discoveries of Schoenberg and the past—thus profiting by the retroactive elements in Schoenberg's work—the genius of Webern is concerned with the possibilities for the future inherent in his work, and thus succeeds in projecting the particularly novel and radical elements.[5]

During their lifetimes, Webern was the most obscure of the three, for neither did he have the crusading zeal of Schoenberg nor did he write a work that became as popular as *Wozzeck*. The few performances he heard of his music were at meetings of the International Society of Contemporary Music.

On the other hand, since his death his compositions have attracted a great deal of attention. His complete works have been recorded, an honor paid to few composers, and young composers all over the world have listened to his music for inspiration and guidance. Some critics have gone so far as to call the 1950's the "Age of Webern."

The son of a mining engineer, Anton Webern was born in Vienna. As a boy he lived there and in the mountain communities where his father worked. He entered the University of Vienna in 1902 to study under Guido Adler, the famous musicologist, and received his Ph.D. four years later, his dissertation being a study of Isaac's *Choralis Constantinus*. In 1904 he became Schoenberg's first pupil and this was the turning point of Webern's life as it was to be for Berg several years later. For the next thirty years the three worked together, exploring the possibilities of the unknown territory, each making his own discoveries.

In 1911 Webern married and started a career as a conductor in several small cities in Germany and Austria. He joined the army in 1915, but after his release a year later because of weak eyes, he settled in a suburb of Vienna where he lived for the next twenty-seven years. In order to support his family he conducted amateur groups, which included both a chorus and an orchestra, and taught a few composition students. During the twenties he assisted Schoenberg in organizing and conducting a series of concerts devoted to contemporary music, and later served as advisor and reader for a music publisher and conducted the Austrian radio orchestra. In the thirties he began to be recognized as a conductor and was invited three times to conduct the BBC orchestra in London.

In spite of this activity, Webern and his family lived in near poverty through all of these years. His frequent letters to friends asking for their help in securing an appointment with an adequate stipend are pathetic, and remind one of similar letters written by Mozart to his friends in Vienna. "How I could work," Webern writes, "if I had a little financial security!"

He remained in Vienna during World War II until 1945, when the bombings reached their height. He then took his family to Mittersill, a mountain village not far from Salzburg. On the night of September 15th, 1945, he stepped out of the house to smoke a cigarette before going to bed. A strict curfew was in effect and a soldier, seeing the light, shot and killed the composer. This tragic act terminated the life of one of the most influential composers of the century.

When Europe's cultural life resumed after the war, it soon became apparent that Webern had a few disciples who had remained underground, so to speak, in the years when the totalitarian governments of Hitler and Mussolini had suppressed advanced art such as his. Once the war was over, articles and books appeared calling attention to him, and occasionally his music was performed. Interest in his style was widespread, from England, Italy, and even France, where the prevailing aesthetic had been strongly neoclassic, to Germany and Austria. Looking for new ideas, young composers of all countries found them in Webern's works, and soon an international Webern "school" existed. The principles underlying his music became the starting place of a new avant-garde.

One of the most surprising champions of Webern's music was Igor Stravinsky, supposedly the leader of an ideal of music diametrically opposed to Webern's. In 1958 he wrote:

> Of the music of this century I am still most attracted by two periods of Webern: the later instrumental works and the songs he wrote after the first twelve opus numbers and before the Trio—music which escapes the preciosity of the earlier pieces and which is per-

haps the richest Webern ever wrote. . . . Webern is for me the *juste de la musique* and I do not hesitate to shelter myself by the beneficent protection of the Muse of his not yet canonized art.[6]

This was not lip service; Stravinsky's compositions of the fifties were strongly influenced by Webern's.

WEBERN'S COMPOSITIONS

The lifework of this composer who has become such a force consists of thirty-one compositions (the longest lasts ten minutes), the prevailing dynamics of which are pianissimo, and whose scores consist of many more rests than notes. The complete works can be played in less than three hours.

The prewar compositions, including the first eleven opus numbers, have already been mentioned. These pieces have several characteristics that are constantly featured in all his works: they are extremely short; the melodies consist of wide, "dissonant" intervals; there are many rests; the predominant dynamic scale is the softest imaginable; they are pointillist in style, the musical line progressing note by note from solo instrument to instrument; the most subtle ranges and combinations of instruments are used; and effects such as mutes, harmonics, and flutter-tonguing are constantly employed.

For many listeners the first impression of these pieces is one of total chaos. The little islands of sound, appearing, disappearing, separated by pools of silence, seem to be signals sounded at random. It is only after repeated hearings, after painstaking analysis (or studying someone else's analysis) that total, meaningful impressions of the music are gained. What seemed to be complete chaos is now understood as an intensely organized pattern. The organization, the skeleton, as it were, is all that remains, for all the flesh—chords, sequences, bridge passages and the sound of massed instruments—is eliminated.

The principle underlying all of Webern's music is economy. He starts with a few tones and builds a piece on them. It follows that these intensely concentrated pieces are most often contrapuntal. Some of Bach's fugues are also concentrated and economical but in comparison with Webern's compositions they are loose and rambling structures.

This ideal of extreme purity, of reducing music to its absolute essentials (any further reduction would result in complete silence) was characteristic of one of the important trends that shaped a considerable amount of twentieth-century art. There was a school of painting, for example, headed by a Russian named Malevitch who, according to Sheldon Cheney, "so purified painting that there was nothing left that the public recognized as art."[7] He painted a picture called *White on White* which consists of an almost white rectangle painted on a white background. This is perhaps a *reductio ad absurdum* of the movement, but the serene nonobjective paintings of Mondrian approach the spirit of Webern's economical pieces. Twentieth century architecture, perhaps the most characteristic art of the period, also is economical. Perret and Le Corbusier, Gropius and Mies van der Rohe, and Nervi—their works are as bereft of ornament and unessential detail as the compositions of Webern.

The compositions of Webern written after World War I are:

Op. 15 Five Sacred Songs (1923)
Op. 16 Five Canons for voice, clarinet, and bass clarinet (1924)
Op. 17 Three Sacred Folksongs (1924)
Op. 18 Three songs for voice, clarinet, and guitar (1925)
Op. 19 Two songs for chorus (1926)
Op. 20 Trio for violin, viola, cello (1927)
Op. 21 Symphony for small orchestra (1928)
Op. 22 Quartet for violin, clarinet, saxophone, and piano (1930)
Op. 23 Three songs (1934)
Op. 24 Concerto for 9 instruments (1934)
Op. 25 Three songs (1934-5)
Op. 26 *Das Augenlicht* (*The Eye's Light,* cantata; 1935)
Op. 27 *Variations for Piano* (1936)
Op. 28 String Quartet (1938)
Op. 29 First Cantata (1939)
Op. 30 *Variations for Orchestra* (1940)
Op. 31 Second Cantata (1943)

Webern's interest in songs is obvious from this list of works. In them, the voice line gives a continuity absent in earlier instrumental works. These songs were probably influenced by *Pierrot Lunaire,* not only in timbre but also in the intricate contrapuntal relationships between the instruments and the voice. This tendency toward strict structural plans comes to a climax in Opus 16, the canons for soprano and clarinets. In the Five Canons, the first song begins:

EXAMPLE 86*

The clarinet and voice, it will be seen, are in canon at the distance of a measure and at the interval of a major second. At the same time, the bass clarinet is in inverted canonic relationship persisting without deviation to the end. The wide melodic line and prominence of sixths, major sevenths, and minor ninths are characteristic, while vertical combinations are often made up of these same intervals. Although there is no theme that unifies the piece as a whole, there is a rhythmic pattern ♩ ♩|♩. ♪♪♩|♩ ♩ that recurs twice, giving additional organization to the composition.

The second canon, also inverted, is written for two parts: the

EXAMPLE 87

soprano and one clarinet. The numerous precise dynamic indications should be noted, for they are imitated in the second voice along with the notes in many of Webern's pieces (see Example 87).

The third canon is a straightforward, three-voice piece with a very subtle rhythmic relationship between the entrances of voices—another characteristic of the composer.

EXAMPLE 88

The final two canons are similar in structure to those already described.

Interesting as they are, the question of the appropriateness of such complicated structures for songs can be raised. Are the words reflected in the music? Yes, in a general way. For instance, the rugged affirmation of the first, *Christus factus est pro nobis*, contrasts completely with the gentle lullaby *Dormi Jesu* which follows it.

Opus 16 is a useful introduction to Webern's style because we find here many of the traits which characterize all of his music. To be noted particularly is the tightness of structure resulting from an underlying plan that accounts for dynamics, articulation, and phrasing as well as the progress of the melodies. Other traits characteristic of the composer are the contrapuntal texture, the use of preferred intervals, and the uncompromising writing for the voices.

The canons were written in 1924. With his next composition Webern moved to the twelve-tone idiom along with Schoenberg and

Berg who took the crucial step at the same time. This did not result in any drastic change in style, for many characteristics of such writing—atonality, contrapuntal texture, and developing variations, for instance—were already prevalent in their music.

The Symphony, op. 21, was written four years after the canons and shows Webern's continuing interest in contrapuntal writing. The work is in two movements, the first a modified sonata form and the second a set of variations. The word "symphony" is misleading since this is chamber music; the only instruments used are clarinet, bass clarinet, two horns, harp and string quartet.

The opening of the first movement (Example 89) shows the extremely pointillistic manner in which the instruments are treated. They seldom play more than a few connected notes; often they emit single sounds separated by rests. The result is a thin web of sound of constantly changing color.

EXAMPLE 89

While this opening sounds as if the tones had no connection with each other, they are actually cunningly plotted. Example 89 has been written in order to show the structure of the movement, which is in the form of a double canon. Canon 1 starts in the second horn (5 notes), proceeds to the clarinet (4 notes), and then to the cellos (4 notes). This is answered (in contrary motion) by the first horn, bass clarinet, and viola. While this proceeds, Canon 2 is given to the harp (1 note), cello (3 notes), second violin (1 note), and harp (2 notes); it is answered (again in contrary motion) by the harp, viola, first violin, harp, horn, and harp.

Another dimension is added to the complexity of the piece in that these notes are also in twelve-tone relationships. Thus, the twelve notes in the upper score of Example 89 form the basic row (O) and the canon in contrary motion is an inversion (I). Canon 2 is a retrograde inversion (RI) while its answering voice is a transposition of the retrograde (R).

The opening measures of *Variations for Piano* show Webern's predilection for mirror forms (Retrograde-Inversions in twelve-tone terminology):

EXAMPLE 90*

The numbers indicate the relationships to the row and show that the second half is played in the left hand while the right hand plays the first half. These seven measures are followed by a three-measure phrase that in itself is a mirror, the first and last measures being reversed. The return of the opening material follows, except that the right hand now plays what the left hand played before. All of this is followed by a middle section that is a "variation" of the first section, and eventually figures similar to those of the opening return.

The second of the three movements is a strict canon in contrary motion. It is most difficult to play and it is difficult to hear since the two melodies, consisting of leaps, are continually crossing. As in the Symphony, op. 21, the ear tends to follow the line as a unit instead of as two melodies.

Familiarity with the piece will reveal that instead of a spattering of random tones over the keyboard there is, rather, a most intricate structural pattern. At four points—Measures 1, 9, 13, and 19—the two voices arrive at the note *a*. While all the other notes go up and down by the same intervals, these measures form focal points on either side of which the elaborate structures are formed.

The third movement is the most extended, and at the same time the easiest to follow. It consists of a theme followed by five variations. The theme has three parts, the second of which reverses the relationship of the two hands. The third part is a retrograde of the first, so that it ends on the same tone with which it began. The variations are similar in structure, but differ greatly in expression.

After repeated hearing of the *Piano Variations* some of the patterns become apparent to the listener. One hears the wonderful symmetry, the highs being answered by lows, and the foldings and unfoldings of tension and repose. Obviously Webern is not an expressionist depicting the chaos of the modern world, because his quiet patterns play themselves out with the inevitability of the movement of the stars in a galaxy. He is more like a mathematician or a theoretical physicist, plotting structures that are so complex that the relationship of the parts eludes most people. There is great beauty in such formulas for those who can read and hear them.

SUGGESTED READINGS

Berg: *Alban Berg, the Man and his Music* by H. F. Redlich (New York, 1957) is the only full-length study of the composer in English. An analysis of individual works will be found in Leibowitz (*op. cit.*).

The Violin Concerto is treated by Mosco Carner in *The Concerto*, edited by Ralph Hill (London, 1952). "*Wozzeck*, a guide to the words and music", by Willi Reich in the *Musical Quarterly, Vol.* XXXVIII, No. 1 (January 1952) is recommended, as its the essay on the same work in Kerman's *Opera as Drama* (New York, 1956).

Webern: No book-length study has appeared in English as yet. The second volume of *Die Reihe* (English edition, Theodore Presser, Philadelphia, 1958) is devoted to Webern and contains articles by eighteen European scholars. The booklet published in conjunction with the recording of his complete works (Columbia K4L-232) by Robert Craft is excellent.

	France	Germany & Austria	Other Countries	Other Arts, Events
1930	Milhaud: *Maximilien* Roussel: *Bacchus et Ariane* Stravinsky: *Symphony of Psalms*	Hindemith: Concerto for Viola Webern: Quartet for Violin, Clarinet, Saxophone and Piano	A. Hába: *The Mother* Shostakovich: *Golden Age*	Auden: *Poems* T. S. Eliot: *Ash Wednesday* Faulkner: *As I Lay Dying* T. Wolfe: *Look Homeward, Angel*
1931	Ravel: Piano Concerto in G Stravinsky: Violin Concerto		R. Thompson: Symphony #2 Bartók: Piano Concerto #2 Walton: *Belshazzar's Feast*	Calder: Mobiles
1932	Stravinsky: *Duo Concertant* for violin and piano	Hindemith: *Philharmonic Concerto*		Picasso: *The Mirror*
1933		Strauss: *Arabella*	Harris: Symphony 1933 Shostakovitch: Piano Concerto	Adolf Hitler becomes Chancellor of Germany
1934		Webern: Concerto for 9 Instruments	Prokofiev: *Lieutenant Kije* Bartók: String Quartet #5	

	France	Germany & Austria	Other Countries	Other Arts, Events
1935	Stravinsky: Concerto for 2 Pianos Honegger: *Jeanne au Bucher* Messiaen: *La Nativité*	Berg: Violin Concerto Hindemith: *Der Schwanendreher* Webern: *Das Augenlicht*	Prokofiev: Violin Concerto #2 Prokofiev: *Romeo and Juliet* Gershwin: *Porgy and Bess* Vaughan Williams: Symphony #4	
1936	Milhaud: *Suite Provençale* Stravinsky: *Jeu de Cartes* Poulenc: Mass	Schoenberg: Violin Concerto Schoenberg: String Quartet #4 Hindemith: Three Sonatas for Piano Orff: *Carmina Burana*	Harris: Symphony #2 Prokofiev: *Peter and the Wolf* Shostakovitch: Symphony #4	Spanish Civil War begins
1937	Poulenc: *Tel jour, telle nuit*	Berg: *Lulu* (1st performance)	Bartók: *Music for Strings, Percussion and Celesta* Shostakovitch: Symphony #5 Piston: Symphony #1 Copland: *El Salón México* Barber: *Essay for Orchestra*	Picasso: *Guernica* Germany: Exhibition of Degenerate Art
1938	Stravinsky: *Dumbarton Oaks Concerto*	Orff: *Der Mond*	Copland: *Billy the Kid*	Sartre: *Nausea*
1939	Milhaud: Symphony #1	Webern: Cantata #1	Harris: Symphony #3 Walton: Violin Concerto Shostakovitch: Symphony #6 Britten: *Les Illuminations* Dallapiccola: *Canti di Prigionia* Prokofiev: *Alexander Nevsky*	Outbreak of World War II

1940	Poulenc: *Banalités*; Stravinsky: Symphony in C	Hindemith: Violin Concerto; Webern: *Variations for Orchestra*	Harris: *Folk-song Symphony*; Piston: Violin Concerto; Shostakovich: Piano Quintet	United States and USSR enter World War II
1941		Hindemith: Symphony in E♭; Strauss: *Capriccio*	Copland: *Quiet City*; Creston: Symphony #1; Schuman: Symphony #3; Copland: Piano Sonata; Prokofiev: *War and Peace*; Shostakovich: Symphony #7	
1942	Messiaen: *Visions de l'amen*	Schoenberg: Piano Concerto	Schuman: Symphony #4; Copland: *Lincoln Portrait*; Copland: *Rodeo*; Prokofiev: Piano Sonata #7; Martinu: Symphony #1; Carter: Symphony #1	Camus: *The Stranger*
1943	Milhaud: *Bolivar*	Orff: *Catulli Carmina*; Hindemith: *Ludus Tonalis*	Hanson: Symphony #4; Vaughan Williams: Symphony #5; Shostakovitch: Symphony #8; Harris: Symphony #5; Bartók: Concerto for Orchestra; Martinu: Symphony #2	Sartre: *The Flies*
1944	Poulenc: *Les Mamelles de Tirésias*	Hindemith: *Symphonic Metamorphoses*	Stravinsky: Sonata for two Pianos; Piston: Symphony #2; Barber: *Capricorn Concerto*; Copland: *Appalachian Spring*; Prokofiev: Symphony #5	Brecht: *Mother Courage*; Allied invasion of Europe

CHAPTER XII

BARTÓK

(Debussy) restored a feeling for chords to all musicians. He was as important as Beethoven who revealed to us progressive form, and as Bach who introduced us to the transcendence of counterpoint. I always ask myself, could one make a synthesis of these three masters and create a vital contemporary style?

BÉLA BARTÓK, SPEAKING OF DEBUSSY

One of the most original and influential voices of the twentieth century was that of the Hungarian composer, Béla Bartók. Although aware of and influenced by the current musical trends in Paris and Vienna, he was a follower of neither Stravinskian neoclassicism nor Schoenbergian expressionism. His musical language was his own, formed of indigenous elements, a thorough knowledge of the main-stream of music, past and present, and his own personality.

As with many composers, Bartók's gift for music was discovered when he was still a child. His mother, the widow of the director of a school of agriculture in a provincial Hungarian town, was his first piano teacher. Upon the death of her husband she became a school teacher, moving from town to town until 1893, when mother and son settled in Pressburg and Bartók began serious study of piano and composition. In 1899 he was accepted as a student at the Royal Conservatory in Budapest, receiving a thorough education as pianist and composer. The piano remained of greatest importance through all his life, for not only was he a virtuoso who gave concerts throughout Europe, but also piano teaching was his principal occupation, and the largest group of his compositions was for this instrument.

As early as 1904 he started collecting Hungarian folksongs, an interest that was to be life-long and that was to have a strong influence on his compositions. His contributions and publications in the field of comparative musicology, the science devoted to collecting and analyzing folk music and music of primitive cultures, are of major importance. He made countless trips to all the Hungarian provinces, recording songs and instrumental music. Later researches carried him further afield; in 1913 he went to Roumania and Arabia, in 1932 to Egypt, and in 1936 to Turkey. In the last years of life, when in the United States, he returned again to the publication of this material.

Among other things proven by this research was the fact that the type of music commonly thought of as "Hungarian" was actually gypsy music as performed in restaurants and cafés of Central Europe. The *Hungarian Rhapsodies* by Liszt and the *Hungarian Dances* by Brahms are based on this type of gypsy music, for before Bartók authentic Hungarian music was uncollected and unknown.

In 1907 Bartók became professor of piano at the Budapest Conservatory, and except for leaves of absence to give concerts or to collect folk music, he remained in the capital city for the next thirty years. During most of this time he received almost no recognition from his compatriots as a composer, and it was not until the late 1920's that some notice came from abroad. A ballet, *The Wooden Prince,* and an opera, *Duke Bluebeard's Castle,* were the first works to win any acclaim at home and in Germany.

In the years between the world wars, Bartók increased his activities as a concert pianist, playing in the United States as well as throughout Europe—most frequently performing one of his two piano concertos. The Swiss conductor Paul Sacher became his particular champion and introduced several of the more important orchestral works.

The rise of Hitler and the collaboration of Hungary with Nazi Germany finally made it imperative that Bartók leave his native country, not on religious grounds, but because of his love of freedom and his outspoken hatred of Nazism. He came to the United States in 1940 and, except for a short return trip to Hungary to settle his affairs, remained here until his death in 1945.

The American years must have been bitter; after all, he was an exile from a fallen country, he was impoverished, and his health was precarious. He received an appointment from Columbia University to continue his folk-music research, he played concerts occasionally, and he worked on some commissioned compositions. Had it not been for illness, he probably would have been able to endure these years of exile and to resume his career. However, as his health grew worse his financial problems increased. A grant from ASCAP provided for medical care, but in spite of this he died of leukemia in 1945.

Since that time he has become recognized as one of the giants of twentieth-century music. His music has been performed more frequently than it ever was during his life. Biographies and studies of his musical idiom have been published, and elements of his style have entered into the vocabularies of younger composers. Practically all of his works have been recorded and many of them are frequently heard in concerts. It is most unfortunate that Bartók did not live another decade so that he might have enjoyed this recognition of his life's work.

BARTÓK'S COMPOSITIONS

Bartók's period of composition extended from 1903 to 1944. Because his style of writing underwent gradual changes, it is convenient to group his compositions into style periods. Throughout Bartók's entire career, the central, unifying core is his nationality, expressed musically by the use of elements of central European music—scales, rhythms, and melodies. While this feature is stronger in some works than in others, it is absent from none of them.

Period 1: 1903-1908

The compositions of the first period are student works that show the formative influences and youthful ideals of a composer with great talent. *Kossuth* (1903), a long, patriotic symphonic poem, pays homage to Liszt and Strauss. Two Suites for Orchestra (1905 and 1907, rewritten in 1920 and 1943 respectively) show his admiration for Strauss and Debussy. This initial period is terminated by the first String Quartet (1908), which reveals the influence of Brahms as well as other mentors.

Period 2: 1908-1926

The most important works of this period are:

STAGE WORKS
> *Duke Bluebeard's Castle* (1911)
> *The Wooden Prince* (ballet; 1914-16)
> *The Miraculous Mandarin* (1919)

CHAMBER MUSIC
> String Quartet #2 (1915-17)
> Sonata for Violin and Piano #1 (1921)
> Sonata for Violin and Piano #2 (1922)

PIANO
> Two Roumanian Dances (1909-10)
> *Allegro Barbaro* (1911)
> *Suite,* op. 14 (1916)

In the *Allegro Barbaro* Bartók made sounds as rude and startling as any other composer's in those brave years preceding World War I. In implication and influence it was as revolutionary as Stravinsky's *Le Sacre du Printemps* (1913) and Schoenberg's *Three Pieces for Piano* (1909). With it, all notions that music should be pretty, charming, or beautiful disappear, and brute force and angry vehemence take their place. Such expression is achieved by treating the piano as a percussion instrument to be struck and hammered instead of carressed or cajoled to "sing." The texture of the piece is chordal, and the chords consist of clusters of seconds, although the basic tonality is never lost.

This mood of intransigence and iconoclasm characterizes many second-period works. Examples are the opera, *Bluebeard's Castle,* and the ballet, *The Wooden Prince.* The two sonatas for violin and piano are important. They too are wild and rhapsodic, with wide leaps in the violin melodies, constantly shifting meters, and chords of strong dissonance in the piano.

Second-period works are not numerous, since Bartók, discouraged by the lack of interest in his music, stopped composing between 1915 and 1919. It was during these years that he devoted himself to the collection of folksongs.

Period 3: 1926-1937

This is the richest and most important of Bartók's style periods, for it includes some undisputed masterpieces of twentieth-century music. Stylistically, the most important change over previous works is a new prevalence of contrapuntal texture. Key works of the period are:

> *Mikrokosmos* (1926-37)
> String Quartets 3-5 (1927, 1928, 1934)
> Piano Concerto #2 (1930-31)
> *Music for Strings, Percussion and Celesta* (1937)
> Sonata for Two Pianos and Percussion (1937)
> Violin Concerto (1937-38)

Two of these works will be described.

String Quartet #4 (1927) has all the boldness and strength of the works immediately preceding, but at the same time the contrapuntal and formal aspects are developed in an entirely new manner. Among the five movements there are thematic connections as follows:

$$I \quad \underline{II \quad III \quad IV} \quad V$$

The form, then, extends to the work as a whole, beyond individual movements, in the manner of some of Beethoven's later sonatas.

The first movement glorifies Bartók's favorite interval, the minor second. It is used both melodically and harmonically, most of the melodies having a narrow compass resulting from a series of chromatic seconds, and most of the chords consisting of clusters of the same interval. Until one is accustomed to the effect, it is rather startling to hear such angry violence coming from the string quartet ensemble, for which so much literature has been written in more "polite" language.

After a bold introduction of a few measures, the principal motive of the movement is heard from the cello:

EXAMPLE 91*

A few measures later, the theme is presented in inversion against itself, ending in a characteristic cluster consisting of the following notes played *szforzando,* fortissimo—*b*-flat, *b, c, c♯, d, d♯ e:*

EXAMPLE 92

The viola begins a new figure making prominent use of harmonics. Under it, in the cello part, another conjunct, few-note theme centering on G♯ is heard. Other voices imitate the cello's theme with characteristic rhythmic freedom, the figure starting on various parts of the measure and making an extraordinarily rich texture. The section ends with another explosive cluster. Example 91 appears in original and inversion simultaneously.

These are the chief elements making up the movement, which almost never lets down from its height of anguished expression. To add to the violence there are long glissandos by all the instruments introducing a shrieklike effect. In spite of this vehemence of expression the form of the movement is that of the classical sonata, with a clear-cut recapitulation and coda. The motto theme, in a Phrygian variant, is played again in the final measures by all the instruments in unison.

The second movement is a miracle of string writing, possibly influenced by a somewhat similar movement in Berg's *Lyric Suite*, already discussed. The tempo is breathlessly fast and the instruments are muted. The effect is unearthly, for one cannot hear individual tones but only "flashes" of sound.

Regardless of the effect, the movement is made up of individual tones cunningly arranged in clever patterns, the main theme a rising and falling chromatic figure. There is much contrapuntal ingenuity in the interplay of the themes, and the cluster chords that characterized the first movement are also strongly evident here. The form is A B A with a more static second theme:

EXAMPLE 93

Glissandos and other string effects, such as *ponticello* and alternations of pizzicato and bowed passages, add greatly to the bizarre sonorities.

The third movement is the keystone of this arch-form work. It is static and atmospheric in a Debussyan manner. An unusual effect is introduced at the beginning where the cluster chord played by the three upper strings is played non vibrato. Throughout the movement there are indications from the composer to alternate the non vibrato and the normal vibrato sound.

Below this chord the cello plays a chromatic soliloquy, centered around a few notes, the phrases starting with the typical Hungarian rhythm: ♪♪ . . Later, the first violin takes over with birdlike, twittering sounds, an example of the "night-music"* mood so characteristic of the composer. The first melody returns to the cello, but this time the first violin answers in free canon.

*This is a special kind of Bartók piece that has aptly been called "night music" by Halsey Stevens, taking his cue from a piano piece so named by the composer.

The fourth movement corresponds to the second in its dependence on special string effects. Here the device is the pizzicato, the entire movement being played without bows. Again a special effect is indicated, a pizzicato so intense that a snap is heard as the string hits the finger board. The movement has a strong folk-dance flavor, derived from the syncopated triple meter and modal scales.

The first theme in the viola is in a modified Lydian mode:

EXAMPLE 94

Canons appear at various intervals and at irregular spacings. A little later there is strumming in the cello and viola, and the second theme of the second movement reappears (Example 92). The scale passages recur and the movement ends in further canonic treatments.

The last movement is also dancelike. There are strong polymodal effects in this section. For example, the following accompanying cluster is based on C while the melody above it starts on C♯.

EXAMPLE 95

At a repetition of this material a Stravinsky-like rhythm is "drummed" by the cello:

EXAMPLE 96

The middle section is introduced by raucous clusters in all the instruments, followed by a section that is light and graceful in mood—a mood we might add, that is seldom found in the work. The melody of the first violin has a gypsy flavor with its ornamentation and prominent use of the augmented second:

EXAMPLE 97

Underneath, as an accompaniment figure, the rhythm of Example 91 from the first movement gradually asserts itself, clearly linking the last movement to the first. The vigorous material shown in Example 96 returns and the composition ends with ever-increasing vigor. At the climax, rasping twelve-note clusters are played fortissimo, *col legno* (with the back of the bow). The coda consists of various canonic treatments of material from the first section (see Example 95), but the final gesture of the whole quartet is again the principal motive of the first movement (see Example 92).

Bartók's Fourth String Quartet embodies many of his outstanding style characteristics. The boldness and audacity of the dissonances, the unusual string effects, the rich treatment of contrapuntal devices, the narrow compass of the modal melodies—these are some of the elements of this important composition.

In this, the richest of Bartók's productive periods, there are several other compositions that should be known by every student of his works. Among them are the Violin Concerto, which has been called the most important work in the medium since Brahms', the Sonata for Two Pianos and Percussion, and *Music for Strings, Percussion, and Celesta*—the latter two works showing Bartók's interest in writing for unusual combinations of instruments.

Music for Strings, Percussion, and Celesta is sensuously beautiful and deeply moving. At the same time, it is constructed with the most subtle skill, fulfilling Bartók's desire to combine the beauty of Debussy's sonorities with the formal structure of Beethoven and the counterpoint of Bach.

A fugue, based on a chromatic, narrow-ranged motive played pianissimo, is heard at the beginning of the first movement.

EXAMPLE 98*

Each voice enters, not in the usual tonic and dominant relationship, but according to the following diagram:

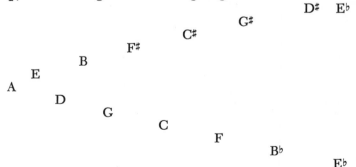

It will be noted that this double series of fifths reaches unanimity on E-flat, the climax of the movement. Afterward, the movement works back to simplicity and the central tonic A through an inverted form of the theme. At the end both forms appear simultaneously.

There is of course much freedom in imitation, since the theme is treated more as a characteristic shape than as an unchanging series of intervals. There are wonderful sonorities throughout—particularly at the end when the celesta adds a shimmer to the combination of the theme and its inversion.

The second movement with its strong rhythmic patterns and modal scales is rooted in the folk music that is the basis of so much of the composer's work. It is cast in a large ternary form, with definite cadence points separating the sections. The opening theme, with its many thirds, is related to the motto theme:

EXAMPLE 99

The strings are separated into two antiphonal groups throughout the movement. After a brief silence this dancelike theme is heard:

EXAMPLE 100

The relation of this theme to the germ theme of the whole becomes apparent if the first note is transposed an octave lower. A close, dissonant canon, a favorite device of the composer, leads to a pronounced cadence on a series of G-major chords.

The development falls into three large sections. The first is built on the theme shown in Example 99. It starts ominously in the lower strings, and soon the whole ensemble is busy with the motive except for the piano and the first group of strings, which play sharply syncopated chords. This is followed by a passage in which the pizzicato strings play modal scale fragments in a close canon. The final section is a fugue, whose subject is related to Example 98. Eventually, the material of the movement's opening is heard again in the original tonality. A free recapitulation and coda follow.

The third movement is a marvelous example of night music where hypnotic sound is the essence, and the xylophone, tympani, and celesta assume an importance rarely granted them. Although the movement seems amorphous and completely atmospheric, it is firmly tied to the whole work through references to the basic theme. An arch-form structure, A B C D C B A, gives it order.

The first section opens and closes with a rhythm tapped out on a high tone on the xylophone, while violas play a fragmentation of the basic theme in imitation. Section B has an eerie sound produced by the celeste and violins playing a derivative of the basic theme against glissandos in the other strings. These slides prepare the way for Section C where there is little besides glissandos for harp, piano, and celesta The music grows in volume, reaching a shattering fortissimo that introduces Section D, consisting of another permutation of the basic theme. The bell-like motive is repeated in different rhythms, manners (pizzicato and *arco*), directions, and textures. This section returns to a pianissimo and then the movement reverses itself. Elements of Sections B and C are combined in the next section where tremolos take the place of glissandos and the violins play the version of the basic theme heard in Section B. The movement ends with the tapping on the xylophone.

EXAMPLE 101

The last movement is the simplest in structure and most direct in expression. A series of boisterous folk dances are heard in which the syncopations and modal scales of the main theme are typical. (See Example 101.) In form it is a rondo, with references to the motto theme becoming prominent towards the end.

In many ways *Music for Strings, Percussion, and Celesta* completely embodies the composer's ideals. In it he treats his cultural heritage—the scales and rhythms of Central Europe—with the sophistication and artistry of a master twentieth-century composer.

PIANO MUSIC

Bartók's piano works call for special attention. He was closely associated with the instrument at all periods of his life as a concert virtuoso, teacher, and editor of publications of classic composers. Furthermore, he composed for the piano from the beginning until the end of his career. Between 1897 and 1926 he wrote and published some thirty collections and individual works for piano. These vary from simple settings of Roumanian and Hungarian dances to a difficult sonata (1926). Between 1926 and 1937 Bartók worked on *Mikrokosmos*, a set of 157 piano pieces published in six volumes. The pieces are grouped according to their difficulty, from simple pieces for beginners to extremely difficult compositions for virtuosos. The complete work gives an insight into Bartók's particular musical world; not only is it an encyclopedia of pianistic figures but also it is just as much a catalog of his compositional devices, for many pieces seem to be sketches for more extended compositions.

The three piano concertos have entered into the repertoires of concert pianists and are counted among the most important written in the past fifty years. The chamber works with piano, such as the two violin and piano sonatas, and the Sonata for Two Pianos and Percussion have also immensely enriched the literature.

Period 4: c. 1937-c. 1945

In the compositions of Bartók's last years a marked stylistic change occurs. Much of the violence and complication of the earlier works disappear and are replaced by serenity and lyric charm. For this reason they have become the most popular of his works. Principal compositions of the time are:

> String Quartet #6 (1939)
> *Divertimento for Strings* (1939)
> Concerto for Orchestra (1943)
> Sonata for Violin Solo (1944)
> Piano Concerto #3 (1945)
> Viola Concerto (unfinished; 1945)

Because of their relative simplicity these compositions will offer no problem to anyone familiar with the earlier works.

STYLE CHARACTERISTICS

Elements of Central European folk music impregnate much of Bartók's composition. Although this is primarily true of the earlier works, it nevertheless applies to the last period as well. Most obvious of these influences are the modal scales already mentioned. Free metric patterns, avoiding the symmetry of the four-bar phrase are also to be traced to the same source. Melodies of narrow compass, with word-inspired rhythms, are also frequently heard (see examples previously given).

Bartók's music often sounds violent and angry because of the numerous harsh dissonances. This is particularly true in the works written before 1939, which certainly lack all trace of charm in the usual sense. He makes frequent use of clusters of minor seconds, for which he is said to have been inspired by the American composer Henry Cowell who toured Europe in the twenties, playing his own music. Melodies doubled in sevenths and played fortissimo gave Bartók the reputation of being one of the boldest of twentieth-century composers. For some time he was accused, along with Stravinsky, of writing "ugly" music. Toward the end of his life, Bartók wrote more ingratiating music, and the Concerto for Orchestra as well as the Third Piano Concerto are conservative in their use of dissonance.

While many works of the first and second period are predominantly harmonic and gain their effects from the harsh sounding chords, the texture of third- and fourth-period compositions is most frequently contrapuntal. This is particularly true in the string quartets, and Bartók's skill as a contrapuntist is shown in the inversions and rhythmic variants that characterize so many passages. He wrote counterpoint of highly dissonant character, of course, and the clashes between voices are uncompromising.

On the other hand, Bartók did not write in a consistently contrapuntal manner. That is to say, contrapuntal writing is alternated with passages or whole movements that are harmonically static in a Debussyan style—pieces in which sheer sound seems to be the most important element. Mysterious sonorities take the place of any kind of manipulation and involved relationships between voices.

While Bartók often used a highly chromatic idiom, he never entirely lost sight of tonality. His tonality is not based on cadence chords, but rather on the preferential use of certain tones, repeated often enough to give a feeling of a tonal center. An *ostinato* figure, rotating around a focal tone for instance, sometimes gives tonal stability, even if the other voices are strongly centrifugal.

The extended works of Bartók show an almost classically formal concept. While he did not write any symphonies (except for a lost student work), the six quartets are a good indication of his attitude toward form. They are in contrasting movements, usually in the traditional order of fast, slow, scherzo, and fast finale. Sometimes in later works five movements are used, arranged in arch form (see the analysis of the Fourth Quartet). "Motto" themes appear in more than one movement, and theme transformations are found in the extended compositions. Within movements he uses elements of sonata, rondo, and minuet and trio types of organization.

For this reason, and owing to the fact that his themes are often little more than strongly rhythmic motives, the similarity to the compositional techniques of Beethoven has often been mentioned. In his boldness and intransigence of expression he also reminds one of Beethoven.

In the realm of musical color, or timbre, Bartók is a great master in discovering the potentialities of individual instruments as well as in their unusual combinations and groupings. His treatment of the piano and the string quartet in a harsh, percussive manner has been mentioned. He was fond of unusual string effects, including extensive use of harmonics, multiple stops, pizzicatos, and striking glissandos. The penchant for unusual combinations can be seen in his Sonata for Two Pianos and Percussion as well as in *Music for Strings, Percussion, and Celesta*. Timbre is so important for Bartók that he sometimes writes evocative compositions that are scarcely more than a fabric of sounds suggesting insect buzzings or bird calls. An example of such "night music" has been cited in the discussion of *Music for Strings, Percussion, and Celesta*.

The question raised by Bartók in the citation at the head of this chapter is answered by his works, for they do combine the color of Debussy, the all-pervading sense of form of Beethoven, and the contrapuntal texture of Bach. His style is original but not eccentric, for it is based on principles that have marked great music of all times. In general classification he is closer to the expressionists than he is to the neoclassicists, but at the same time, because of his strong roots in the folk idiom of his country, he does not approach Schoenberg's pinnacle of subjectivity.

SUGGESTED READINGS

The authoritative study is *The Life and Music of Béla Bartók* (New York, 1953) by Halsey Stevens. A biographical study of the American years is Agatha Fassett's *The Naked Face of Genius* (Boston, 1958). The Autumn and Winter, 1949, issues of *Tempo* are devoted to Bartók and contain biographical and analytical material, as well as a comprehensive bibliography.

WEBERN

BERG, WITH A PORTRAIT OF HIMSELF BY SCHOENBERG

"WOZZECK," Act III, Scene 1

BARTÓK

HINDEMITH

PROKOFIEV

SHOSTAKOVICH

VAUGHAN WILLIAMS

BRITTEN

245

COPLAND

HARRIS

PISTON   SESSIONS

HANSON

THOMSON

CHAPTER XIII

HINDEMITH

A composer's horizon cannot be far-reaching enough: his desire to know, to comprehend, must incite, inspire, and drench every phase of his works.   HINDEMITH

Paul Hindemith has had an extraordinarily rich life in music, for there is scarcely a field he has not touched, from the most practical to the most theoretical. He performs on many instruments, ancient and modern, and plays the viola with the mastery of a great artist. A prolific composer of music of all dimensions and for many media, he is also a conductor who has led many of the world's great orchestras. As an inspiring teacher he has influenced a generation of composers, and his textbooks in basic musicianship and harmony are widely employed. Furthermore, he is a theorist in the real sense in that his elaborately developed theory of the relationship of tones is one of the few that is comprehensive enough to include complex contemporary styles along with the music of the past.

Hindemith has played many roles, and the public has thought of him successively as a brash young radical, a wild expressionist, an unfeeling neoclassicist, a mature, respected, neoromantic master, and finally, a reactionary. Each of these labels has been appropriate at one time or another.

He was born in Hanau, central Germany, and attended the Frankfurt Conservatory. He was a spectacularly

249

gifted student of the string instruments and composition and at the age of twenty was already concertmaster of the Frankfurt Opera and violist in a leading string quartet. After a year in the army in World War I, he plunged into the hectic musical life of post-war Germany.

This was an exciting time and place in which to come of age in the arts, for Germany's cultural life in the period after the war and before Hitler's time was unequaled anywhere. The country was torn with a cruel inflation and its very existence was threatened by one political crisis after another. Colonies were lost and industrial areas were expropriated, leaving thousands of Germans penniless, their life-savings dissipated by inflation. In spite of this general insecurity, the arts flourished. Opera houses and symphony orchestras were established by ephemeral governments in over a hundred different cities—this in spite of the fact that Germany is not as large, say, as Texas—and money was found to produce lavish new operas. It is characteristic, for instance, that Berlin and not Paris was the scene of the première of Milhaud's elaborate *Christophe Colomb* in 1930. Art and music schools were re-established and theatrical production was revolutionized by the imagination and skill of Max Reinhardt and others.

A typical product of the time was the Bauhaus, a school of design and architecture whose aim was to strip away the vast accumulation of styles and ornaments from past ages, and return to basic, austere simplicity and honesty of expression. Disciples of the Bauhaus eventually changed the appearance of everything from packages to cities throughout much of the world.

The term *neue Sachlichkeit* (new objectivity) was used to designate this "no-nonsense" attitude which opposed the intense subjectivity of the expressionists. *Neue Sachlichkeit* found its expression in the bitter, satirical portraits of George Grosz; in the gaunt, cube-form, glass buildings of Gropius; and, for a time, in the music of Hindemith.

In 1927 Hindemith was called to Berlin to be a professor of composition at the *Hochschule für Musik,* and remained there until Hitler came to power and decreed that dissonant, "modern" music was degenerate and forbade any more performances. Hindemith and his music became openly involved in the struggle when Wilhelm Furtwängler, Berlin's distinguished conductor, insisted on playing his compositions after they had been condemned.

Seeing no future for himself in Germany, Hindemith left the country. He spent two years in Ankara, Turkey, organizing a state system of music education and toured widely as a conductor and violist, making several trips to the United States. In 1940 he became a professor of theory and composition at the School of Music at Yale University and remained there for thirteen years. In 1953 he returned to Europe, settled in Switzerland, and continued his busy life of composing, conducting, teaching, and writing about music.

HINDEMITH'S COMPOSITIONS

Hindemith's main compositions include: three full-length operas—*Cardillac* (1926, revised 1952), *Mathis der Maler* (*Matthias, the Painter,* 1938), *Die Harmonie der Welt* (*The Harmony of the World,* 1957); five short operas; three ballets, including *Nobilissima Visione* (1938) and the *Four Temperaments* (1944); large orchestral works including the *Philharmonic Concerto* (1932), Symphony in E-flat (1941), and *Symphonic Metamorphoses on a Theme of Weber* (1944); productions for amateurs; choral works with orchestra and *a cappella;* concertos for piano (two), cello (two), horn, and violin, and several for string instruments with chamber orchestra; six string quartets and other chamber music; sonatas for almost every orchestral instrument with piano; three sonatas for piano solo; *Ludus Tonalis,* a set of preludes and fugues for piano; and songs with piano and with instruments.

This is a long and comprehensive list of works including large and small, serious and casual, difficult and easy compositions. Hindemith resembles Milhaud in that there is no gradual evolution of style to be traced in his music after he achieved a personal style in the late twenties. Before that time he experimented widely and wrote in many of the idioms of the day; these compositions constitute his first style period.

Period 1: 1917-1927

It is not at all surprising that Hindemith's rich gifts and vigorous curiosity led him to experiment in many different styles in his youthful works. The first compositions stem from the late romantic style of Reger and Strauss, and are characterized by rich, dissonant harmony, and thick contrapuntal textures. Typical early works include the string quartets and the sonatas for violin and piano, Opus 11. A very dissonant, expressionistic phase follows, examples of which are the song cycle, *Die Junge Magd* (*The Young Girl;* 1922) for contralto, flute, clarinet, and string quartet, and an opera, *Mörder, Hoffnung der Frauen* (*Murder, the Hope of Women;* 1921) whose libretto was written by Kokoschka, the expressionist painter. The piano suite, *1922,* consisting of "March," "Shimmy," "Night Piece," and "Rag-time" shows the influence of jazz, but Hindemith's brutally dissonant and heavyhanded treatment of the popular idiom was very different from Milhaud's light-hearted approach. The directions that he wrote to the performer in the score are typical of his youthful iconoclasm:

DIRECTIONS FOR USE

Don't pay any attention to what you learned in your piano lessons!

Don't spend any time considering if you should play D# with the fourth or sixth finger.

Play this piece very savagely, but always rigidly in rhythm like a machine. Consider the piano as an interesting kind of percussion instrument and treat it accordingly.[1]

One of the most successful compositions of the period was *Eine Kleine Kammermusik* (*Miniature Chamber Music;* 1922). Pert and irreverent, it is surprisingly close in spirit to music then being written in Paris. The first movement opens with two planes of harmony and "slips" from one tonality to another—idioms typical of the twenties (see Example 102).

Succeeding movements continue this light-hearted mood; the second recalls a hurdy-gurdy, while the third is a nocturne with suggestions of the blues. The fourth movement is an acrid scherzo. There are many measures of irregular length in the final movement, and the strident dissonances in the coda are obtained by combining two disparate factors: a pedal in the bassoon and horn, and a series of parallel chords built in fourths played by the treble instruments (see Example 103).

EXAMPLE 102*

Playful

CLARINET

HORN

BASSOON

EXAMPLE 103

Very Fast

Modest as it is, *Eine Kleine Kammermusik* is important in Hindemith's development, for it shows his emancipation from the overly serious, romantic style of the first works.

Period 2: 1927 to the present

By the time Hindemith left Frankfurt for Berlin in 1927 he had passed through his experimental phase and had arrived at a carefully worked out theory of composition as well as a philosophy of the function of music. He continued to write pieces of all dimensions, but his musical style remained essentially the same from then on.

Sensing that the complexity and dissonance of the early works had alienated many music lovers, he deliberately lightened the texture and simplified the expression of succeeding compositions. There was a strong socialist movement in Germany at the time, which led to the establishment of orchestras and choruses for working people. Hindemith wrote music for these amateur groups on down-to-earth, timely subjects. For example, one of his cantatas commemorated Lindberg's flight.

These pieces are examples of *Gebrauchsmusik* (everyday music, useful music, functional music), a term that has become permanently attached to Hindemith in much the same way that the label "Les Six" is still applied to Milhaud and his friends long after they have changed orientation. Much later, in the United States, Hindemith explained the origin of the term. He tells of using it in a casual way in conversation with a group of choral conductors:

> Some busybody had written a report on that totally unimportant discussion, and when years later I came to this country, I felt like the sorcerer's apprentice who had become the victim of his own configurations: the slogan *Gebrauchsmusik* hit me wherever I went. It had grown abundant, useless, and disturbing as thousands of dandelions in a lawn. Apparently it met perfectly the common desire for a verbal label which classifies objects, persons, and problems, thus exempting anyone from opinions based on knowledge.[2]

Only a small number of Hindemith's compositions were "functional" in that sense. His general simplification of style and growing interest in contrapuntal textures rather than in dissonant chords, however, became a constant feature of his writing. The term *neoclassic*, or more appropriately, *neobaroque*, already encountered in the discussion of Stravinsky's music, is often applied to these compositions, as well as the phrase *back-to-Bach*. In form and texture many of his pieces of the late twenties and thirties resemble those of Bach. The most Bach-like composition is *Ludus Tonalis* (*Musical*

Diversions, 1943), a twentieth-century *Well-Tempered Clavier* that consists of a set of twelve fugues each in a different tonality and separated by interludes. The whole set is preceded by a prelude and terminated by a postlude, which is a retrograde version of the opening piece.

The sonatas for piano and various wind instruments are examples of *Gebrauchsmusik* in the best sense. Noting a lack of solo repertoire for the orchestral instruments, he wrote sonatas for most of them. These compositions filled a need, and have become popular.

Concurrent with these modest, "practical" compositions, Hindemith occasionally wrote large, serious works. The two operas make no concessions to popular taste or to amateur production. They have had few performances, but their "symphonic syntheses" (Hindemith's term) are often heard on symphony programs.

One of the best known of Hindemith's compositions is *Mathis der Maler*. Mathis, the hero of the opera, is Matthias Grünewald (born 1503), North German painter of the famous Isenheim Altar in Colmar, Alsace. Each of the three movements represents a panel of the triptych.

The first movement is called *"Engelkonzert"* ("Concert of the Angels"). The picture that inspired the piece shows a group of angels playing instruments. In the foreground, before the Virgin and Child, is a smiling, blond angel playing the viola da gamba. The atmosphere is one of radiant happiness, reflected in the music through the prevailing consonance and dancelike rhythms. There are frequent chromatic alterations and shiftings of key center. For example, at the beginning this melody is heard in clarinets and bassoons over a widespread G-major chord:

EXAMPLE 104*

CLARINETS

After a cadence, the trombones intone a medieval melody against which the violins move in a lilting counterpoint. The *cantus*

*Copyright 1934 by B. Schott's Soehne, Mainz.

moves to the horns and then to the woodwinds. The beginning melody is heard again and the introduction comes to a close followed by the first theme of a modified sonata form:

EXAMPLE 105

The use of modal scales, major and minor thirds, and the sudden shift of tonality at the end should be noted.

After this theme is imitated by various instruments in various keys, a second theme closely related in rhythm and mood is heard in the violins.

EXAMPLE 106

The second theme is treated in much the same manner as the first. It is heard in augmentation and then cadence chords stop the motion.

The closing theme appears in the flutes. It, too, has a strong rhythmic resemblance to the first theme, which soon reappears as a countermelody:

EXAMPLE 107

The exposition ends with cadence on *b*.

The development consists of contrapuntal treatment of the three exposition themes, and at the climax, the Gregorian melody of the introduction is added to the bustling countermelodies.

The recapitulation does not start in the original tonality of G. Instead, Example 105 is heard in various keys and instruments. The second theme is not heard in its expected place since the closing theme appears next, but in the coda all three themes are exploited once again.

The second movement is entitled *"Grablegung"* or "The Entombment" and is based on the central panel of the exterior of the triptych. It is a somber, realistic scene depicting the figure of Christ hanging heavily on the Cross, with the grieving figures of the two Marys, John, and John the Baptist at his feet.

This movement is quite short and is based on a slow, conjunct theme. The changing tonal centers are characteristic of the composer:

EXAMPLE 108

Later a new theme in the oboe starts with two skips of a fourth, a favorite melodic device:

EXAMPLE 109

The first theme then returns in the full orchestra.

The last movement, the "Temptation of St. Anthony," is the most exciting. The picture itself is an amazing scene, full of fantastic birds, reptiles, and demons attacking the Saint. In the sky above, God is represented in the act of sending Michael to aid the suffering Anthony.

The music starts with a chromatic recitativelike passage in the strings interrupted by roaring dissonances played by full orchestra. The rhetorical introduction comes to an end; the movement proper begins with this theme in the strings:

EXAMPLE 110

The introductory material has anticipated this theme. Notable here is the fact that it contains eleven of the twelve notes of the chromatic scale. The theme is treated freely by the entire orchestra against a "panting" rhythmic motive in the background. Contrast is offered by a conjunct oboe solo, and by crashing dissonances.

After a slow middle section, a strongly syncopated brass passage ushers in the concluding section. At the height of an exciting climax the main idea of the movement returns in its original tonality. Rhythmically altered and augmented, this time it is played by the trombones.

The coda begins with a *fugato* during which the deliverance of Anthony is suggested by the hymn "Lauda Sion Salvatore" discernable above all the hubbub. The piece ends with great impressiveness in a choralelike alleluia played *mit aller Kraft* (with full strength) by the brass.

HINDEMITH AS A THEORIST

It is well known that conventional harmonic theory breaks down when applied to certain styles of contemporary music. For example, it is impossible to analyze Bartók's chords or to use Roman numerals to designate chord progressions in music no longer tonal in the old sense. This state of affairs disturbed the orderly, systematic Hindemith who felt the need of a more inclusive theory of music, one that would give order to and establish a classification system for even the most complicated chords.

In order to do so, he went back to the basic physical fact of music, the overtone series. By a process of logic (but one that has not been universally accepted) he arrived at a series of tones establishing their relationship with one another:

EXAMPLE 111

This series establishes the relationships of the tones with the fundamental, C. Thus, the further a note is to the right, the more distant is its relationship.

Although all twelve notes of the chromatic scale are given here, this is in no sense a Schoenbergian tone-row, for the series has nothing to do with any particular composition. However, it should be noted that all the notes are present and consequently the concept of a seven-note diatonic scale with five chromatic notes no longer applies. All twelve are included here, in an ordered relationship, allowing the composer to use any tone without modulating.*

Next Hindemith establishes a series of intervals arranged from the simplest to the most complex.

EXAMPLE 112

*The phrase *diatonicized chromaticism* has been used to describe this concept by Mosco Carner in his book, *Twentieth Century Harmony*.

On the basis of these two series it is possible to weigh the degree of dissonance or tension of any combination of tones. Once this is done the use of dissonance is no longer arbitrary. Now it is possible to say that one combination is more or less dissonant than another; therefore, it can be used with full understanding of its effect. As Hindemith explains:

> Armed with the concept of harmonic fluctuation (i.e., the range of tension from a major triad to the most dissonant tone-cluster and its calculated application), . . . we no longer have to leave determination of the degree of harmonic complexity of each chord to the combined effect of melodic lines which are not binding on the harmony. On the contrary, this concept enables us to understand the factor of harmonic complexity according to its own laws, so that we can place each harmony in that position in which its tonal effect will be most favorable. This means of evaluation admits in principle every possible harmony (even the most complicated) just as formerly, when instinct alone was the criterion.[3]

Hindemith's theory is not easy to understand, and certain inconsistencies in its development have not gone unnoticed by critics. Students who are interested should read his *Craft of Musical Composition,* the translation of *Unterweisung im Tonsatz* (1937).

Whether the theory is completely valid or not, it is interesting for the insights it gives into the composer's personality, for Hindemith is not content merely to write a tremendous number of significant scores and be actively engaged in their performance; his inquiring mind demands a rational foundation for his music, the absence of which has not troubled many other composers.

It is possible to see the effects of Hindemith's theoretical convictions in the two versions of *Das Marienleben (The Life of Mary),* a song cycle written to poems by Rainer Maria Rilke, the German poet. The original setting was written in 1923, but twenty-five years later he rewrote and recast the songs and published the new version with an extended preface explaining the reasons for the changes.

All of the changes were made in the light of the theoretical principle he developed in the meantime, his theory of tonal relationship, and the exact weighing of dissonances. This principle gave him control of all aspects of composition, and in the new version nothing is left to chance. The fifteen songs are arranged in four groups according to the subject matter of the poems. Each has its appropriate metrical and tonal organization and its dynamic and expressive high point, which are calculated and plotted for the whole cycle.

In rewriting the songs according to these principles Hindemith simplified the vocal lines and made their relationships with the piano more consonant. In the preface (1948) he writes:

> A quarter-century ago, it was widely believed that we were witnessing the dawn of a new age of counterpoint. The composer who wished to write contrapuntal music needed only, it was thought, to invent lines that made sense in themselves. For the harmonies resulting from their combination, and for the logical sequence of those harmonies Heaven would provide.[4]

Hindemith, of course, held these views invalid when he wrote the second version.

In a few songs, when the subject matter makes it reasonable to do so, instrumental forms such as *passacaglia* and *theme and variations* are used. Melodic phrases recur from one song to another as leitmotifs when they share a common idea.

Of particular interest is the linking of the order of tonal relationships (given in Example 111) to ideas expressed in the poems. For example, a relationship is established between concepts expressed in the poems and the keys that are used. Ideas that are remote from the central concept (Christ) are expressed in keys remote from the central tonality of the whole.

Although the poems are concerned primarily with Mary, she gains her importance through being the mother of Jesus. Christ, then, is the central figure of the cycle; the key of E is associated with Him. The complete relationship of keys with concepts is given here.

E   Christ
B   Mary
A   Celestial beings (angels)
C♯   The inevitable, fixed and unalterable
G♯   Anything that lies outside of our power of conception
G   Idyllic
C   Infinity and the Eternal
F♯   Acknowledgment of the smallness one feels in the face of the exalted
D   Trust and confidence
A♯   Everything in the domain of human feelings that at first op-

poses itself to the believing acceptance of all the wondrous happenings

F   Everything that moves us by its mistakenness or short sightedness to regret and pity

D♯   The greatest purity[5]

Hindemith explains how he worked with these relationships:

> When in composing one has once trod the path of tonal symbolism here described, one may easily succumb to the fascination of all the many possible relations between ideas and tonalities. At first one will perhaps be satisfied to avoid writing tonal constructions that would contradict the sense or the interpretation of a phrase in the text. But one soon comes to seek and consciously insert such constructions as will confirm and enhance it, and one ends by not writing down a single chord that would not play its part in this tonal exegesis of the text. To confirm this statement I will mention as one example among many, the theme of No. 14 (Death of Mary II). The tonal contemplation of the death of Mary there set down would lead us to approximately the following series of thoughts and feelings: we are made aware of the entrance into infinity (C, Measure 1), which, with its utter inexorability (C♯, Measures 2-3) but yet with its infinite gentleness (diffuse G, Measure 4) fills us with a feeling of our own minuteness (F♯, Measures 5-6). Although we trust fate (D, Measure 7) we are nonetheless troubled by a slight feeling of lack of understanding (B-flat), etc.[6]

This quotation would seem to be a *reductio ad absurdum* of an interesting idea and Hindemith himself admits that "I do not expect that in this tendency to freight musical sound so heavily with ideas I will encounter any too enthusiastic agreement." One can imagine what Stravinsky's reaction to such an approach to music would be!

The songs in *Das Marienleben* cover a wide gamut of emotion, from the sweet, gentle rhythms of Number 1, The "Birth of Mary," to the brilliance of Number 9, "The Wedding at Cana"; from the intimacy of Number 3, "The Annunciation," to the abstractness of Number 2, "The Presentation of Mary in the Temple"; and from the joy expressed in Number 6 "The Annunciation to the Shepherds," to the grief of Number 11, "Pietà." Technically and expressively the songs make great demands on singer and pianist alike, and regardless of the theory behind it, *Das Marienleben* is one of the most important song cycles of the period.

STYLE CHARACTERISTICS

The melodies that were quoted in the discussion of *Mathis der Maler* are typical in that they move over a firm tonal base but also include many "foreign" tones. Of course, in Hindemith's realm of expanded tonality they are not foreign, but simply more distantly related. These examples do not stress the melodic trait that he uses so often it becomes a mannerism—his fondness for the interval of the fourth. Three examples are added here; others can be found in any of his compositions:

EXAMPLE 113a*

Example 113b†

EXAMPLE 113c

Hindemith also has a favorite metrical pattern, expressed by 6/8 and 9/8 signatures. The Violin Sonata in E is typical. Its first movement flows easily and quietly in 9/8 with a constant eighth-note motion in either the violin or the piano, reminiscent of Bach. The last movement is a fast 6/8 with frequent hemiolas and augmentations. This preference for triple meter is perhaps related to Hindemith's interest in medieval music. In other moods, he writes march and dance rhythms.

Hindemith's vocabulary and treatment of chords are consistent with his theory. He uses any combination of tones, no matter how dissonant, but always returns to simple consonance at cadences. Thus, his compositions are far removed from the constant dissonances that characterize Schoenberg's works. Tonal consonance is still the norm for Hindemith; dissonance is used for special effects. As pointed out in the discussion of the composer's theory of music, his use of dissonance is always carefully controlled.

He often writes in a contrapuntal texture; *Mathis,* for example, contains *fugatos* and other types of imitative writing. The many sonatas for orchestral instruments with piano resemble Bach's chamber sonatas in that they proceed in three lines, one in the solo instrument part and two in the piano part. Hindemith's counterpoint is often dissonant, but like his harmonies, the relationship of voices becomes consonant at the cadences.

Hindemith prefers chamber groups and *ad hoc* combinations to the conventional orchestra. His *Concert Music for Piano, Brass, and Harps* is typical, as are the variously scored compositions called *Kammermusik.*

Hindemith is very fond of baroque forms and textures, often writing canons and fugues, chamber sonatas, and sets of variations. His compositions called sonatas are more often than not built on the baroque rather than the classic plan.

At several points in this discussion comparisons have been made between the music of Hindemith and Bach, and there are also similarities in the careers of the two. Both were practical musicians, happy when performing on any of a number of instruments or when conducting student or professional groups. In the music of both men there is a good deal of what Germans call *Spielfreudigkeit,* or joy in sheer music-making. Both wrote incessantly without radical changes in style after they grew out of their first youthful exuberance. For that reason it is difficult to assign dates to their works on a stylistic basis. Both wrote simple compositions for instructional purposes as well as large, serious masterpieces. Both could be objective and casually expressive in their compositions, and both could on occasion write music of deep, symbolic meaning.

SUGGESTED READING

There is no full-scale study of Hindemith and his music in English. The following articles are recommended: "Paul Hindemith and Neo-Classic Music" in *Music and Letters,* January 1932; William Hymanson's "Hindemith's Variations" in the *Music Review,* February 1952; and Rudolf Stephan's "Hindemith's *Marienleben*: an Assessment of its Two Versions," *Music Review,* November 1954. Norman Cazden's "Hindemith and Nature" in the *Music Review,* November 1954, is a well worked-out rebuttal of Hindemith's theoretical views.

A catalog of Hindemith's works was published by Schott in London in 1954. This is particularly valuable because Hindemith stopped assigning opus numbers to his works after he reached Opus 50 in 1930.

Hindemith's lectures given at Harvard published as *A Composer's World, Horizons and Limitations* (Cambridge, 1952) is recommended for the insights it gives to his thinking. His theory is expressed in *The Craft of Musical Composition* (English Ed., 1941). H. W. Heinsheimer's *Menagerie in F Sharp* (Garden City, N. Y., 1947) gives an accurate and amusing picture of the musical situation in Austria and Germany between the wars.

CHAPTER XIV

SOVIET RUSSIA

The Soviet artist is an engineer of human souls.   JOSEF STALIN

In the preceding chapters the main currents of twentieth-century music have been discussed, and the two principal lines of development, the French and the German-Austro-Hungarian, have been defined. It is within this orbit that most of the important innovations and additions to the vocabulary of music have been made.

In this chapter the contributions of Russia—and in following chapters those of England and the United States—will be surveyed. It will be noted that composers of these countries have been influenced to greater or lesser degrees by Debussy, Stravinsky, or Schoenberg, depending on their contact and sympathy with them, and on the strength of the musical tradition of their respective countries.

The achievements of Russia are particularly interesting. Because of the physical isolation of this huge country, it was a late arrival to the European cultural scene, but by the middle of the nineteenth century it had made great contributions to the arts of music and literature. By that time Russian musicians had become thoroughly familiar with the music of Western Europe and were also becoming aware of the wealth of their indigenous folk material. Before the outbreak of the First World War, Russia rivaled the musical activity of other European countries with her composers, opera companies, orchestras, and the virtuoso performers trained at the great conservatories in Moscow and St. Petersburg. It has already been mentioned that composers of Western Europe were influenced by Moussorgsky, Rimsky-Korsakov, and Scriabin.

The Russian Revolution of 1917 ushered in a social upheaval whose magnitude and consequences are still undetermined. Years of political chaos and of vast changes in the social order followed. Russia's participation in the Second World War threatened her existence, but her emergence after the war as a world power brought the once isolated nation into the center of the world arena.

Throughout all the tremendous changes experienced by Russia since the beginning of the century, the cultivation of music and musicians has never ceased. Whether under the czars or the Central Committee, the conservatories have continued to nurture musical talent; operas, ballets, and concerts have been given without interruption.

Russian artists have learned that their chief function is to glorify the State or to edify or amuse their fellow citizens. Edicts have been issued that prescribe the proper styles for music, painting, and literature. Individualistic artists who do not comply are cast aside—but those who follow the recommendations are handsomely rewarded.

In spite of these restrictions, Russian composers have made contributions to twentieth-century music which cannot be ignored. Out of many, the two figures best known to the West are Serge Prokofiev and Dmitri Shostakovich, both of whom have been in and out of official favor several times.

PROKOFIEV, 1891-1953

Prokofiev is a man of both East and West, for he spent many years in Western Europe before returning to his native country. He was born in the village of Sontsovka, where his father was the superintendent of a large estate. Because they were far removed from any cultural center, his well-educated parents personally supervised their son's schooling; his mother, an accomplished pianist, also provided his musical education. The boy's talent was unmistakable and he started composing little pieces when he was five. When eight, he was taken to the opera in Moscow and upon returning home he attempted to write an opera. When Serge outgrew his mother's teaching, the composer Glière was engaged to spend the summers of 1902 and 1903 with the family, to guide the boy in his compositions. In 1904 mother and son moved to St. Petersburg so that Serge could enter the Conservatory. The thirteen-year-old boy submitted four operas, two sonatas for piano, a symphony, and numerous piano pieces to the examining committee! For the next ten years he was a restive student, finding it difficult to accept the discipline of even such distinguished teachers as Lyadov and Rimsky-Korsakov. There was no question as to his ability as a pianist, for he quickly developed into a virtuoso.

During these years before World War I, St. Petersburg showed considerable interest in new Western music. Prokofiev was attracted to the new idioms and soon became known as a composer whose music rivalled Stravinsky's and Bartók's in its ruthless dissonance. He made a trip to London in 1914 to attend the opening of Diaghilev's season and to hear *Le Sacre*. Here he met the great impresario who commissioned him to write a ballet. Hoping to obtain a production as sensational as Stravinsky's latest work, Diaghilev recommended another subject from Russia's savage past. The war prevented the production of the ballet, but the music Prokofiev wrote, *The Scythian Suite*, proved that Diaghilev had found a composer equal to the task.

Prokofiev had nothing to do with the Revolution of 1917 and left on a world tour as a pianist-composer before the year was over. He made his debut in New York in 1918 and for the next fourteen years lived the life of a touring virtuoso pianist, making seven tours of the United States. When not on tour he lived for several years in a mountain village in Bavaria, but in 1923 he settled in Paris and remained there for a decade.

At that time Stravinsky and neoclassicism ruled the music circles of Paris. As Prokofiev's compositions were not in the same vein they made little impression there. Only his two Diaghilev commissioned ballets, *Le Pas D'Acier* (*The Steel Leap*, 1924) which glorified the industrialization of new Russia, and *The Prodigal Son* (1929) were favorably received.

After a few visits to his native country where his concerts and music were greeted with great enthusiasm, Prokofiev returned in 1932 to the USSR to stay. He remained there for the rest of his life except for two more tours of the United States in 1937 and 1938. He apparently cooperated fully with the Soviet ideas of the role of the arts, and when necessary accepted his reprimands and apologized to the Central Committee for musical transgressions. He wrote a number of propaganda works; in one of them, a cantata, he used excerpts from the writings of Marx, Lenin, and Stalin for the text. It is interesting to note that this work was not a success with either critics or the public.

In spite of occasional reprimands by the State, the last two decades of Prokofiev's life were highly productive and filled with honors. He won several Stalin prizes, the highest accolade that Russia bestows, and generous financial rewards for his operas, ballets, and film music. His last symphonies, concertos, and piano sonatas are among the important achievements of our time, in spite of the fact that they came out of an environment in which most composers of the West would find it impossible to work.

PROKOFIEV'S COMPOSITIONS

A summary of Prokofiev's principal works includes seven operas, six ballets, incidental music for plays and films, nine cantatas, six symphonies, five piano concertos, two violin concertos, one cello concerto, a small amount of chamber music, a long list of compositions for the piano which includes eight sonatas, and many songs. The three phases of Prokofiev's life, his student days, his years abroad, and those after his return to Russia, constitute the three style periods in which these compositions will be discussed.

Period 1: 1908-1918

During the first period Prokofiev's music was dominated by his strong iconoclasm and dislike of late-romantic chromaticism and overrefinement. Many of his early pieces are for piano, of which the well-known *Suggestion Diabolique* (1908) is a characteristic example. It reveals an area of expression that will often be met in his later works—a penchant for grotesque, sardonic, "dark" emotions. Also characteristic is his treatment of the piano as an instrument to be pounded instead of caressed. The driving rhythms and blatant melodies doubled in minor ninths howl defiance at delicate sensitivity as thoroughly as any composition written at this early date. Other important piano works of the time are *Sarcasms, Fugitive Visions,* and the brilliant *Toccata.* These early piano pieces reveal many of the characteristics of Prokofiev's style of writing for the instrument, and they call for performers of stamina and dexterity to execute the flying leaps, repeated chords, and brilliant passage work.

The attitude expressed in these piano pieces—that of a bad boy delighting in making rude noises and poking fun at his elders—can also be recognized in the ballet music entitled *Chout (The Buffoon)* and the opera based on Dostoevski's story *The Gambler.*

The best-known work of Prokofiev's early period is the *Classical Symphony* (1917) which shows quite another side of his musical personality. In this evocation of the eighteenth century, the savagery of the *Scythian Suite* is absent and delicacy and lyricism reign. These more ingratiating traits become increasingly prominent in the composer's later works.

Period 2: 1918-1932

These are the years Prokofiev spent away from Russia. They were disappointing years, however, for he did not acquire a circle of enthusiastic pupils such as that enjoyed by Schoenberg, nor did the spotlight of publicity play upon him as it did upon Stravinsky. He was regarded primarily as a pianist rather than a composer. As a matter of fact, many of the compositions of the time are not very ingratiating, for the verve of the earlier pieces is lost and the pure lyricism of the later works has not yet been achieved. There are some notable exceptions, however, such as his delightful fantasy opera *The Love for Three Oranges* first produced in Chicago in 1921. The two Diaghilev ballets and the Third Piano Concerto are also highly successful compositions.

This popular Third Piano Concerto is one of the composer's happiest inspirations, and it brings together many of his most characteristic style elements. It starts with a solo clarinet singing a gentle melody of Russian tinge:

EXAMPLE 114*

Soon a bustling, busy C-major passage is heard in the strings leading to the entrance of the solo piano that presents the main theme:

EXAMPLE 115

Interest in this subject lies largely in its rhythm, although there is a characteristic harmonic "slip" to a distantly related key at its conclusion. The orchestra and soloist engage in brilliant interplay until the second theme enters. Here is Prokofiev in his mock-serious, tongue-in-cheek mood:

EXAMPLE 116

A chromatic closing theme leads to the development, which is concerned exclusively with the slow theme of the introduction, a rather unusual and original procedure.

With the recapitulation, the roles of the piano and orchestra are reversed. Now the soloist plays the scalelike passage—one of the most exciting pages of the whole concerto repertoire as the pianist nimbly traverses the keyboard. The second theme receives a more pungent "wrong-note" harmonization and brilliant passage-work brings the movement to a close.

The quiet second movement is in complete contrast to the forthright opening movement. The flute and clarinet present the melody which is the basis for the variations that follow:

EXAMPLE 117

The first variation starts as a piano solo in a distant key with the melody harmonized by rich chromatic chords. The next variation begins with tempestuous scales in the piano while the trumpet plays fragments of the main theme in another key. This variation is quite free, but the prim, plagal cadence at the end restores decorum. Three contrasting free variations follow, and then the theme returns in its original form in the flutes while the soloist plays staccato treble chords, forming a charming conclusion to the movement.

The third movement is rich in contrasts. The main theme, whose periodic return gives the movement a modified rondo form, has a characteristic rhythmic irregularity:

EXAMPLE 118

There is a contrasting, slow middle section with a broad, singing melody, resembling an American Negro spiritual:

EXAMPLE 119

In contrast to this there is a new melody which, in its slides and general outlines, is in the "blues" tradition:

EXAMPLE 120

The vigorous opening material returns and the concerto comes to a crashing close with both orchestra and piano pounding C-major chords. Throughout the movement, the utmost in virtuosity is demanded of the pianist. Prokofiev wrote it for himself, and his fingers and wrists of steel are legendary.

Period 3: 1932-1953

The works of Prokofiev written after his return to Russia show a great variety of forms and genres. At one extreme there are the popular patriotic songs and marches written for special occasions, such as the *Cantata for the Twentieth Anniversary of the October Revolution.* Then there are simple works such as *Peter and the Wolf* which have endeared the composer to millions of people around the world. His music for a film, *Lieutenant Kije,* and his ballets, *Romeo and Juliet* and *Cinderella,* have also met with wide approval. In these works the lyric elements assume an importance they did not enjoy in earlier works. The opera *War and Peace,* the Fifth and Sixth symphonies, and the later sonatas for piano and for piano and violin are the mature works of a master composer.

The Piano Concerto just discussed reveals Prokofiev the athlete, the extrovert, while the Second Violin Concerto, written in 1935 after his return to the Soviet Union, reveals Prokofiev, lyricist of the first order. This composition has become one of the most popular twentieth-century concertos because of its singing melodies and idiomatic writing for the violin.

The concerto starts with the unaccompanied violin playing the principal theme. A characteristic shifting of the eighth-note figure from a weak to a strong beat should be noted:

EXAMPLE 121

Allegro moderato ♩ = 108

mp

VIOLIN SOLO

Also, the remote key of B minor in which the orchestra enters a few bars later is another example of the composer's fondness for contrasting well-defined but distantly related keys.

After a rhythmic and harmonic development of the principal theme, the soloist announces the second theme which is even more cantabile than the first. It too slips into a far distant tonality:

EXAMPLE 122

Meno mosso ♩ = 80

p

The development section is spacious in dimension. It is built principally on the first subject, which usually appears in the orchestra while the soloist plays decorative figurations. The second theme is referred to and then a *piu mosso* built on the first theme prepares for the recapitulation in which the relaxed themes are heard again.

The second movement is even more songlike. Over a modest broken-chord figure played by the strings, the solo violin spins a long melody reminiscent of Mendelssohn:

EXAMPLE 123

Andante assai

p

The movement is organized as a large ternary form, rich in secondary themes and lovely combinations of solo woodwinds with the solo violin. A special characteristic is the extremely high *tessitura* of the solo instrument.

The last movement returns to the composer's boisterous, rough style. The opening theme has the character of a grotesque peasant-dance:

EXAMPLE 124

Allegro ben marcato

f SOLO VIOLIN

In form, it is a sonata-rondo of never-flagging vitality. There are pungent dissonances, frequent changes of meter, and measures of 7/4 and 5/4. Adding to the tension are the many long passages played high on the G-string bringing forth a forced, strident sound from the solo instrument.

STYLE CHARACTERISTICS

As a young composer Prokofiev took a stand against the ultrachromatic style of Scriabin and the fragmentary suggestiveness of Debussy, writing music that was forthright, clear, and blunt. While his compositions mellowed somewhat as he matured, directness of expression has always been their chief characteristic. For example, he preferred the key of C major at a time when the music of other composers was black with accidentals.

Attention has already been called to the lyric, singing quality of many of his melodies, and such a work as his Fifth Symphony, starting with a beautiful flowing line, is permeated with melodies to a degree unusual in twentieth-century music. These melodies frequently consist of small intervals, with an occasional soaring to an upper octave. Prokofiev habitually writes balanced, four-bar phrases which he builds into symmetrical periods; such regularity helps to account for the directness of expression. Occasionally the regularity is disturbed when a melody is repeated but starts on another part of the measure. Example 121 is characteristic. He often uses the modal scales familiar to all Russians, with a special preference for the mixolydian.

Prokofiev prefers strong, obvious rhythms and has written

many marches (the "March" from the *Love for Three Oranges* is an example), and dance-inspired compositions. In fast movements he frequently repeats a simple eighth-note ostinato figure to build huge climaxes. An exception to his usual habit of using regular rhythms is found in the last movement of his Seventh Sonata for piano where an exciting 7/8 meter prevails.

Prokofiev's music is firmly tonal, and his chords are built in thirds. He is conservative in his attitude toward dissonances, for he uses them to establish points of tension and not as the normal harmonic climate. Occasionally he writes short polytonal passages and sometimes he uses the major and minor third simultaneously or in close connection. A striking example of the latter is at the beginning of the Sixth Sonata for piano:

EXAMPLE 125*

One particular harmonic device, used by Prokofiev so often that it has become one of his most characteristic traits, is that of starting a passage in one key and then suddenly shifting to a distantly related key without any transition or preparation. Examples of this are ubiquitous. Two that come to mind are found in the introduction to *Peter and the Wolf* and in the opening theme of the Third Piano Concerto. Since Prokofiev's style is essentially harmonic and rhythmic, counterpoint plays but a small role.

His treatment of the piano as a percussion instrument has already been mentioned. This is not his only technique, of course, for he also writes beautifully delicate effects for the instrument. When writing for orchestra he shows the mastery of scoring that one would

*Copyright 1946 by Leeds Music Corporation, New York.

expect from a pupil of Rimsky-Korsakov. Unlike many of his contemporaries, he usually uses the full symphony orchestra, showing particular sensitivity for the solo woodwind instruments. While he is not often interested in novel effects, the "Battle on the Ice" movement from *Alexander Nevsky* is striking in its unique coloring.

In the organization of his compositions Prokofiev is content to use the time-tested forms of the classical period. In an interview published in the *New York Times* in 1937, Prokofiev said:

> I strive for greater simplicity and more melody. Of course, I have used dissonance in my time, but there has been too much dissonance. . . . We want a simpler and more melodic style for music, a simpler, less complicated emotional state, and dissonance once again relegated to its proper place as one element in music, contingent principally upon the meeting of the melodic lines.
>
> Music, in other words, has definitely reached and passed the greatest degree of discord and of complexity that it is practicable for it to attain. . . .
>
> Therefore, I think the desire which I and many of my fellow composers feel, to attain a more simple and melodic expression, is the inevitable direction for the musical art of the future.
>
> However these questions are considered, it is obvious that there is an immense desire to win back to simplicity, to reach again, as it were, a clear-cut spot in the forest and chart the course of music anew. And here is a striking theme: there is a return to classic forms which I feel very much myself.[1]

SHOSTAKOVICH 1906-

A more representative composer of the USSR is Dmitri Shostakovich, who, in contrast to Prokofiev, received all of his training in Russia after the Revolution of 1917. Further, he has spent little time outside of its borders since then. He was born in St. Petersburg in 1906, and as is so often the case with composers (Prokofiev, Bartók, and Poulenc, for example) his mother was a well-trained pianist who guided his first experiences in music. At the age of thirteen, two years after the Revolution of 1917, Shostakovich entered the conservatory in his native city, where he was a brilliant and cooperative student, graduating as a pianist four years later. He continued his studies in composition, working under Steinberg, a pupil of Rimsky-Korsakov.

During the 1920's, interest in the new music of Western Europe continued in St. Petersburg, and key works such as the ballets of Stravinsky, Berg's *Wozzeck,* the symphonies of Mahler, and works of Schoenberg and Milhaud were heard and discussed. These performances were of great interest to the composition students whose training for the most part was academic and conservative. Shostakovich's early pieces, such as his *Three Fantastic Dances* and the satirical ballet *The Golden Age* (the well-known "Polka" originated here) show his awareness of aggressively dissonant, but good-humored, "wrong-note" music.

In 1925 he completed his first symphony. It is a remarkable composition, and although it shows the influence of composers with such contrasting traits as those of Stravinsky and Mahler, it is much more than a mere student piece. It was performed immediately in Russia and soon after in Europe and the United States, bringing world-wide attention to the highly gifted young composer. It is little wonder that the symphony made such an impression, for in spite of its eclecticism it established a strong musical personality. Of note are the transparent treatment of the orchestra (it is rare that there are any mass effects); the sardonic first theme; the sudden, unprepared modulations; the biting sarcasm of the scherzo; the poignant, melancholy oboe solo of the slow movement; the threatening trumpet calls that clash polytonally; and the mood of anxiety and terror of the last movement later transformed into the grandiose, triumphant peroration of the final pages. These are all areas of expression and effects that become constant factors in Shostakovich's mature style. The First Piano Concerto and the preludes for piano also made very favorable impressions at home and abroad.

With such as auspicious start, one would think that Shostakovich's career would be untroubled and secure, and in the long run this has proved to be true. Today he is one of Russia's most honored citizens, but he has nevertheless been seriously criticized twice by the official spokesmen of the Communist Party. His opera *Lady Macbeth of Mzensk* (1934) brought on the first reprimand. Although well received by the public it was suddenly withdrawn and accused of the most heinous of musical crimes. It was deemed to be "formalistic"—

the convenient word of condemnation used in Soviet Russia to imply that a work is either not sufficiently propagandistic or that it is too much influenced by the "decadent" music of the "decadent" West. The sordidness of the story and the *Wozzeck*-influenced dissonant music did perhaps make *Lady Macbeth* something less than an inspirational work. Shostakovich publicly accepted the reprimand and promised to mend his musical ways. He continued teaching at the Moscow Conservatory, a position of the highest honor, and went on composing. With his Fifth Symphony (1937) he assumed the position of Russia's most highly respected composer.

He was considered so valuable that he was not allowed to join the army during the Second World War and was told to continue composing and make his contribution to his country through music. Complying, he wrote his gigantic Seventh Symphony (*Leningrad*) during the siege of his native city. This work describes the heroism of the Russian people at a crucial moment in their history. Interest in it was world-wide; for example, both the New York Philharmonic and the Boston Symphony vied for the honor of playing the first performance in this country. The score was microfilmed and flown by a devious route over North Africa (so as to avoid war-torn Europe) to New York where it was copied and played by Toscanini and the New York Philharmonic on a well-publicized nation-wide broadcast. The composer's picture appeared on the cover of *Time*, wearing the uniform and hat of a Stalingrad fire-fighter, an "honor" bestowed on few composers.

Since that time Shostakovich has written four more symphonies. The Eighth Symphony is another heroic work, heavily expressive of the sorrows of war. The Ninth is comparable to Beethoven's Eighth in that it is an untroubled, cheerful composition, a relaxation between large, serious works. His Tenth (1953) is another full-scale work which won the New York Critics Award in that year. The Eleventh (1958) is subtitled *The Year 1905* and its four movements commemorate an ill-starred but prophetic uprising of the people against the Czar. Other works of the 1950's are *Twenty-Four Preludes and Fugues* (1951), Violin Concerto (1955), and the Second Piano Concerto (1957).

Soviet Russia is difficult to understand in every way, but especially in the treatment of her artists. Shostakovich reportedly receives the equivalent of $7,500 to $10,000 for each symphony he writes, plus royalties from recordings. He has been honored with six Stalin Prizes of $25,000 each. He has an apartment in Moscow and a country house and drives an expensive automobile. This is a scale of material compensation unmatched in the West for a composer of noncommercial music.

In spite of this, at a "World" Congress of Intellectuals held in Warsaw in 1948 (after the *Stalingrad Symphony*), Shostakovich's music, along with that of Prokofiev, Khatchaturian, and Miakovsky, was condemned once again for being formalistic and not simple enough for the masses to enjoy. A report of the meeting has been published in a fascinating little book called *Musical Uproar in Moscow* by Alexander Werth. In it one can read the speeches of composers comparable in status to our Tin Pan Alley writers, such as:

> Comrades, it seems to me that this discussion has gone off the rails. I work in the field of Russian folksong. I am very frequently in contact with the People in the real sense of the term. . . . Let us look at our symphonic music. Here some big names have established themselves, both at home and abroad. But I must say that the works of these composers are alien and completely incomprehensible to our Soviet People. There are still discussions round the question whether Shostakovich's Eighth Symphony is good or bad. Such a discussion is nonsense. From the point of view of the People, the Eighth Symphony is not a musical work at all; it is a "composition" which has just nothing to do with musical art whatsoever.[2]

Another critic condemned the Seventh Symphony because he felt that in it Shostakovich's depiction of the threatening Germans was more graphic than his expression of the heroism of the Russians.

At the conclusion of the meeting, the Central Committee issued a decree that condemned the formalist tendency in Soviet music as being anti-People and leading to the liquidation of music and called upon Soviet composers to become more conscious of their duties to the Soviet people.

Shostakovich publicly accepted his reprimands. In his speech which closed the meeting he said:

> In my work, I have had many failures even though, throughout my composer's career, I have always thought of the People, of my listeners, of those who reared me; and I always strive that the

People should accept my music. I have always listened to criticism, and have always tried to work harder and better. I am listening to criticism now, and shall continue to listen to it, and shall accept critical instructions. . . . I think that our three days discussion will be of the greatest value, especially if we closely study Comrade Zhadanov's speech. I, no doubt like others, should like to have the text of his speech. A close study of this remarkable document should help us greatly in our work.[3]

SHOSTAKOVICH'S COMPOSITIONS

Most of the important works of Shostakovich have been mentioned in the preceding pages. A summary by categories follows. That he is primarily a symphonist is attested to by the eleven symphonies (1926-1958). The two piano concertos and the numerous works for piano solo show his interest in that instrument. He has written no operas since *Lady Macbeth,* but he has provided music for a number of films and plays. The chamber music is important, especially the Piano Quintet (1940), the Second Trio (1944), and two string quartets (1938 and 1944).

Written in 1937 after the reprimand caused by *Lady Macbeth,* Shostakovich called his Fifth Symphony a "Soviet artist's reply to just criticism." It brought the composer back into favor, and in many ways is his most representative composition. A large-scale symphony, it begins with a brooding, slow-paced movement in sonata-form. Two elements make up the first thematic group—a jagged, tortuous melody, presented in canon, and an ominous four-note descending scale fragment:

EXAMPLE 126a

Moderato ♪=76

p 1ST VIOLINS

These two factors are the subject of a discourse carried out in the transparent orchestration already noted in the First Symphony.

The second theme is a widespread melody heard over a throbbing rhythmic figure. Except for its range, it has the effusiveness of a Puccini aria:

EXAMPLE 127

1ST VIOLINS

p espress.

The four-note opening theme breaks into the calm, low in the brasses, as the development begins. It permeates this section and is heard in many guises and colors. Shostakovich treats his orchestra in planes, keeping each section busy with rhythmic figures or thematic derivatives, and often the groups create polytonal clashes. The turbulence resulting from this opposition of forces comes to a climax with a simultaneous presentation of the rhythmic figure of the opening bars sounding against the second theme played by the brasses.

The greatly shortened recapitulation starts with a powerful unison treatment of the first theme-group material, followed by a magnificently expansive statement of the second theme, this time in the parallel major key. Its canonic treatment between the flute and horn is of particular interest. As the movement sinks to its close, the opening melody is heard, inverted, in the flute. Low trumpets and a tinkling celesta add a final touch of color.

The boisterous scherzo of the second movement is characteristic of the grotesque, satirical mood so often found in Russian music.
It is achieved here through the shrill E-flat clarinet in the opening
statement, the frequent shifting of tonalities so that a passage starting in one key ends in another, and parodies of popular styles. In
form it follows the traditional minuet-and-trio pattern. The solo violin
is featured in the trio in an atmosphere of old régime sentiment. The
third movement is an impressive, deeply moving largo. The violins
are divided into three sections and the violas and cellos into two sections each, providing the warm string sound that characterizes the
opening. Several chantlike themes are used. The first is static

EXAMPLE 128

while the second, although closely related, is more urgent:

EXAMPLE 129

A third theme, first heard in the flute, recalls the principal theme of
the first movement. After this material is repeated in various orders,
the oboe starts the central portion of the movement with this contrasting theme:

EXAMPLE 130

284 / Part Two: 1914-1945

The woodwinds offer a relief from the predominantly string tone of the first section, but soon the first two themes recur, working up to a climax of high tension, again reminiscent of Puccini. An abbreviated return of the opening section, including Example 126 from the first movement, brings the movement to a close.

The last movement is a wild burst of energy. It is marchlike and the pounding, recurring rhythms give it a savage strength. The first theme is blared by the trumpets, trombones, and tuba:

EXAMPLE 131

This is followed immediately by a frenetic dance:

EXAMPLE 132

These themes are developed into tremendous outpourings of sound which are eventually interrupted by a hymnlike horn call which ushers in the quiet middle portion. The vigorous opening theme recurs and the coda, consisting of a chorale version of Example 131 in major, played in the horns, brings this heroic symphony to a close.

The Fifth Symphony closely links Shostakovich with his Russian heritage, for Rimsky-Korsakov and Tchaikovsky are the ancestors of music like this. Revolutions and radical changes in government apparently are not strong enough to destroy continuity of cultural patterns.

STYLE CHARACTERISTICS

Since there are many similarities between the styles of Shostakovich and Prokofiev, a detailed exposition of the younger composer's music will not be given. This does not mean that the music of the two composers is indistinguishable. Each has his own style, but both share a common background of experience and general orientation to music.

Particularly in his early works, Shostakovich, like Prokofiev, showed his scorn of the past by writing satirical, grotesque caricatures of nineteenth-century popular music. The "Polka" from his ballet *The Golden Age* and the waltz in the third movement of his First Symphony are examples, characterized by the wrong-note harmonizations and the obviousness of the "um-pah-pah" accompaniment figures.

The younger composer also shares Prokofiev's fondness for music of large dimensions and effects. His symphonies contain wide-spanned, exalted melodies, insistent rhythmic figures (♩ ♫♩ ♫ is a favorite pattern), elegiac slow movements, rough but good-humored scherzos, and vigorous finales. In his later works Shostakovich goes beyond Prokofiev in expansiveness.

Shostakovich is the greater colorist in orchestral writing. One thinks of special effects such as a blatant trumpet at the end of the First Piano Concerto, the glissandos for the violins in the Fifth Symphony and the many witty instrumental characterizations in the operas. One important difference in their styles is the result of Shostakovich's interest in counterpoint. Prokofiev did not write any formal fugues, but his younger colleague wrote a set of preludes and fugues for piano and the opening movement of the Piano Quintet is an extended fugue. The canonic beginning of the Fifth Symphony also shows his interest in contrapuntal textures.

In spite of the fact that he spent most of his life in his own country, the music of the younger composer is more eclectic, more influenced by Western composers such as Mahler, Stravinsky, and Berg, than is Prokofiev's. Nevertheless, the strongest influence on both of these composers and their lesser-known compatriots is their rich heritage of nineteenth-century Russian music. Perhaps because its composers were forbidden to use experimental idioms, perhaps because they were by nature conservative—for whatever reason—the music that has come out of the country that has experienced the most radical social changes in the early twentieth century has been the least experimental.

SUGGESTED READINGS

On Prokofiev, Israel V. Nestyev's *Serge Prokofiev, His Musical Life* (New York, 1946) is a Soviet-slanted, but thorough, study. The chapter "SRG SRGVTCH PRKFV" in Nicolas Nabakov's *Old Friends and New Music* (Boston, 1951) gives interesting insights into the personality of the composer.

On Shostakovich, two biographies are: Ivan Martynov's *Dmitri Shostakovich: The Man and His Work* (New York, 1947), and Victor Seroff's *Dmitri Shostakovich: The Life and Background of a Soviet Composer* (New York, 1943). The article "Dmitri Shostakovich," by Nicolas Slonimsky in the *Musical Quarterly*, Vol. XXVIII, 1942, and another by Hugh Ottaway, "Shostakovich: Some Later Works" in *Tempo*, Winter 1959, cover early and recent works.

There are several books covering a wider field of modern Russian music. Among them are *Eight Soviet Composers* by Gerald Abraham (London, 1944), *Realist Music; 25 Soviet Composers* by Rena Moisenko (London, 1949); and *Handbook of Soviet Musicians* by Igor Boelza (London, 1943). Also to be mentioned is Nicolas Slonimsky's article, "The Changing Style of Soviet Music," in the *Journal of the American Musicological Society*, Vol. 3, No. 3, 1951, and his translations of various official decrees on music in *Music Since 1900 (op. cit.)*. *Musical Uproar in Moscow* by Alexander Werth (London, 1949) gives an account and translation of the speeches at the important World Congress of Intellectuals in 1948.

CHAPTER XV

ENGLAND

I usually feel content to provide good plain cooking and hope that the proof of the cooking is in the eating.

RALPH VAUGHAN WILLIAMS

During the first half of the twentieth century, England once again became a producer of significant music after two hundred years of subservience to German and Italian music and musicians. While her musical achievements had been of prime importance in the late Middle Ages and the Renaissance, after the death of Purcell in 1695 there were no other outstanding native composers. From that time on foreign composers dominated the scene—Handel in the eighteenth century, and German symphonists from Mendelssohn to Brahms, and Italian opera composers from Bellini to Verdi, in the nineteenth.

However, because of a unique feature in English music—the great interest in choral singing—English composers throughout these years wrote countless cantatas and oratorios on Handelian or Mendelssohnian models for the numerous regional and national choir festivals.

In the Edwardian era, a respectable if not highly original group of composers emerged. Like their contemporaries in the United States (discussed in Chapter V), they tended to follow either the conservative ideals of Brahms or the progressive directions of Wagner and Strauss. However, the most important English composer of this generation, Edward Elgar (1857-1934), was virtually self-trained. His

Enigma Variations for orchestra (1899), the massive oratorio *The Dream of Gerontius* (1900), and the Violin Concerto (1910) have proved to be late romantic works of lasting value that are still performed, even outside England.

With the composers of the next generation, England entered the twentieth century. These men were aware of the new continental musical currents (many of them studied in France), but there were two indigenous activities, the results of which gave their music a unique "English" quality. The first was the founding of the English Folk Song Society in 1898. This was a group dedicated to collecting and publishing the treasure of native melodies which up to this time had gone unnoticed, and which, had they been noticed, would have been beneath the interest of serious composers. The young composers of the opening decades of the century were profoundly influenced by the modal melodies they found here, so unlike the tension-filled, chromatic melodies they had been taught to admire and write, and they were also attracted to the gentle 6/8 meter that underlay many of the tunes. Both of these elements became prominent in many of their compositions.

The other noncreative activity that affected the music of this generation of English composers was the editing and publishing of another forgotten national treasure, sixteenth-century vocal polyphony. The madrigals of Weelkes and Morley as well as the masses and motets of Byrd and Taverner, now made available, opened the eyes and ears of the young English composers to rhythmic subtleties and harmonic practices that were also far removed from the textbook rules they had studied. Thus the English composer of the early twentieth century had a heritage far different from that of his colleagues across the Channel—a heritage often apparent in his music.

VAUGHAN WILLIAMS, 1872-1958

Among the large number of English composers active in the first half of the century, none is more important than Ralph Vaughan Williams. In the extent and variety of his compositions, in his slowly formed, highly personal style (based on the English tradition, but not reactionary), in his teaching activities—no contemporaneous English composer approached his stature.

There was nothing spectacular about his career; although he studied the piano, violin, and harmony as a child, he was never a professional performer. Upon graduation from Charterhouse, a public school, he entered the Royal College of Music and studied composition with Sir Hubert Parry, whose advice to his students was, "Write choral music as befits an Englishman and a democrat."[1] Although he went to Munich to hear the *Ring*, the young composer was "painfully illiterate" as far as the general literature of music was concerned. In his autobiographical sketch he tells of the amazement he felt when, at the age of twenty, he heard Beethoven's *Appassionata Sonata* for the first time.[2]

Vaughan Williams' years of apprenticeship were many. After graduating from the Royal College of Music, he took degrees at Cambridge, and following this he settled in London as a church organist and choir master. In 1896 he went to Berlin to study with Max Bruch. After his return to England, he joined the Folk Song Society and came to know the music that was to leave such a strong mark on his own. He started teaching composition at the Royal College after serving in World War I, and except for a few months of study with Ravel in Paris and three trips to the United States in 1923, 1932, and 1956, he remained there for the rest of his life. Vaughan Williams composed constantly and modestly, relying on the advice and counsel of a few colleagues, frequently rewriting his compositions on the basis of their criticism. In his autobiography he singles out and pays special tribute to his friend and fellow composer, Gustav Holst, who for many years acted as his mentor. Such acknowledgements are rare in the world of composers.

His works were performed occasionally at choir festivals, and in 1914, when he was over forty, his sprightly *London Symphony* made a favorable impression. Over the next forty years the musical world gradually came to realize that he was a composer who grew in maturity from year to year, that he did not follow changing continental styles, and that he did not repeat himself. Throughout his sixties, seventies, and eighties, he continued to compose works of ever-increasing power and unpredictability, and when he died at the age of eighty-six, he left an impressive list of compositions of all dimensions.

VAUGHAN WILLIAMS' COMPOSITIONS

Among his works are the operas *Hugh the Drover* (1911-1914), and *Sir John in Love* (1929) (the composer's setting of the Elizabethan tune *Greensleeves* in this opera has become well known), a chamber opera *Riders to the Sea* (1937), and the ballet *Job* (1931). There is also incidental music to plays and films, a wealth of sacred choral music of which the *Mass in G Minor* is the most extensive, choral works with orchestra, and part songs. He wrote nine large symphonies, shorter orchestral pieces, concertos, a small amount of chamber music, and nearly one hundred songs.

The *Fantasia on a Theme by Thomas Tallis* (1908, revised in 1913 and 1919), scored for string quartet and double string orchestra, is an example of his "English" style. The first decade of the century saw the creation of much feverish music on the continent—such works as *The Firebird, Erwartung,* and *Elektra*—but this contemporaneous English piece breathes an air of timeless calm and dignity. It is neither dissonant nor complex. Instead, it is rich in many-voiced string sonorities with antiphonal effects that resemble vocal writing.

The series of triads that opens the piece establishes the modal atmosphere at once:

EXAMPLE 133

The first phrase of the Tallis theme is heard in the lower strings, answered by a refrain in parallel triads (see Example 134). Such harmonizations are frequently found in the composer's later works.

This material is repeated in the higher strings with a flowing

EXAMPLE 134

accompaniment in the second violins. After a cadence, the various phrases of the Tallis melody are taken up, one after the other, according to the pattern of the seventeenth-century *fantasia* and *ricercare*. Solos alternate with the group in ever-changing combinations.

With the *Tallis Fantasia,* English music shook off two centuries of German domination and tapped a rich source of native musical beauty. If he had done nothing more than write mellifluous fantasias on Elizabethan melodies, Vaughan Williams' place in twentieth-century music would have been important, though modest. Instead, he developed a musical style that was not only national and personal, but of international significance.

The nine symphonies, spaced throughout his life, mark various stages in the development of his style. The first three have descriptive subtitles. The first, with chorus, is the *Sea Symphony* written in 1912. In 1914 the *London Symphony,* a wonderful evocation of the city in all its moods, was performed; this was followed in 1922 by the *Pastoral.* The Fourth (1935), Fifth (1943), and Sixth (1948) symphonies do not have titles, but their stormy dissonances and somewhat forbidding nature reveal a constantly developing musical style. The seventh symphony, called *Sinfonia Antartica* (1952) is an extension of music the composer wrote for a film, *Scott of the Antarctic*. The Eighth (1956) and Ninth (1958) symphonies are not programmatic and their fresh vitality gives no hint that they are the works of an octogenarian.

The Sixth Symphony is a far cry from the composer's early "English" style. This is a mid-twentieth century statement, complex and dissonant in harmony, strong in rhythm, rich in melody and orchestral effects, and equivocal and disturbing in expression.

The symphony is in three connected movements with an epilogue. A headlong, impetuous, bitonal introduction leads to a restless first theme:

EXAMPLE 135*

The rushing figures of the introduction continue as accompaniment after the theme enters. Following the seriousness of the opening, the second theme is a complete surprise, for it is a bouncy jazz tune played over an "oompah" bass:

EXAMPLE 136

*Copyright 1948 by Oxford University Press, London.

A series of syncopated, "swinging" melodies follows until this warmly lyrical closing theme is heard:

EXAMPLE 137

p *cantabile*

It is obvious that the composer is fond of this material. He lingers over it, repeating it in ever-richer versions. He seems to leave it reluctantly for the short development and recapitulation and then returns to it as soon as he can.

A tympani roll and a note held in the double basses join the first and second movements—an ominous march with many military overtones, suggested by prominent trumpets and drums. The chromatic principal theme seems scarcely able to raise itself out of the gloom:

EXAMPLE 138

Moderato

The theme eventually rises to more sonorous altitudes, and then parallel-chord harmonizations, reminiscent of the early Tallis piece, appear. Tympani and muffled snare drum add to the funereal solemnity. In the contrasting middle section, a hollow-sounding fanfare alternates with unison string passages. Gradually the rhythmic figure of the opening section becomes prominent and the muted opening material returns.

The third movement is entitled "Scherzo" but it is no lighthearted frolic. It is a piece of diabolical energy, resulting from strong rhythms and dissonant counterpoint, but most of all from the extreme exploitation of the *diabolus in musica,* the augmented fourth. Here is the opening:

EXAMPLE 139

The trio features the tenor saxophone in a rather maudlin melody.

The Epilogue is an eerie, disturbing piece of music, resembling the opening of Bartók's *Music for Strings, Percussion, and Celesta* in its fugal texture, involuted chromatic theme, and muted-string color.

EXAMPLE 140

Unlike the Bartók opening, however, which develops to a climax in volume and then subsides, this movement has but one dynamic—pianissimo—and continual warnings: *senza crescendo* (without crescendo). The canons, inversions, and augmentations progress in this dim atmosphere, and after the demonic energy of the earlier movements this quiet, mysterious close produces a profound effect.

The Sixth Symphony was by no means the last work of this grand old man of English music. The two symphonies that followed are warm, genial works which sum up the lifework of one of the major composers of the period.

BRITTEN, 1913-

During the long years of Ralph Vaughan Williams' career, a number of younger English composers came into prominence, among them Gustav Holst (1874-1934), John Ireland (1879), Sir Arnold Bax (1883), Arthur Benjamin (1893-1960), Edmund Rubbra (1901), Sir William Walton (1902), Lennox Berkeley (1903), and Alan Rawsthorne (1905). The most spectacularly gifted composer of the younger generation, however, and the most widely performed, is Benjamin Britten (1913). All musical prodigies are compared to Mozart, but the parallels in careers and similarities in creative personalities between Britten and Mozart are striking. Like Mozart, Britten started to compose while still very young; he has continued without pause. He, too, composes with tremendous facility, working out compositions in his mind and then transferring his thoughts to notation no matter where he is—backstage or in airplanes. He has written operas as well as instrumental music, sacred as well as secular choral works, pieces for children and pieces for sophisticates. Britten's style is eclectic and one can hear in his compositions traces of composers as disparate in style as Purcell and Berg. He seems to sum up, and to have at his disposal, all of the musical techniques and idioms of his time just as Mozart made thorough use of the ideals and vocabulary of his age.[3]

There are few important biographical details apart from the dates and events related to the performances of his compositions. Britten was born in the village of Lowestoft in Suffolk where his father was a dentist and his mother was an enthusiastic choir singer and secretary of the local choral society. He studied piano and viola as a child and worked in composition with Frank Bridge. When he was sixteen he won a scholarship at the Royal College of Music where he continued his work in composition with John Ireland and in piano with Arthur Benjamin. After graduation he started to write music for documentary films and plays, an occupation for which his facility and ability to reflect situations in music eminently suited him. His work for the theater brought him in contact with W. H. Auden, the poet and dramatist, and when the latter left England for the United States shortly before the war, the young composer followed. Britten remained for three years, but then gave up his idea of becoming an

American citizen and returned to wartime England. After some years he settled in the fishing village of Aldeburgh where he lives (when not on tour), composes, and directs a summer music festival.

BRITTEN'S COMPOSITIONS

Britten's operas form an impressive group of works and they can be counted among the most successful of their time. They have all survived their premières and are performed regularly in the opera houses of the world. They are *Peter Grimes* (1945), *The Rape of Lucretia* (1946), *Albert Herring* (1947), *Let's Make an Opera* (1948), *Billy Budd* (1951), *Gloriana* (1953), *The Turn of the Screw* (1954), *Noye's Fludde* (*Noah's Flood*, 1957), and *Midsummer Night's Dream* (1960). He has also written a number of song cycles for solo voice and instruments, such as *Les Illuminations* for high voice and strings (1939); *Serenade* for tenor, horn and strings (1943); *Nocturne* for tenor and small orchestra (1958); and *Songs from the Chinese* for voice and guitar (1959). *The Ceremony of Carols* for boys' voices and harp (1942) and *The Young Person's Guide to the Orchestra* (1946) have achieved world-wide popularity. He has also written the *Sinfonia da Requiem* (1940), concertos for violin and for piano, and numerous works for chamber music combinations.

The première of *Peter Grimes* on June 7th, 1945, was a momentous day in England's musical life; critics and the public alike felt that after two hundred years an English opera had been written which would hold its own, not only at home, but on operatic stages anywhere. They were not mistaken; *Peter Grimes* has become one of the most successful twentieth-century operas, despite its lack of easy charm and light entertainment value.

The libretto, based on a poem by George Crabbe (1754-1832), offers no opportunity for glamorous costumes or elaborate settings. It is a psychological drama, the tragedy of a "little man," an unimportant, harassed fisherman, played against the background of sea and village. Peter Grimes is an "outsider" and recluse; poor, friendless, suspected of maltreating the apprentice boy who works for him. When the boy dies at sea, Grimes is brought to trial. He is exonerated, but the village still does not accept the solitary Grimes, with the exception of Ellen Orford, a widow. Grimes is driven with the ambition to make enough money to win the respect of the village and to marry Ellen. He takes on another apprentice. There is evidence that he is cruel to the boy and when Ellen remonstrates, he strikes her. Forced by Grimes to go fishing in the midst of a storm, the second boy falls off a cliff and is killed. The men of the village are aroused and seek Grimes, but he becomes insane and drowns.

In setting this grim story to music Britten has chosen a form of opera which, while showing the influence of many composers and styles, is perhaps closest to Verdi's *Otello*. This means that it is neither consistently through-composed in the manner of *Tristan* or *Pelléas,* nor is it divided into recitatives and arias as is *Figaro* or *Rake's Progress.* As in Verdi's later operas, Britten's opera proceeds primarily in arioso-recitative passages with the action pausing occasionally for freely formed arias. There are also occasional "set pieces" such as the round sung in the pub on the stormy night and the village dance. The choruses and ensembles are especially important, another feature that removes *Peter Grimes* from late Wagnerian ideals.

The orchestra is treated with great flexibility; accompanying the singers, characterizing the people in the story, and depicting what is happening on stage. In the interludes that separate the scenes, it takes over completely, providing compositions of great power and beauty. The "Four Sea Interludes," frequently heard in concerts, will be discussed, showing their significance in the opera.

The first interlude is played immediately following the Prologue (the trial of Peter), and serves to introduce the scene of the first act, the village beach and street "on a cold gray morning." The bleakness of the scene is portrayed in an unaccompanied melody, high in violins and flutes, interrupted from time to time with clarinet, harp, and viola arpeggios, like gusts of wind:

EXAMPLE 141*

*Copyright 1945 by Boosey & Hawkes.

Below, major chords played by the brass are heard, contradicting the mode of the melody:

EXAMPLE 142

These three factors continue as the villagers come onstage and the chords thus become associated with the people. With these basic elements—melody, arpeggio, and chord—the sea and man, the theme of the opera, is established.

The second interlude, "Sunday Morning," occurs in the opera as a prelude to Act II. The scene is the same as before, but now it is "a fine sunny morning with church bells ringing." It must be difficult for a composer to write festive, outdoor-music with bells and not think of the Coronation scene from *Boris Godounov*. Britten does not resist the association. This interlude starts with overlapping thirds played *fp* (loud attack and then immediately soft) by the horns. The effect is bell-like, and the bright syncopated woodwind figures sound like overtones:

EXAMPLE 143

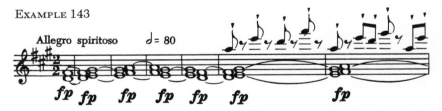

A *cantabile* melody, later the theme of the Sunday morning aria sung by Ellen, interrupts the tone-painting.

The third interlude is a nocturne, serving as a welcome relief after the tense scene that precedes it. Once again, the musical means are extremely economical. They consist of diatonic chords in the bas-

soons and lower strings and a halting melody in the cellos. In the
opera, this quiet interlude is followed immediately by a barn dance,
and the raucous village music which breaks into it makes a vivid contrast, not unlike the village-inn scene in *Wozzeck* in which the out-of-
tune piano breaks into the high tension of the preceding interlude.

The last section of the orchestral suite depicts a storm at sea.
Here is a blustering, savage piece, strong in irregular rhythms and
tympani accents, interspersed with progressions in parallel seconds and
fifths for trumpets and trombones. Near the end an expansive phrase,
associated with Grimes' hope for salvation through his love for Ellen,
is heard:

EXAMPLE 144

This interlude is integrated directly into the scene that follows as are
all the others.

The most important interlude (not included in the concert
suite) is a *passacaglia,* the basis of which is a theme sung by Grimes
after he strikes Ellen. When he realizes the enormity of his act he
sings:

EXAMPLE 145

God have mer -   cy upon me!

Once again a similarity to *Wozzeck* comes to mind, as Berg's hero
sings a passage expressing his misery:

EXAMPLE 146

WOZZECK:

wir   ar - me Leut!

The similarities to Berg's masterpiece do not end here. The central character in both operas represents the underdog, the under-privileged member of society who, through lack of opportunity, has no control over his fate. Wozzeck's ironic remark that it is difficult for the poor to be virtuous is echoed many times by Grimes. In both works tremendous compassion is raised for these unfortunate, timeless people. An interesting sidelight is the fact that the authors of the two librettos, Crabbe and Büchner, were contemporaries of the early nineteenth century.

Besides these similarities in the basic stories and in the impact of the two operas, there are also similarities in the over-all musical structures as well as in details. Both composers achieve continuity by writing important orchestral interludes that connect the scenes. As Kerman points out, in speaking of *Wozzeck*, these sections give oppor-tunity for the music to expand after the terseness demanded by a realistic setting of the words.[4] The use of "abstract" forms, such as the *passacaglia*, to provide a structural framework for dramatic scenes is also found in the two operas, but of course, much more consistently in Berg's. Both composers have the ability to characterize personages and situations with few notes (the Captain in *Wozzeck* and the lawyer Swallow in *Peter Grimes*), and both move from low life (the scenes in the pub and the beer hall, each with its appropriate music) to high pathos. Britten as well as Berg achieves tremendous, shatter-ing, musical effects with the simplest musical means, as shown by the terrifying drum beat that accompanies the villagers' search for Grimes and the mournful fog horn (tuba) that accompanies his last soliloquy.

Emphasis upon similarities does not mean that *Peter Grimes* is derivative from *Wozzeck*, and therefore a second-rate opera. Knowl-edge of such points of contact helps to classify Britten as a creative type. He is not a composer who holds originality to be of prime im-portance. He is reported to have said, "I do not see why I should lock myself inside a narrow personal idiom"[5]—an attitude completely at odds with that of many of his contemporaries who seek a highly personal style. That this attitude is right for Britten is proved by the success of his later operas. Several have entered the repertoires of leading opera houses (a tribute given to few twentieth-century operas) and within a year after its première in 1960, *Midsummer Night's Dream* promised to be his most popular.

SUGGESTED READINGS

A general survey of the period can be found in *British Music Of Our Time,* edited by A. L. Bacharach (London, 1946), as well as in Norman Demuth's *Musical Trends in the Twentieth Century* (London, 1951). Two books devoted to Ralph Vaughan Williams and his music are: *Ralph Vaughan Williams* by Hubert Foss (contains short autobiography by the composer; New York, 1950), and *The Music of Ralph Vaughan Williams* by Frank Howes (London, 1954).

Two valuable books on Britten are: *Benjamin Britten, A Commentary on his Works from a Group of Specialists,* edited by Donald Mitchell and Hans Keller (New York, 1953), and *Benjamin Britten, a Sketch of his Life and Work* by Eric Walter White (London, 1954).

CHAPTER XVI

MUSIC
IN AMERICA

*The way to write American music is simple. All you have to do
is to be an American and then write any kind of music you wish.*

VIRGIL THOMSON

The most important fact about American music of the mid-
twentieth century is its diversity and vigor. In contrast to
the situation in the early 1900's, when interest in and performance of music was largely limited to metropolitan
centers and an American composer was a *rara avis,* by 1950
music was being written, played, and listened to across
the land by ever-increasing numbers of people. This is not
to say that our composers immediately found audiences
and fame but, rather, that at least their chances for
recognition and performances were as favorable here as
in any other place. The growth of music departments in
colleges and universities with their composers-in-residence
and festival concerts helped to establish the American
composer as a valuable and respected member of his com-
munity.

This chapter will be devoted to six American composers born close to the turn of the century. These men still
went to Europe in the twenties for advanced study and
stimulation, but when they returned they did much to create
genuine twentieth-century American music. It will be

immediately apparent that no American "school" or "sound" resulted. On the contrary, representatives of most of the major style trends will be found and a wealth of music of strong personal imprint.

COPLAND, 1900-

Copland's background is thoroughly American. He was born in Brooklyn to immigrant Russian parents, attended public schools, worked on Saturdays in his father's department store, and took his first piano lessons from his older sister. When his interest in music became predominant and he decided to become a composer, his parents were surprised, but they did not hinder his ambition.

After graduating from high school, Copland studied piano and harmony in New York, but he was more interested in the Strauss, Wolf, Debussy, and Ravel scores he found in the public library. During the summer of 1921 he went to France to attend the newly opened American School of Music at Fontainebleau. After overcoming his misgivings about studying with a young woman, he enrolled in the classes of Mlle. Nadia Boulanger, and became the first of a long series of Americans to work under this remarkable teacher. Finding the musical life of France stimulating (this was during the early twenties, it must be remembered), and encouraged by the acceptance of a piano piece by Durand, Debussy's and Ravel's publisher, he remained in Paris for the next two years.

The young composer returned to New York in 1924, and Mlle. Boulanger introduced his Symphony for Organ and Orchestra with the New York Symphony Orchestra early in 1925. It was after this performance that Walter Damrosch, the conductor, said to the audience, "Ladies and gentlemen! If a young man at the age of twenty-three can write a symphony like that, in five years he will be ready to commit murder."[1] This remark shows the total lack of sympathy for, and understanding of new music, on the part of New York's most prominent musician.

However, Copland received a Guggenheim Fellowship, the first to be awarded to a composer, and he returned to France for another stay. With this move the pattern of his life became established—residence in or near New York was interspersed with frequent sojourns in

Europe, Mexico, Hollywood, South America, and the Far East. Copland is typically American in his cosmopolitanism, in his restless energy, and in his wide-ranging interests. He has been an untiring promoter of new music; organizing concerts (Copland-Sessions concerts 1928-1931); composers' societies (American Composers Alliance); festivals (Yaddo); and schools of music (Tanglewood). Although he has not held a full-time appointment at a college or university, he lectured for several years at the New School for Social Research in New York and filled guest appointments at Harvard and other universities. He has composed music for Hollywood movies, traveled as a cultural ambassador, written books and articles, conducted, and performed as a pianist.

COPLAND'S COMPOSITIONS

Since Copland, along with many other twentieth-century artists, has progressed through clearly defined style periods, it will be helpful in discussing his compositions to place them in the groups defined and named by Julia Smith in her study of the composer.[2]

Among the works written while he was still a student of Boulanger, the *Passacaglia* for piano (1922) is the most significant. Built on an expressive chromatic theme, this composition shows the disciplined workmanship he acquired from his teacher.

EXAMPLE 147*

Other early works are the Symphony for Organ and Orchestra (rewritten in 1928 without the organ, as the First Symphony), and a ballet *Grohg*, which later was incorporated in his *Dance Symphony*.

The principal works of Copland's first period (1925-1929) called "French-Jazz" by Julia Smith are: *Music for the Theatre*

*Copyright 1922 by Editions Maurice Senard; international copyright secured by Editions Salabert, Paris.

(1925), Concerto for Piano (1926), *Vitebsk* (1928), and *Symphonic Ode* (1929). These compositions were written after his return to New York and during the second European sojourn. Outstanding musical traits are the use of jazz idioms and rhythms, aggressive dissonances, and Jewish melodies in *Vitebsk,* which was written for piano, violin, and cello.

Music for the Theatre is a vital composition that clearly reveals Copland's background—that of a young American who knew authentic jazz as well as the sophisticated jazz stylizations of Milhaud and Stravinsky. The piece was not written for any particular production; it is "theatrical" in a general way. It opens with the trumpet playing a nervous, free-ranging melody with frequent repeated notes —an example of what Arthur Berger has called Copland's "declamatory" style.[3] Resembling wordless recitative, synagogue cantillation, or the wandering improvisation of a jazz musician, this type of melody is frequently encountered in Copland's works. A theme consisting of three descending notes (3-2-1 of the major scale) is introduced; it is used again by the composer in later compositions. A strongly syncopated middle section follows, and then the movement closes with references to the opening soliloquy.

The second movement, "Dance," recalls a jam session as one instrument after another comes into prominence. The rhythm is convulsive, and a distorted version of "East Side, West Side" is heard. This movement is close to real jazz—much closer than anything written by Milhaud, Stravinsky, or Hindemith. "Interlude" is in blues style, opening with an English horn solo. "Burlesque," which follows, reminds one of the music of Les Six with its music-hall flavor, and "Epilogue" returns to the mood and musical material of the opening.

There is no light-hearted gaiety in the compositions of the second or "Abstract" period (1929-1935). The principal compositions are: *Piano Variations* (1930), *Statements* for orchestra (1932-1935), *Hear Ye! Hear Ye!* a ballet, (1934), and *Short Symphony* (1932-33), later rewritten as a sextet (1937). These are difficult, austere works in which the working out of musical ideas to their logical conclusions seems to be the main concern of the composer.

The composition that most completely embodies this trend is the *Piano Variations,* an uncompromising statement of a serious young composer. The piece abounds in accented fortissimos in the

piano's most percussive registers. Among twentieth-century compositions exploiting the "spiky" aspects of the instrument, none is more
severe. The theme is:

EXAMPLE 148*

*press down silently

*Copyright 1932 by Cos Cob Press, Inc.; renewed 1959. Copyright and renewal
assigned to Boosey & Hawkes, Inc.

The conflict between C-sharp, the tonic, and C-natural—both melodically and harmonically (Measure 2)—is an example of the Stravinskyan type of dissonance often used in this piece. Further influence of Stravinsky is expressed in the frequent octave transpositions of melody notes, the unrelenting doublings in major sevenths and minor ninths, as well as in the theme itself, which shows similarities to the theme of the Octet (Example 60).

The variations are skillfully tied together so that their effect is cumulative. In early sections the piece moves in a steady quarter-note motion (in measures of constantly changing length), but later on, notes of shorter time value add momentum. The moods vary from the granitic sonorities of the beginning to a playful scherzo; from brilliant toccatas to solemn hymns. Throughout the piece there is neither figuration nor accompaniment figures; everything is essential and sparse.

The *Variations* are highly expressive, moving, harshly dissonant, and rigorously constructed. They are an example of what the distinguished critic, Paul Rosenfeld, meant when he said that Copland's music "resembles nothing so much as steel cranes, bridges, and the frames of skyscrapers."[4]

In the mid-thirties, Copland made one of those abrupt shifts in style which have marked the careers of many present-day artists and composers. This particular about-face was caused in part by his growing social consciousness resulting from the economic depression of the thirties. Copland was not alone in this particular development; many artists, writers, and musicians of the time felt that they should leave their ivory towers and communicate more directly with "the people." He turned away from the forbidding austerities of his recent compositions and wrote music that was easy to perform and to listen to.

His operetta for children, *The Second Hurricane* (1937), and *An Outdoor Overture* (1938), for high school orchestras, are true examples of the *gebrauchsmusik* ideal. *A Lincoln Portrait* (1942), for narrator and orchestra, is perhaps the composition most obviously aimed at mass appeal. Another piece that found an immediate audience was *El Salón México* (1937), a rhapsody on Mexican folk and street tunes. Unlike similar pieces of the romantic era (for example, Enesco's *Roumanian Rhapsody*), in which folk-tunes were made glamorous by their colorful orchestral dress, in Copland's composition the vulgarity and humor of the tunes are emphasized by the brashness of the orchestration. Twentieth-century devices such as measures of varying lengths, dissonance, and polytonality add to its attractiveness.

Next, Copland wrote a series of ballets on American themes, in which he exploited popular and folk music of his own country. Among these are: *Billy the Kid* (1938), *Rodeo* (1942), and *Appalachian Spring* (1943-44). In the first two he employed authentic cowboy and Western tunes, but as in *El Salón México* the simple melodies are presented with all the sophistication of an urbane contemporary composer. Jazz and ragtime rhythms, "vamps," unexpected silences—all contribute to the boisterous high spirits of these popular compositions. *Appalachian Spring* is another matter. Concerned with the courtship and wedding of a Shaker couple in rural Pennsylvania in the early nineteenth century, Copland employs simple, old hymn-tunes, triadic harmonizations, and a modest orchestra, resulting in a score of quiet beauty. Among his excellent film scores are those for *The Heiress, Of Mice and Men, The Red Pony,* and *Our Town.*

Having learned that he could write music that had wide appeal did not cause Copland to renounce his original orientation completely. After 1940 he occasionally wrote compositions that were neither functional nor "travel souvenirs." In these mature compositions, such as the Piano Sonata (1941), the Third Symphony (1946), Clarinet Concerto (1948), the songs, *Twelve Poems by Emily Dickinson* (1950), Piano Quartet (1950), and *Fantasy* for piano (1958), he reverted to a more austere idiom, but these later compositions are never as stark as the *Variations.* One frequently hears traces of the cowboy tunes and hymns he came to know when he wrote the ballets.

The Third Symphony is a full-scale work. Written without the external conditioning provided by a ballet or movie scenario, it is one of Copland's most personal statements.

The first movement is calm and hymnlike, showing the influence of the Shaker hymns Copland discovered while preparing to write *Appalachian Spring.* It starts with a disjunct, unharmonized melody in the violins, flutes, and clarinets, which immediately establishes a quiet, early-morning feeling:

EXAMPLE 149*

Molto moderato

VIOLINS, FLUTES, CLARINETS
IN THREE OCTAVES

At first there is a steady march of quarter notes, but the pace becomes more animated with the addition of eighth notes. A four-
square, contrasting second theme is introduced by the trombones:

EXAMPLE 150

This theme is heard in various choirs of the orchestra with ever-
increasing dynamics and busier accompaniment figures, until a noisy
climax is reached and the quiet opening melody returns.

The second movement reminds one of the cowboy music of
Copland's western ballets. After some introductory fanfares related
to Example 149 the main theme appears:

EXAMPLE 151

This is a "perky" (the composer's word) scherzo, with a contrasting
middle section. At the end, the main theme is presented again in

*Copyright 1947 by Boosey & Hawkes, Inc.

octave doublings throughout the whole orchestra with noisy punctuation in the tympani.

The third movement also starts with a variant of Example 149 in the strings after which the principal theme is heard in the flute:

EXAMPLE 152

This theme permeates the movement.

The last movement starts with a fanfare the composer had written during World War II, which serves as an introduction to a sonata-form movement. The main theme, presented by the oboe, is strongly rhythmic and reminds one of bird twitterings when it is presented contrapuntally in the high woodwinds:

EXAMPLE 153

This is a gay movement, bright with syncopation and rushing figures. The development section begins with a reference to the opening fanfare, but soon the busy figuration resumes. A new theme (Copland calls it his second theme, although its introduction in a development section is unusual) has a strong Latin American rhythmic feeling:

EXAMPLE 154

After a recapitulation of the opening theme there is an extended coda in which allusions are made to various elements of the whole symphony. At the end there is a blazing statement of the hymnlike melody heard at the beginning.

During the nineteen fifties, Copland, along with many other composers of his generation, showed his interest in serial music by writing some compositions organized according to twelve-tone principles. This tendency is most pronounced in the *Fantasy* for piano, but even here, according to the composer, he "made liberal use of devices associated with that technique rather than writing rigorously controlled twelve-tone music."[5] The *Fantasy* is a serious piece, lasting a half hour, written "to suggest the quality of fantasy, that is, a spontaneous and unpremeditated sequence of events that would carry the listener irresistably (if possible) from the first note to the last, while at the same time exemplifying clear and somewhat unconventional structural principles."[6]

This important piece is written on the following ten-note row:

EXAMPLE 155

The unused two tones are employed in the cadences.

In spite of its serial organization, the *Fantasy* is readily recog-

EXAMPLE 156*

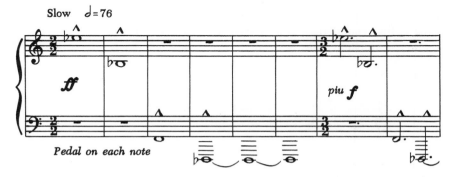

*Copyright 1957 by Boosey & Hawkes, Inc.

314 / Part Two: 1914-1945

nized as a composition by Copland. The beginning (Example 156) suggests the *Piano Variations,* written almost thirty years previously.

Copland is one of the most interesting and significant American composers of his generation. He has achieved a genuinely personal musical style, not by exclusion, but by including European as well as American elements. His activities as teacher, writer, and entrepreneur have been extensive and his leadership unquestioned.

HARRIS, 1898-

In contrast to Aaron Copland, the New Yorker and cosmopolite, Roy Harris was born in Oklahoma, grew up in rural California, and has spent most of his life on college campuses, far removed from metropolitan centers. Furthermore, while Copland was a dedicated musician and began to compose while still in his teens, Harris did not discover music until after he was discharged from service in World War I.

He was in Los Angeles at the time, and began his studies with Arthur Farwell, a composer and energetic champion of American music who recognized the unusual talent of his student and encouraged him to submit one of his first compositions, the *Andante* for orchestra, to the Eastman School of Music's 1926 Festival of American Music. The piece was selected to be played; Harris went East and recognition rapidly followed. A Guggenheim Fellowship took him to Paris where he worked for a short time with Nadia Boulanger. After returning to the United States, he started a long career of teaching, serving for various lengths of time at Colorado College, Cornell University, Peabody (Nashville), Pennsylvania State College for Women, Indiana University, and the University of Puerto Rico.

During all of these years he composed constantly, and in the thirties his music was frequently performed both at home and abroad. A sign of his prestige is the fact that at this time when there were few recordings of "serious" American music, he was well represented in the catalogs. Always an admirer of Russia, Harris during World War II dedicated his Fifth Symphony to our then ally; it was performed with great success in Moscow.

HARRIS' COMPOSITIONS

Roy Harris is primarily a composer of instrumental music. He has written seven symphonies (1933-1951), a concerto for two pianos (1946), and a violin concerto (1950). Chamber works include three string quartets (1930-1939), a piano quintet (1937), a sonata for violin and piano, and three sonatas for piano. Perhaps his best known composition is his arrangement of the Civil War song, "When Johnny Comes Marching Home."

Harris' Third Symphony (1939) did much to establish him as an important American composer. A short work, taking about seventeen minutes to perform, it is built on an original structural plan consisting of five sections played without pause.

The first section, described by the composer as "tragic, low string sonorities," starts with a long-spanned melody suggesting a Gregorian chant by its modal flavor and steady movement in quarter notes arranged in asymmetrical groups:

EXAMPLE 157*

The intervals become larger and other voices are added, at first in parallel, organumlike chords. Eventually, as other choirs of the orchestra enter, the texture becomes polyphonic until a climax in volume is reached.

Without any pause, the second section, described as "Lyric, strings, horns and woodwinds" begins with a change in timbre when the solo flute enters above sustained strings. Its melody outlines the notes of an augmented triad, F-A-C♯-F, previously heard at the climax

*Copyright 1939, 1940 by G. Schirmer, Inc., New York.

of the first section. This linking of one section to the next through a common theme is characteristic of the symphony. In this section the music continues to move in steady quarter notes in antiphonal passages between the woodwinds and strings with occasional punctuation by the horns. Once again a climax of volume is reached.

The mood changes completely in the third movement, described as "Pastoral—woodwinds with a polytonal string background." Over shimmering, impressionistic figuration in the strings, this English horn melody is heard:

EXAMPLE 158

The figuration continues for two-hundred measures while individual woodwinds, brass, and then combinations of wind instruments are heard in answering phrases. Toward the end of the section these melodic entries become closer, the note values are shortened, and the dynamics increased.

At the height of the climax, a new theme, angular and brusque, is heard in the strings. This is the principal theme of Movement IV, described as "Fugue—dramatic":

EXAMPLE 159

Later, the theme of the second movement (Example 158) is added to the lively syncopated polyphony.

Long melodies reminiscent of the opening announce the last section, described as "Dramatic, tragic." The coda is marked by a pedal in the tympani and a somber slowing of pace. The symphony ends on a somewhat theatrical note.

Harris' music has always been strongly modal, and in recent years he has worked out a theory of modes that has become the basis of his later composing. He arranges seven modes in an order from "dark" to "light." The former are those whose tones form small, or diminished, intervals with the final or tonic. For instance, the Locrian mode is the darkest in Harris' opinion, because the intervals formed between B, the final, and the other tones are with one exception diminished or minor:

EXAMPLE 160

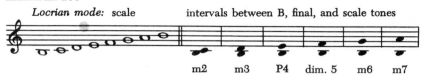

The "lightest" mode is the Lydian, for in contrast to the Locrian all of the intervals between the final and the other notes are with one exception major, or augmented:

EXAMPLE 161

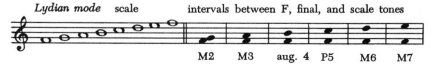

The other modes are arranged between these two, according to their degree of "lightness" or "darkness." The Dorian comes in the middle as a neutral mode, since its intervals are of the same size and quality when inverted.[7] Harris' Quartet #3, a series of preludes and fugues, is organized according to this theory, each piece becoming "darker" than the preceding.

Harris has also worked out a theory of chords, considering them to be "bright" when they resemble the overtone pattern in structure, or "dark" when they differ from it. He has gone so far as to label chords "dark luminous," "bright luminous," "savage bright," "savage dark," etc. These theoretical ideas of the composer have not had wide acceptance among musicians, but they give an interesting insight into his somewhat mystic, contemplative personality.

One of the reasons for Harris' quick acceptance by a relatively large audience lies in the basic simplicity of his music. There is none of the sophisticated, tongue-in-cheek quality prevalent in the music of some of his contemporaries; instead, sincerity and earnestness are felt in everything he writes. The long melodies, mild dissonances, clear differentiation between the choirs of the orchestra, strong, asymmetrical rhythms—above all, the adherence to a basic tonality—give a heartening "American" sound to his music. Furthermore, the America suggested is not that of nervous, neurotic cities, but an America of the plains and wide-open spaces. A decade that was attracted to the paintings by Grant Wood and John Stuart Curry found similar qualities to admire in the music of Roy Harris.

Since Harris has not sustained the prominent position he held in the thirties and forties, his final position in American music of the first half of the twentieth century is impossible to gauge. Nevertheless, it is safe to say that his has been one of the most individual and "American" voices of the time.

PISTON, 1894-

Roy Harris can be classified as the rugged individualist, the sometimes rough, but sincere American who created his own musical language with a minimum of contact with the long heritage of music. Walter Piston is a completely different type of composer. He can be classified as a neoclassicist in that his music is conservative in form and restrained in expression, and shows a predominance of baroque textures and the skilled control of a master craftsman.

Piston's roots and home are in New England. His grandfather, an immigrant from Italy who settled in Maine, was named Pistone. The composer was born in Rockland, Maine, in 1894 and moved with his family to Boston in 1905. Throughout his high school days he showed casual interest and talent in music, but he did not decide to become a composer until after he had worked as a draftsman and spent a year studying painting. During that time he played the violin in dance and theater orchestras. Later, during World War I, he was a saxophonist in an army band stationed at the Massachusetts Institute of Technology.

Upon his release from the Army in 1920, he entered Harvard as a music student. Graduating four years later, at the age of thirty, he went to Paris to study with Nadia Boulanger. He stayed there for two years and upon his return started to teach in the music department at Harvard University, remaining there until his retirement from teaching in 1960. Throughout these years he taught a large number of young composers, and his textbooks on harmony, counterpoint, orchestration, and analysis have been widely used.

One of the most respected of American composers, Piston has been honored with a Pulitzer Prize, a Guggenheim Fellowship, a New York Music Critics Circle Award, and several honorary doctorates.

PISTON'S COMPOSITIONS

Piston is primarily a composer of absolute orchestral and chamber music. He has written but few vocal compositions, no operas, and except for one ballet, no works for the theater.

The catalog of his works includes: six symphonies (1937-1955), a piano concerto (1937), two violin concertos (1940 and 1959) and a viola concerto (1958). Among the many chamber works are: sonatas for violin and piano, violin and harpsichord, flute and piano; a quintet for piano and strings; a woodwind quintet; a *divertimento* for nine instruments; and several string quartets.

The Sonata for Violin and Piano is characteristic of Piston's economical, somewhat austere style. Written in 1939, it is in the three conventional movements of the classical sonata design he so often employs. The first movement, in clear sonata form, is in an equivocal major-minor tonality on F. This is the main theme, stated over complex, nonfunctional harmonies:

EXAMPLE 162

A canon between violin and piano leads to a restatement of the theme, this time firmly established on the tonic, F.

The second theme contrasts strongly with the first, a situation often found in Piston's clear-cut forms. The new theme is sprightly and dancelike, alternating 5/8 meter with 3/4:

EXAMPLE 163

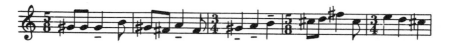

There are lively canons between violin and piano, and the development is largely polyphonic with dissonant counterpoint. The recapitulation follows, with the expected tonal shifts so that the F tonality is maintained throughout.

The second movement is in the key of B minor, an augmented fourth higher than F, the key of the first and last movements (the first movement began with a signal-motive consisting of these notes). This movement is darkly expressive, in spite of the fact that it is built from very simple musical ideas; for instance, the chief melody is nothing more than a minor scale sounded over an ostinato:

EXAMPLE 164

The nimble last movement shows many of Piston's traits—the clear-cut contrast between sections, contrapuntal ingenuity (inversion of the second theme in the recapitulation), and *fugato* development. The piano part, as in earlier movements, has mainly a linear texture that avoids elaborate figuration or rich chords. It may be compared to Bach's writing for the keyboard instrument in his accompanied violin sonatas.

Piston's Fourth Symphony, written on a commission from the University of Minnesota in 1951, is a good example of the composer's mature style. It is warmer and more lyrical than the sonata just discussed and suggests that the austerity felt in the early works disappeared as the composer grew older. This symphony is neither dramatic nor heroic in expression; words such as "amiable," "economical," "restrained," or "witty," might well be applied to it.

The first movement, marked *piacevole* (peacefully) starts with a long, graceful melody in the violins soaring over a compass of more than two octaves. The interval of the fourth is prominent and occasional unexpected dissonances add bite:

EXAMPLE 165*

Piacevole

VIOLINS

The flowing motion is interrupted by chords in the brass. Eventually a narrow-compassed chromatic theme is heard in the clarinets:

EXAMPLE 166

CLARINET

pp

The first theme appears again, followed by the second, as the form reveals itself to be baroque binary (A B A B).

The second movement is marked *ballando* and is a vigorous, gay rondo with an over-all structural pattern A B A C A B A. All sections are dancelike. The first, in spite of its irregular measure lengths $\left(\begin{smallmatrix} 3 & 7 & 5 \\ 4 & 8 & 8 \end{smallmatrix}\right)$, has a Spanish fandango character:

EXAMPLE 167

Fast

WOODWINDS

The next begins with an um-pah-pah waltz "vamp" introducing an old-fashioned, sentimental melody:

EXAMPLE 168

CELLOS, BASSOON, BASS CLARINET

espr.

The next digression sounds like a reel or a hoe-down, with swirling violin figures over syncopated chords in the bass. The earlier sections all reappear and the movement ends with brilliance and *éclat*.

The slow movement, marked *contemplativo,* is less obvious because the main theme, presented by the clarinets, is not based on a clear tonality as are the themes of the previous movements. This theme contains ten different tones:

EXAMPLE 169

Contemplativo (♪ = 92)

CLARINET

The two additional tones, G-flat and D, are heard immediately afterward from cellos and clarinets. However, this is not a twelve-tone composition since there are underlying tonal centers in most of the sections. A contrasting middle part starts with a flute solo. An ever-increasing number of imitative entries build to a climax. At the height of volume and dissonance the original theme returns in the horns with octave transpositions of some of the notes. The last movement returns to the noisy brilliance of the second. The syncopated main theme exploits the interval of the augmented fourth:

EXAMPLE 170

VIOLINS, VIOLAS, HORNS, BASSOON.

By way of contrast the second theme, presented in canon, is diatonic and smoothly flowing:

EXAMPLE 171

The two compositions just discussed are characteristic of their composer in the way they combine old and new elements. Classical sonata form provides the framework, and baroque polyphony the texture, while harmony, key relationships, and rhythm are of the twentieth century. The whole is welded together with the sure hand of a master craftsman. Herein lies the neoclassical quality of Piston's music.

SESSIONS, 1898-

Roger Sessions stands in the same relationship to expressionism as Piston to neoclassicism. This statement is meant to be more suggestive than precise, but it does point to a difference in approach on the part of these two important composers. For Sessions, composition is not a matter of working out expressive designs in carefully controlled forms. On the contrary, music is a medium for the expression of highly serious musical thoughts and convictions in compositions that are necessarily difficult and challenging to perform and listen to.

Sessions was born in Brooklyn, but his ancestors had lived in New England since Colonial days. His mother, a pianist who had studied in Leipzig, guided his first musical experiences. After she took her fourteen-year-old son to a performance of *Die Meistersinger,* he resolved to become a composer. A brilliant youth, he entered Harvard the same year. After his graduation the outbreak of World War I prevented a projected trip to France for study with Ravel.

Unable to go abroad, Sessions went to the Yale School of Music for graduate study. This was followed by his teaching at Smith College where he remained from 1917 until 1921. The major musical influence on him during those years was the Swiss composer, Ernest Bloch, with whom he studied. When Bloch went to Cleveland to head the Institute of Music, Sessions followed, and later joined the faculty.

In 1925 he made his first trip to Europe and remained until 1933, with occasional visits to the United States. Subsidized by his family and various fellowships during these eight years, Sessions showed his independence of thought by avoiding Paris and the Boulanger circle and, instead, spent his time in Italy and Germany. Returning home in 1933, he resumed his activity as a teacher, working in Boston, in New York, at Princeton University, at the University of California, and since 1952, again at Princeton.

SESSIONS' COMPOSITIONS

Sessions has never been a prolific composer and the list of his works is not long, but there are no insignificant or "little" works among them. Among the orchestral music is the Suite arranged from music he wrote for a college production of Andreyev's play *The Black Maskers;* four symphonies (1927-1958); a violin concerto (1935); and a piano concerto (1956). There is a one-act opera, *The Trial of Lucullus* (1947), and the full-length opera *Montezuma* (1947), neither of which has had professional production. Among the chamber music are two string quartets (1936, 1950), a duo for violin and piano (1942), and a string quintet (1957). In addition, there is a sonata for violin solo (1953), two sonatas for piano (1930 and 1946), a collection of piano pieces called *From My Diary,* and a set of chorale preludes for organ.

Sessions' Second Symphony is a good example of his "difficult" style. It must be remembered, however, that what seems difficult in music is a relative matter, depending on the background and experience of the listener. Compared to a symphony by Harris or Hanson, Sessions' symphony *is* difficult, but if one brings to it a background that includes familiarity with Schoenberg's or Berg's orchestral works, it offers no special problems. On the contrary, such listeners would feel at home in the first movement, for here the rushing strings, jagged chromatic melodies, muted trumpets playing dissonant chords, strident xylophone, and the highly charged atmosphere suggest the *Five Pieces for Orchestra.*

The first movement is in sonata form. The opening melody, divided between first and second violins, is treated contrapuntally, recurring from time to time in inversions and augmentations (Ex. 172). The second theme, related to Example 172, introduces a quieter section and provides opportunity for the shimmering color of the elusive woodwind figures that accompany the solo violin (Example 173). The energetic contrapuntal development of these themes is the content of the movement which eventually dies away on a pizzicato, low in the strings.

The second, very short movement, *"Allegretto Capriccioso,"* is a grotesque march with a sly Lydian theme. Stated in the oboe and English horn, its humorous refusal to be bound to one tonality is apparent at once (Example 174).

The third movement breathes the atmosphere of the third act of *Tristan* with low strings in a slow, wavelike motion underlying poignant chromatic melodies in low woodwinds. As in the other

EXAMPLE 172*
Molto agitato

EXAMPLE 173

Tranquillo ♩ = 54

EXAMPLE 174

Allegro capricciaso ♩ = 80

movements, polyphony is the usual texture with sinuous, highly-charged melodies.

The last movement bubbles with energy and optimism. It is a rondo with a theme reminiscent of the music of Les Six:

EXAMPLE 175

The development the theme receives is more involved, however, than in most French music of that era. Here the larger-than-life, Beethovian boisterousness persists to the end. This symphony, like most of Sessions' works, is warm-blooded and expressive of a wide gamut of emotions.

Sessions has defined his aims in the following statement:

> I reject any kind of dogma or platform. I am not trying to write "modern," "American," or "neo-classic" music. I am seeking always and only the coherent and living expression of my musical ideas. ...I dislike rhetoric, overemphasis, vulgarity, but at the same time believe that perfection in art is a sort of equilibrium which can be neither defined nor counterfeited....I have no sympathy with consciously sought originality. I accept my musical ideas without theorizing.[8]

HANSON, 1896-

Howard Hanson was born in Wahoo, Nebraska, to Swedish-American parents. After graduating from a local Lutheran college, he studied composition with Percy Goetschius at the Institute of Musical Art in New York, and in 1916 accepted a position in the music department of the College of the Pacific in California. Three years later, the twenty-three-year-old instructor was made Dean, and when twenty-five he was awarded the Prix de Rome. During the three years he lived in Italy, he composed his first symphony, the *Nordic,* a work more expressive of Scandinavia's gray clouds than of the azure skies of Rome. This independence from surroundings and outer influences gives insight into Hanson's creative personality. In contrast to those composers who have responded to every new current and every whim of fashion, he has been undeviating in his goal —to write highly romantic music.

He returned to the United States in 1924 to become director of the recently established Eastman School of Music and in the following decades gradually assumed a position of leadership in American musical life. An untiring champion of American music, Hanson started the annual festivals of contemporary music in Rochester which have given performance opportunities to hundreds of composers representing all schools of musical thought. As a teacher he has influenced scores of students, many of whom have become composers of stature. His activities in national and international musical organizations—often as president—have further spread his influence.

HANSON'S COMPOSITIONS

During the years he devoted to creating a school of music and working for the cause of American music, Hanson composed a large number of works. These include: five symphonies, *The Nordic* (1923), *The Romantic* (1930), The Third (1938), *Sinfonia da Requiem* (1943), and *Sinfonia Sacra* (1955); and a number of symphonic poems, *Pan and the Priest* (1926), *Lux Aeterna* (1926), and *Mosaics* (1958). He has also written a piano concerto (1948), an organ concerto (1926), and numerous works for chorus and orchestra: *The Lament for Beowulf* (1926), *Three Songs from Drum Taps* (1935), *The Cherubic Hymn* (1949), and *The Song of Democracy* (1957). His opera *Merry Mount* (1933) was commissioned and performed by the Metropolitan Opera.

In his compositions Hanson reveals a consistent and undeviating point of view. He is loyal to the principles of tonality and uses dissonances to build climaxes. His melodies have unashamed and immediate appeal and his orchestrations are rich and colorful. That these are "old-fashioned" traits has never disturbed him.

The Second Symphony, subtitled *Romantic,* is Hanson's most popular and characteristic work. Written in the 1930's, Stravinsky was simultaneously working on the *Symphony of Psalms,* Schoenberg on *Moses und Aron,* and Copland on the *Piano Variations.* It has little to do with such music and suggests rather the symphonies of Sibelius. The first movement opens with an adagio introduction in which the basic theme of the symphony is immediately presented:

EXAMPLE 176

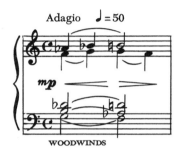

This motive (and its inversion) is used throughout the introduction as an ostinato. Trumpets and an imperious horn call usher in the principal theme of the movement, played by the horns against brilliant accompaniment figures:

EXAMPLE 177

*Copyright 1932 by the Eastman School of Music. Carl Fischer Inc., New York, sole agents for the world.

This is presented in canon, works up to a climax, and leads directly to a contrasting second theme in the oboes:

EXAMPLE 178

Another quiet melody that serves as the closing theme follows. The restrained development is primarily concerned with the principal theme with one section exploiting the two fourths of Example 177 in an impressionist manner. A full recapitulation, including all three themes, follows.

The second movement, *andante con tenerezza,* presents a simple melody that is related to the themes of the first movement in the prominence of the interval of the third:

EXAMPLE 179

No other composer discussed in this chapter would claim paternity to such a theme. Hanson develops it lovingly, including a setting for strings *divisi.* The contrasting middle section refers to the motto theme as well as to the closing theme of the first movement.

Most of the material of the last movement is related to themes already presented. It is a brilliantly orchestrated piece with a middle section recalling *The Rite of Spring* in its irregular rhythmic patterns:

EXAMPLE 180

Allegro con brio

p CELLOS *pizz.*

Hanson is fond of such patterns and they are frequently found in other compositions, showing that even he could not resist Stravinsky's rhythms. There is a brilliant coda with polychordal dissonances, finally resolving into a blazing D-flat chord.

Hanson's position in twentieth-century American music can be accurately ascertained from the *Romantic Symphony*. It shows how far removed he is from neoclassic austerity or daring experimentation. Instead of reducing his orchestra to a thin, unblending group of instruments, his motto seems to be "the more the better," and some of his most successful compositions are for full orchestra, chorus, and soloists, culminating in shattering climaxes.

It has been said of Brahms that he composed "as if Liszt and Wagner never existed." Perhaps Hanson is a twentieth-century parallel; the music of many of his contemporaries has not existed for him.

THOMSON, 1896-

If Howard Hanson represents the conservative, neoromantic, twentieth-century American composer, Virgil Thomson is his complete antithesis. The former's music is serious, expressive, and highly personal; the latter's is witty, sophisticated, and highly objective.

Virgil Thomson was born in Kansas City in 1896. He studied music and played the organ while still a school boy, and after brief, noncombatant service in World War I, continued his studies at Harvard. He made his first trip to Europe in 1921 with the Harvard Glee Club, but instead of returning with the group, remained in Paris to study with Nadia Boulanger. He returned to graduate from Harvard in 1923 and spent the next two years in New York where he continued his studies in composition and began his career as a church organist, choir master, and critic.

In 1925 he went back to France and remained there until 1940 when the imminent German occupation forced his return to the United States. He then became music editor of the *New York Herald Tribune*, and a powerful force in raising musical standards and shaping musical taste. Like Schumann, Berlioz, and Debussy—other composer-critics—he combined high musical standards, based on a thorough technical knowledge of music and performance, with an urbane and witty prose style. His critiques are among the few that make good reading in book form. He left this position in 1954 to devote all of his time to composition and lecturing.[9]

THOMSON'S COMPOSITIONS

A list of Thomson's compositions would give little indication of their style and content; their generally noncommittal titles give little indication of their originality. For instance, who would expect to hear a tango in a *sonata da chiesa* or gospel hymns in a symphony? There are a great many piano works, including four sonatas, numerous etudes, and over fifty "portraits"—character sketches of friends and acquaintances who "sat" for their piece in the same way they would sit for a painted portrait. The composer's interest in the organ accounts for the numerous works for that instrument; of these the best known is *Variations on Sunday School Tunes* (1926). There are two symphonies (although what Thomson calls a sonata or symphony is likely to have little in common with what the term usually connotes). He has written two string quartets and two sonatas for violin and piano; two operas on librettos of Gertrude Stein, *Four Saints in Three Acts* (1928), and *The Mother of Us All* (1947); a ballet, *The Filling Station* (1937); music for documentary films; and incidental music for plays.

Anyone familiar with the critical writings of Virgil Thomson will recognize similar qualities in his music—urbanity and sophistication, lack of reverence, and a refusal to be proper and dull. He shares these attributes with Les Six and Erik Satie, and if a pigeon-hole classification is required, he can be considered their American equivalent.

During his long residence in France, Thomson was in close association with many painters and writers of avant-garde inclinations. Among them Gertrude Stein was most important, and some of his most successful compositions have been the operas and the cantata *Capital, Capitals* (1927) that he wrote to her puzzling, highly amusing words. Miss Stein used utterly simple words, took them out of their usual order and function, and repeated them in unpredictable patterns. The result is nonsense if one expects language to "say something," but amusing and fascinating if one can lose his preconceptions of the nature and usual function of words.

Thomson's *Variations on Sunday School Tunes* will illustrate his style of writing. The first four bars show both a "wrong note harmonization" and a completely incongruous syncopated "break" (Example 181). The first variation consists of a rhythmic distortion of the hymn tune presented in the pedals. The next is given *in toto* (Example 182). This straightforward piece of nonsense is not unlike lines by Miss Stein such as "They never knew about it green and they never knew about it she never knew about it they never knew about it they never knew about it."

Later variations consist of elementary canons on motives of the hymn tune, excruciating clusters played full organ (sounding all the worse because they are sounded on the organ, usually the most respectable of instruments), elaborate pedal cadenzas, dissonant, bitonal harmonizations, and a pompous, grandiose finale.

Thomson is not always facetious. His scores for the documentary film *Louisiana Story* and the ballet *Filling Station* consist of simple and effective harmonizations of folksongs and his *Stabat Mater,* for voice and string quartet, and *Five Songs from Blake,* for baritone and orchestra, show unusual care in word-setting.

He frequently uses gospel hymns in his compositions, as well as tangos (as a movement of a *sonata da chiesa,* or as a dance in *Four Saints*), sentimental waltzes, and academic fugues. No matter what the idiom, it was probably chosen because of its incongruity and shock value. Such an attitude adds a welcome touch of levity to

an age in which many works of art express deep anxiety, but it is doubtful whether it results in masterpieces. Thomson would be the first to say that he is not interested in writing masterpieces.

*Copyright 1955 by H. W. Gray Co., New York.

YOUNGER COMPOSERS

Because of the frequent performances and recordings of their music and because of their significant activities as teachers, administrators of schools of music, and critics, the six composers discussed in this chapter are the leading American composers at mid-century. They became known as young and promising composers; they now hold positions of highest prestige and honor. Following these men are legions of younger composers (many of them their pupils) who together form the powerful school of twentieth-century American music.

Of the generation of composers born around 1910 the following must be mentioned. Samuel Barber (b. 1910) received his training at the Curtis Institute in Philadelphia. His first compositions, such as *Essay for Orchestra* and *Adagio for Strings* (1938), showed a warm lyricism in a generally conservative idiom. The lyricism has remained in his succeeding works, even after he adopted a more astringent style. Important later works are *Capricorn Concerto* for flute, oboe, trumpet, and strings (1944), the orchestral suite *Medea* (1947), and the opera *Vanessa* (1956). Closely associated with Barber is Gian Carlo Menotti, born in Italy (1911), but also educated at the Curtis Institute. He has written some of the most successful operas of our time. They include *Amelia Goes to the Ball* (1937), *The Old Maid and the Thief* (1939), *The Medium* (1946), *The Telephone* (1947), *The Consul* (1950), *Amahl and the Night Visitors* (1951), and *The Saint of Bleeker Street* (1954). The popularity of Menotti's operas is due as much to his strong sense of theater (he writes his own librettos) as it is to his eclectic and dramatically effective scores.

William Schuman (b. 1910) studied with Roy Harris and in 1945 became president of the Juilliard School of Music. He has written six symphonies, chamber music, the ballets *Night Journey* (1948) and *Judith* (1950), and a comic opera, *The Mighty Casey* (1953). John Cage (b. 1912) has been a leader of avant-garde tendencies. His compositions for "prepared piano" and those based on chance elements are discussed in the next chapter. Elliot Carter (b. 1908) holds a special position in this group of composers. A student of Walter Piston and Nadia Boulanger, he has developed slowly and is not as widely known as his contemporaries already mentioned. Nevertheless, since 1950 he has assumed a position of prime importance, primarily through his two string quartets (1951 and 1960). Many critics and musicians believe that he will be judged the outstanding American composer of his time. Attention is called to one younger man, Leon Kirchner (b. 1919) in this brief summary. He is a pupil of Roger Sessions, and has also worked informally with Schoenberg and Bartók. This orientation is apparent in his compositions, which include a duo for violin and piano (1947), a string quartet (1949), and a piano concerto (1956).

There are so many other young composers of merit that a complete list would be almost interminable. Thus, while at the beginning of the century America could claim only a few native composers, by mid-century she had achieved a position of leadership in music.

SUGGESTED READINGS

Copland. Two full-length studies have been written: Julia Smith, *Aaron Copland: His Work and Contribution to American Music* (New York, 1955) and Arthur Berger, *Aaron Copland* (New York, 1953). There are numerous periodical articles and the Autumn, 1948 issue of *Tempo* is devoted to his works. Among Copland's own writings, *Music and Imagination* (Cambridge, 1952), and the autobiographical sketch in *Our Modern Composers* (New York, 1941) are of interest.

Harris. No comprehensive study of Harris' style has been published. Among periodical articles, the following are recommended: Arthur Farwell, "Roy Harris" *Musical Quarterly,* XVIII, No. 1, Jan. 1932; Walter Piston, "Roy Harris" *Modern Music,* Jan.-Feb. 1934; and Nicolas Slonimsky, "Roy Harris" *Musical Quarterly,* XXXIII, No. 1, Jan. 1947. The last article is particularly recommended for the analysis of style elements it contains. Harris' own views on compositions can be found in *American Composers on American Music,* edited by Henry Cowell (Palo Alto, 1933).

Piston. "Walter Piston," by Elliot Carter, in *Musical Quarterly,* XXXII, No. 3, July 1946; "Piston's Fourth Symphony," by W. Austin, in *Music Review,* May 1955.

Sessions. Mark A. Schubart, "Roger Sessions: Portrait of an American Composer," *Musical Quarterly,* XXXII, No. 2, April 1946; various reviews of compositions in *Musical Quarterly*. Writings by Sessions: *The Musical Experience of Composer, Performer, Listener* (Princeton, 1950); *Reflections on the Music Life in the United States* (New York, 1956); *The Intent of the Artist*, edited by Augusta Centano (Princeton, 1941).

Thomson. *Virgil Thomson, His Life and Music* by Kathleen Hoover and John Cage (New York, 1959).

Books useful as references are *American Composers on American Music*, a symposium edited by Henry Cowell (Palo Alto, 1933), *Our Contemporary Composers* by John Tasker Howard (New York, 1941), *Composers in America* by Claire Reis (New York, 1947), *American Composers Today* by David Ewen (New York, 1949), *Modern Music-Makers* by Madeleine Goss (New York, 1952), *America's Music* by Gilbert Chase (New York, 1955), and the entries in *Baker's Biographical Dictionary of Musicians,* fifth edition (New York, 1958).

For bibliography, see *Some Twentieth Century American Composers; A Selective Bibliography* by John Edmunds and Gordon Boelzner (New York Public Library, New York. Volume I, 1959; Volume II, 1960).

	France	Germany & Austria	Other Countries	Other Arts, Events
1945	Milhaud: *Suite Française*		Shostakovitch: Symphony #9 Bartók: Piano Concerto #3 Britten: *Peter Grimes*	Hiroshima: first atomic bomb World War II ends United Nations created Rossellini: *The Open City*
1946	Honegger: Symphony #3 and #4	Hindemith: *When Lilacs Last*	Barber: *Medea* Prokofiev: Symphony #6 Menotti: *The Medium* Copland: Symphony #3 Carter: Piano Sonata	Giradoux: *The Mad-woman of Chaillot*
1947	Milhaud: Symphony #4 Poulenc: *Calligrammes*	Hindemith: Piano Concerto von Einem: *Dantons Tod*	Sessions: Symphony #2 Kirchner: Duo for violin and piano Carter: *The Minotaur*	Tennessee Williams: *A Streetcar Named Desire* Camus: *The Plague*
1948	Boulez: *Le Soleil des Eaux* Messiaen: *Turangalila*		Vaughan Williams: Symphony #6 Piston: Symphony #3 Dallapiccola: *Il Prigioniero* Carter: Woodwind Quintet	Pound: *Pisan Cantos* Breton: *Poems* Sartre: *Dirty Hands*
1949	Boulez: String Quartet	Egk: *French Suite*	Blitzstein: *Regina*	Orwell: *1984* Miller: *Death of a Salesman* T. S. Eliot: *The Cocktail Party*

	France	Germany & Austria	Other Countries	Other Arts, Events
1950	Poulenc: Piano Concerto Messiaen: *Ile de feu*	Hans Henze: Concerto	Menotti: *The Consul* Prokofiev: Symphony #7	Korean War begins Riesman: *The Lonely Crowd* Wilder: *Sunset Boulevard*
1951	Honegger: Symphony #5 *Di tre re.* Poulenc: *Stabat Mater*	Stockhausen: *Kreuzspiel*	Carter: String Quartet Menotti: *Amahl and the Night Visitors* Stravinsky: *The Rake's Progress*	
1952	Boulez: Structures	von Einem: *The Trial*	Kirchner: Sonata Concertante for Violin and Piano Stravinsky: Cantata Vaughan Williams: Symphony #7	Beckett: *Waiting for Godot*
1953	Poulenc: Sonata for Two Pianos	Stockhausen: *Studie I* (first electronic composition)	Britten: *The Turn of the Screw* Copland: *The Tender Land* Stravinsky: Septet	
1954	Boulez: *Le Marteau sans Maître* Milhaud: *David*	von Einem: *Meditations*	Barber: *Prayers of Kierkegaard* Dallapiccola: *Variazioni per orchestra* Leuning & Ussachevsky: *Poem of Cycles and Bells for Tape Recorder and Orchestra*	Dylan Thomas: *Under Milk Wood* Hydrogen bomb perfected

1955			Copland: *Canticle of Freedom* Dallapiccolla: *Canti di Liberazione* Kirchner: *Toccata for Strings, Solo Winds, and Percussion*	
1956		Henze: *Five Neopolitan Songs* Stockhausen: *Elektronische Studien*	Maderna: *Serenata No. 2 for 11 Instruments* Menotti: *The Unicorn, the Gorgon, and the Manticore* Schuman: *Credendum*	Eugene O'Neill awarded Pulitzer prize (post-humously) for *Long Day's Journey Into Night* Fellini: *La Strada*
1957	Poulenc: *Les Dialogues des Carmelites*	Blacher: *Music for Cleveland* Hindemith: *Die Harmonie der Welt* (1937-1957) Stockhausen: *Gruppe fur drei Orchester* Stockhausen: *Zeitmasse*	Berio: *Nones* Sessions: *Symphony #3* Stravinsky: *Agon*	Sputnik launched by USSR Anshen & Allen: Chapel of the Holy Cross, Sedona, Arizona Packard: *The Hidden Persuaders* Whyte: *The Organization Man* Camus awarded Nobel for literature
1958	Boulez: *Poésie pour pouvoir* Poulenc: *La Voix Humaine*	Stockhausen: *Pieces for Piano XI*	Copland: *Piano Fantasy* Nono: *Coro di Didone* Stravinsky: *Threni* Varèse: *Poême Electronique*	MacLeish: *J.B.* Williams: *Sweet Bird of Youth* Bergman: *The Seventh Seal*
1959	Boulez: *Improvisations sur Mallarmé*	Hindemith: *Pittsburgh Symphony*	Britten: *Missa Brevis* Stravinsky: *Movements for Piano and Orchestra*	Fidel Castro seizes power in Cuba Moon rocket successfully launched by USSR Frank Lloyd Wright: Guggenheim Museum, New York

PART III

1945-1960

CHAPTER XVII

NEW
DIRECTIONS

It is something of a miracle (and a tribute to man's creative instinct) that immediately after the carnage and tragic waste of World War II a vigorous cultural and musical life resumed. Artistic currents, submerged by totalitarian governments and the war, rushed to the surface. Famous older composers—even Richard Strauss—came out of their retreats with important new compositions, and a number of middle-generation composers, largely unnoticed before the war, now attracted attention. Young men, schoolboys during the war, puzzled and disturbed their elders with the audacity of their new ideas.

THE AGE OF WEBERN

It will be the task of future historians to define the musical styles of the mid-century; however, some tentative observations can be presented here. The most apparent dominant trend seemed to be the development of the styles established by Schoenberg, Berg, and Webern, particularly the last. In France before the war there had been no recognition of twelve-tone music, but now an important group of young French composers became its ardent proponents. During the Nazi years in Germany and Austria the idiom had been forbidden, and former students of Schoenberg and Webern went underground. They now assumed positions of importance, and a vigorous school of dodecaphonists gathered around them. Others, such as Dallapiccola in Italy

345

and Skalkottas in Greece, who had spent student years in Germany, were revealed as mature masters of the idiom. Composers in North and South America, in England, and in Japan wrote serial music. Illuminating analyses of important compositions appeared in books and periodicals, and recordings made the sound of the music available to large numbers of people.

Stravinsky's espousal of the technique* was spectacular and unpredicted. For forty years he had been the unchallenged leader of an ideal of composition held to be the antithesis of Schoenberg's, and their differences were so great that it extended to their social life —there was no communication or friendship between the two great composers when they lived in Southern California. Nevertheless, all of Stravinsky's compositions since 1950 were based on rows and he often expressed his admiration—sometimes in extravagant terms and gestures—for Webern's music.

Many other composers were attracted to these principles of tonal organization. Copland, Barber, Sessions, Piston, Britten, Martin are a few of the mature, well-established composers who turned to twelve-tone techniques. Of course such trends are never unanimous and some composers remained true to their conception of tonality. Hindemith, for instance, opposed the style on conviction and the Russians abstained from adopting it by decree, but much of the rest of the world capitulated.

Acceptance of twelve-tone principles did not mean slavish imitation of the founding-fathers' music. As a matter of fact, the principles were never really crystallized, for they were in a state of constant revision and development from composition to composition. Twelve-tone technique is an "angle of vision," according to Aaron Copland. "Like fugal treatment, it is a stimulus that enlivens musical thinking. . . . It is a method, not a style, and therefore it solves no problems of musical expressivity."[1]

NEW DEVELOPMENTS IN RHYTHM

Along with the interest in new ways of relating tones, some composers devised new systems of organizing rhythms. While *Le Sacre du Printemps* influenced the rhythm of a whole era, now other possi-

*Mentioned in Chapter IX.

bilities were explored, inspired by sources as disparate as the music of the Middle Ages, Oriental music, and mathematical calculation. Some of the ideas resulting from this exploration will be mentioned here.

Boris Blacher, the German composer, devised and used "variable meters" in many of his compositions—a systematic employment of measures of varying lengths. For instance, in a piano sonata (1951) the measures contain eighth notes in the following quantities:

Example 183

etc.

Eventually the pattern is reversed and the measures shorten. Other sequences are built of progressing series such as 2-3-4, 3-4-5, 4-5-6 and reverse; symmetrical series, 2-3-5-8-13; and cyclical variations, 2-3-4-5, 5-3-2-4, 3-2-4-5. Blacher's melodic phrases coincide with these varying measure-lengths, resulting in a highly personal style.

Elliott Carter, a highly respected American composer, works in the opposite direction by freeing his rhythms from regular meter. In his First String Quartet, for instance, the basic pulse rate changes frequently and smoothly from one tempo to another, while the individual parts move with the utmost independence. Normal rhythmic notation is strained to the breaking point in indicating such complex relationships; frequent meter signature changes and metronome equivalents dot the score. Here is an example from the quartet:

Example 184

$\frac{2}{4}$ $\frac{14}{12}$ $\frac{2}{4}$

♩ = 126   ♩.. = 72   ♩.. = ♩

In this example, the sixteenth notes do not change in speed. Therefore in the second measure, where there are seven sixteenths to the unit rather than four, the pulse almost doubles in length. As a result, in the last measure quarter notes take on the new, slower value, and the tempo has "changed smoothly and accurately from one absolute metronomic speed to another by lengthening the value of the basic note unit."[2] This process is called "metrical modulation."

It must be emphasized that Carter's use of new and complex rhythmic patterns by itself does not make him an important composer. He is highly regarded because of the expressive power of his music.

The French composer Olivier Messiaen (b. 1909) has also made use of new rhythmic concepts. Basing his music on models as heterogeneous as Hindu music, the songs of birds, and the Gregorian chant, he employs augmentations and diminutions of rhythmic patterns, not by the usual doublings and halvings, but by the addition or subtraction of fractional values. Here is an example of augmentation by quarter value:

A diminution by 2/3 means that

In the years immediately following the war, a large number of young musicians studied with Messiaen, and among them Pierre Boulez and Karlheinz Stockhausen made further rhythmic explorations. The latter, in a composition called *Zeitmasse* (*Time Densities*; 1957) for oboe, flute, English horn, clarinet, and bassoon, calls for a flexibility of tempos which goes beyond the possibilities of conventional notation. The composer gives the direction, "as slow as possible" from time to time, meaning that the breath-capacity of the instrumentalist playing the phrase determines the speed of all the others, as they adjust to him. Other passages are to be played "as fast as possible." Here, the technique of the leading instrumentalist determines the speed. Other directions are "fast-slowing down" and "slow-quickening." One result of this concept is that the piece will never be played twice in the same manner.

Another idea that developed out of the Messiaen group in the fifties was the expansion of the tone-row concept to include duration values. Pierre Boulez has used the following series of note values to construct a row of durations.

EXAMPLE 185

1.	2.	3.	4.	5.	6.	7.	8.	9.	10.	11.	12.

This series corresponds to the twelve notes of the chromatic scale and a "row" of duration values can be selected from it to give rhythmic organization to a composition.

TOTAL CONTROL

Boulez and his contemporaries did not stop here; having accepted the idea that duration-rows were as valuable as tone-rows, they added rows of dynamics and articulations. Thus, in his Second Piano Sonata, Boulez chose rows from the following series:

EXAMPLE 186

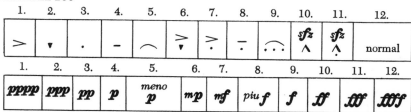

Music that is the result of the permutations and combinations of **these four rows**—tones, durations, dynamics, and articulations—is said to be "totally controlled." That is, every factor is planned by the composer, and the performer need only carry out his precise directions. Of course, the exactness of these orders makes demands on the performer which are almost impossible to execute as, for example, when he is asked to go from a note marked ♪ to another marked ♪. It is remarkable that performers have met the challenge of this music, just as they did in the past when confronted with new and "impossible" music. The Beethoven quartets, the roles of Isolde and Elektra, the Tchaikovsky Piano Concerto are examples of music which were all considered unplayable at one time.

It would be hazardous to say that any masterpieces of totally controlled music have been written as yet. A major problem lies in the fact that the systems of order they embody are far too precise to be perceived by most listeners, and the absence of any familiar elements such as melody and timbre tend to make for aridity.

ELECTRONIC MUSIC

Total control in the full sense could be achieved only by eliminating the human performer. This radical step was accomplished during the 1950's in *electronic music*. This term is used loosely to describe music produced on electronic instruments such as the Theramin or Ondes Martinot which are "played" by moving the hands towards or away from a sensitive tube, resulting in a whining, musical-saw effect. The term also includes electric instruments that simulate the sound of the organ, guitar, or other conventional instruments.

Used more precisely, the term *electronic music* has nothing to do with synthetic instruments. It refers to a kind of music which originated in the Studio for Electronic Music of the West German Radio, in Cologne, and its sound material is produced by electronic devices, recorded on magnetic tape, and heard through loudspeakers. It is this type of electronic music which will be described here.

The basic sound of electronic music is a pure (free from overtones) sinus tone produced by an oscillator. Because there are no limitations imposed by either instruments or humans, any and all pitches within the thresholds of audibility (16 to 20,000 vibrations) are available, instead of the eighty-eight fixed tones that more than suffice for conventional music. Moreover, the possibilities of dynamic levels are greatly increased since every perceptible level of loudness can be accurately specified. Duration and timbre possibilities are likewise unrestricted. Needless to say, Western music up to this time has used only a fraction of these total resources.

The problem for the composer of electronic music is that of constructing order in this new aural universe, and serial music, particularly that of Webern, has provided clues for doing so. Electronic music may rightly be considered a direct outgrowth of the second Viennese school.

EXAMPLE 187* STUDIE II

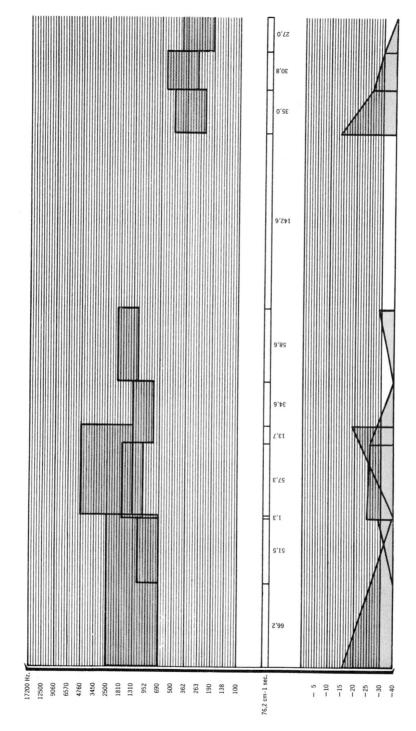

One of the special problems has been the creation of a system of notation. The conventional symbols, geared to the chromatic scale, are useless of course. Example 187 shows a page from Stockhausen's *Elektronische Studien II*. This is not so much a score as "working instructions for the electro-acoustical realization of the composition." The upper section, calibrated from 100 to 17,200, refers to pitch and timbre. The individual pitches used in this composition are chosen from a scale of eighty-one steps with a constant interval ratio of $25\sqrt{5}$ (the tempered scale is based on a ratio of $12\sqrt{2}$), and one hundred and ninety-three mixtures constructed from them. The heavy horizontal lines indicate the high and low frequencies of the first sound mixture to which another overlapping mixture is soon added.

The two horizontal lines in the middle of the page indicate the duration of the sounds in terms of centimeters of tape moving at a specified speed. The triangular shapes at the bottom indicate volume in decibels.

In order to "realize" the composition, i.e. "perform" it, a tape recording would first be made of the one hundred and ninety-three tone mixtures that serve as its basic material. This is the "keyboard," the gamut of sounds from which selections would be chosen and recorded following the instructions of the diagrams.

Electronic music is still in its infancy. A number of first-rate musical minds are excited by its possibilities and future developments might be of importance.

MUSIQUE CONCRÈTE

Electronic music, largely a German development, differs from a parallel French movement called *musique concrète* in the nature of the sound medium employed. In the latter, natural sounds and noises—for example, the wind, a motor accelerating, or a door slamming—are recorded on tape and then treated in all the ways tape can be manipulated—played slower (lowering pitch), faster (raising pitch), backwards (reversing the usual attack-diminuendo pattern), or played in combinations of possible treatments. Compositions are then constructed from this palette of sound.

Musique concrète has its followers in the United States. Vladimir Ussachevsky of Columbia University combines electronic with natural sounds. He has described the "raw material" of his *Piece for Tape Recorder*. He uses "non-electric sounds: a gong, a piano, a single stroke on a cymbal, a single note on a kettledrum, the noise of a jet plane, a few chords on an organ" combined with "electronic sounds: four pure tones, produced on an oscillator, and a tremolo produced by the stabilized reverberation of a click from a switch on a tape recorder."

So far, *musique concrète* has proved to be more useful for background sounds in plays and movies than as the material for "pure" composition. The sounds have an unearthly, eerie quality which lend themselves very well to the expression of supernatural events or to neurotic states.

CHANCE MUSIC

The same decade that saw the development of total-control and electronic music witnessed another, and diametrically opposed, musical experiment. Perhaps repelled by the danger of mechanization, this group of composers investigated the effect of sheer chance on musical composition and performance. The element of chance is present in all composition and performance, but now its effect became obligatory, so to speak. For instance, Stockhausen (the same composer mentioned in connection with electronic music), wrote a piece called *Piano Piece XI* which permits the performer to play the various sections in any order he chooses. When he desires to end the performance, the composer has instructed him to play the last section three times. John Cage, the chief American proponent of chance music, has written a piece for piano printed on several different sheets of paper. He instructs the performer to drop the pages and then play the music in the random order in which it is picked up. In another series of pieces the order of notes was determined by the "pointal imperfections" in a sheet of transparent paper. These were transferred to staff paper, but the durations and clefs were determined by coin throws (heads, treble; tails, bass). The *I-Ching*, a Chinese device consisting of a box from which marked sticks are shaken, determined the manner in which the notes should be sounded on the piano—normally, muted, or plucked on the strings.[4] John Cage's most extreme experiment involved twenty-four radios. They were switched on or off by twelve "performers" who followed their directions with stop watches. The patterned montage which resulted was determined by the type of program being broadcast at the moment.

Experiments such as these would seem to be close to the lunatic-fringe, and one might be tempted to dismiss them as harmless amusements except for the fact that the elements of chance and accident have become matters of interest and investigation in other arts and areas of speculation. Jackson Pollack, for instance, spattered or poured paint on pieces of Masonite without a preconceived plan and the chance result sometimes became a highly expressive "painting." The Abstract-Expressionist school of painting that followed, without doubt the dominant style of the postwar period, is based on this philosophy. The painters of this school do not say that anything produced by chance is necessarily artistically valid, but they believe that *some* chance products might be of value. The art world has accepted the premise wholeheartedly.

Modern mathematics, in its interest in the theory of probability, theoretical physics, and certain schools of philosophy are also studying the "laws" of chance. Perhaps all of these activities point to a revolt of the creative mind against the increasing mechanization of the world.

COMPUTER MUSIC

One of the most recent experimental approaches to music has been the use of an automatic high-speed digital computer in actual composition. In contrast with *electronic music* and *musique concrète,* where new sound media are created, the computer composes pieces that can be played on conventional instruments; a string quartet called the *Illiac Suite,* the result of such a process, has been published.

A computing machine cannot "think," but it can be instructed to make selections and rejections. In one sense, the process of composition is the making of selections and rejections, whether consciously or unconsciously. The composer chooses key, meter, timbre, and type of harmony (not necessarily in that order) and once started, chooses from many possibilities what should follow. The number of possibilities are not limitless, but are determined by the general style in which he is writing. In the Bach style, for instance, the exact probability of a tonic chord following a dominant has been determined, and McHose can write, "In their music the composers of the 18th century use the normal progression about seventy-six percent of the time."[5] Bach of course knew nothing about this; he simply wrote music. Nevertheless, on the basis of his music the "Bach style" can be defined accurately. The same is true of any other style.

Coded instructions can be given to a computer so that it will choose a "possible", i.e. not incorrect, series of musical material. It can even be instructed to reject "impossible" (in terms of a given style) progressions. Therefore, if a computer is fed instructions based on probabilities determined by a given style of music, it can turn out endless "compositions" in the form of a code which can be easily transcribed into musical notation and performed. At this point human sensitivity enters. Through operation of the laws of chance, some of these "compositions" might be "better" than others. The critical judgment of the trained musician can then accept some of the results and reject others, just as a composer continually accepts or rejects his own ideas when he composes.

However, the value of the computer to music is not in its creation of compositions "in the style of" various composers. Nothing would be formed here that could not be done without the machine, although the possibility of creating songs for "juke-box consumption and similar uses, probably at a highly efficient and rapid rate" is an intriguing possibility.[6] Rather, the value of the approach will probably be in the direction of trying out various new possibilities for combining sounds, and thus saving time for the creative musician.

BUT IS IT MUSIC?

Here are some excerpts from reviews of the first performances of four compositions, the names of which will be temporarily withheld:

> The . . . is filthy and vile. It suggests Chinese orchestral performance as described by enterprising and self-sacrificing travelers. This may be a specimen of the School of the Future for aught I

know. If it is, the future will throw the works of Haydn, Mozart, and Beethoven into the rubbish bin.[7]

The . . . was generally regarded as an incomprehensible production, the depths of which (if there really are depths) it was impossible to fathom. This opinion I confess I adopted. After poring for hours over the ponderous pages, the only result was an absolute bewilderment among its mazes.[8]

We now have . . . formlessness elevated to a principle, a systematized non-music, a melodic nerve fever written out on the five lines of the staff.[9]

At first hearing, much, perhaps most, of . . . sounds exceedingly, even ingeniously, ugly. Every now and then one comes across the most ear-flaying succession of chords; then, the instrumentation, although nearly always characteristic, is often distinctly rawboned and hideous; the composer shows a well-nigh diabolical ingenuity in massing together harsh, ill-sounding timbres.[10]

It might be thought that these criticisms selected from Nicolas Slonimsky's *Lexicon of Musical Invective* refer to compositions described in this chapter. On the contrary, they are taken from critiques of a Liszt concerto, Beethoven's *Missa Solemnis, Tristan und Isolde,* and *La Tosca.* Some interesting questions are raised with the realization that well-loved classics such as these met with complete misunderstanding when they were first heard. Will the names of Stockhausen and Boulez become as well known as those of Wagner and Puccini? Will repeated performances of their compositions be listened to by countless thousands of music lovers in the years to come?

While it would be foolhardy to attempt to answer such questions, it should be remembered that *Le Sacre du Printemps, Pierrot Lunaire,* and many of the other compositions discussed in the preceding chapters were also greeted with vituperation. Nevertheless, fifty years later they are being performed to ever-growing audiences. The musical innovations of the first half of the century have been accepted and the battle of "modern music" has been won.

Consequently, we should not be dismayed if new musical horizons are again being explored at mid-century. The attitude expressed by Roger Sessions in summing up a seminar on "the problems and issues facing the composer today," held at Princeton University in 1959, suggests a thoughtful and optimistic stand toward the problem of change in musical style. "One hears a good deal, these days," he said, "of the developing 'dehumanization' of music and the other arts. . . . This is all very well, and not without plausibility; but we are speaking of a movement that is widespread among the younger composers of Europe, that has begun to take root in the United States, and that above all is in constant development and evolution. Many ideas are being tested, and many are quickly discarded. If we regard certain manifestations with raised eyebrows, that is our privilege as members of an older generation, as it is always our privilege to point out flaws in logic. But if it is also our prerogative to insist on the primacy of the creative imagination, and to minimize the decisive importance of theoretical speculation, we are at the same time obliged to abide by our own premises, and look towards artistic results rather than towards the ideas by which these are rationalized. By the same token it is well to remember that art, considered on the most objective level, reflects the attitudes of the individuals that produce it. The danger of dehumanization is a real and patent one, and the individual can, and certainly should, resist any dehumanizing tendency with all his strength. But this cannot, and must not, blind us to the claims of whatever is genuinely new and vital in the arts, or, once more cause us to forget that it is the product, not the process, that is of real importance and that the creative imagination, at its most vital, has revealed itself through many and often surprising channels. There is no reason to believe that it will not continue to do so, as long as creative vitality—which for musicians means above all the intense love of music—continues to persist."[11]

SUGGESTED READINGS

One of best sources of information on electronic music of various kinds is a periodical *Die Reihe*, published in an English translation by Theodore Presser Company, Bryn Mawr, Pennsylvania (in association with Universal Edition, Vienna.) The first issue (German, 1955; English, 1958) was devoted to electronic music and contained articles by many of the composers closely associated with the movement. The third issue, called *Musical Craftsmanship* (German, 1957; English,

1959), discussed problems of electronic music composition. The fourth issue (1958-1960) is devoted to studies of composers in the field.

Computer music is discussed in *Experimental Music* by Lejaren Hiller and Leonard Isaacson (New York, 1959). Messiaen's book *The Technique of My Musical Language* (Paris, 1956) describes his theories. A special issue of the *Musical Quarterly*, Vol. XLVI, No. 2 (April 1960), is devoted to the problems of modern music and contains several articles of value; the "Current Chronicle" section of the same publication regularly contains analyses of new music.

References

Chapter 2

1. Léon Vallas, *Claude Debussy, His Life and Works* (London: Oxford University Press, 1951), p. 86.
2. Oscar Thompson, *Debussy, Man and Artist* (Dodd, Mead & Co., 1937), p. 103.

Chapter 3

1. Ralph Vaughan Williams, "Musical Autobiography," in Hubert Foss, *Ralph Vaughan Williams* (New York: Oxford University Press, 1950), p. 35.

Chapter 4

1. Bruno Walter and Ernest Krenek, *Gustav Mahler* (New York: The Greystone Press, 1941), pp. 198-99.
2. Arnold Schoenberg, "My Evolution," *Musical Quarterly,* 38 (October, 1952), p. 518.
3. Arnold Schoenberg, *Style and Idea* (New York: Philosophical Library, 1950), p. 8.
4. *Ibid.,* p. 13.
5. Schoenberg, "My Evolution," p. 518.
6. Schoenberg, *Style and Idea,* p. 5.
7. *Ibid.,* p. 105.
8. Arnold Schoenberg, *Die glückliche Hand* (Vienna: Universal Edition, 1923).
9. Mark Van Doren, ed., *An Anthology of World Poetry* (New York: Reynal & Hitchcock, 1928), p. 45.
10. James Huneker, *Ivory, Apes and Peacocks* (New York: Charles Scribner's Sons, 1925), p. 93.
11. Igor Stravinsky, *An Autobiography* (New York: Simon and Schuster, 1936), p. 67.

Chapter 5

1. Charles Ives, *Second Pianoforte Sonata, Concord, Mass., 1840-1860* (New York: Arrow Music Press, Inc., 1947), preface.
2. Charles Ives, *The Unanswered Question, a cosmic landscape* (New York: Southern Music Publishers, Inc., 1942), preface.
3. Charles Ives, *114 Songs* (privately printed, 1922), preface.
4. Winthrop Sargeant, *Jazz, Hot and Hybrid* (New York: E. P. Dutton & Co., Inc., 1946), p. 59.

Chapter 6

1. Nicolas Slonimsky, *Music Since 1900* (Boston: Coleman-Ross Company, 1949), p. 642.

Chapter 7

1. Darius Milhaud, *Notes Without Music* (London: Dennis Dobson, Ltd., 1952), p. 85.
2. Jean Cocteau, *Cock and Harlequin*, Rollo Myers, trans. (London: The Egoist Press, 1921), pp. 4 ff.
3. Rollo H. Myers, *Erik Satie* (London: Dennis Dobson, Ltd., 1948), p. 80.
4. *Ibid.*, p. 60.
5. Cocteau, *op. cit.*, p. 6.
6. *Ibid.*, p. 8.
7. Paul Collaer, *La Musique Moderne* (Paris: Elsevier, 1955), p. 156.
8. Milhaud, *op. cit.*, p. 82.
9. Jean Cocteau, "Les Mariés de la Tour Eiffel," Dudley Fitts, trans. (Norfolk, Conn.: New Directions, 1937).
10. Milhaud, *op. cit.*, p. 87.

Chapter 8

1. Milhaud, *Notes Without Music*, p. 117.
2. Milhaud, *Les Choëphores* (Paris: Heugel & Cie., 1947), preface.
3. Milhaud, *Notes Without Music*, p. 127.
4. *Ibid.*, p. 130.
5. Arthur Honegger, *Je Suis Compositeur* (Paris: Editions du Conquistador, 1951), p. 32.
6. *Ibid.*, p. 15
7. *Ibid.*, p. 25.

8. *Ibid.*, p. 117.

Chapter 9

1. Stravinsky, *The Poetics of Music* (Cambridge, Mass.: Harvard University Press, 1947), p. 83.
2. Alexandre Tansman, *Igor Stravinsky* (New York: G. P. Putnam's Sons, 1949), p. 9.
3. Stravinsky, *The Poetics of Music,* p. 52.
4. *Ibid.*, p. 54.
5. *Ibid.*, p. 67.
6. Eric White, *Stravinsky* (London: John Lehmann, 1947), p. 63.
7. Stravinsky, *An Autobiography,* p. 128.
8. Heinrich Strobel, "Igor Stravinsky," *Melos,* 2(Jan., 1921), p. 40.
9. Stravinsky, *An Autobiography,* p. 162.
10. Walter Piston, "Stravinsky's Rediscoveries," in Minna Lederman, ed., *Stravinsky in the Theatre* (New York: Pellegrini & Cudahy, 1949), p. 130.
11. Igor Stravinsky and Robert Craft, *Conversations with Igor Stravinsky* (Garden City, N.Y.: Doubleday & Co., 1959), p. 136.

Chapter 10

1. Anton Webern, "Homage to Arnold Schoenberg," *Die Reihe,* 2(1958), p. 9.
2. Schoenberg, *Style and Idea,* p. 107.
3. René Leibowitz, *Introduction à La Musique de Douze Sons* (Paris: L'Arche, 1949), pp. 111 ff.

Chapter 11

1. Stravinsky and Craft, *Conversations with Igor Stravinsky,* p. 81.
2. *Ibid.*, p. 82.
3. T. S. Eliot, "The Hollow Men," *Collected Poems, 1909-1935* (New York: Harcourt, Brace & Co., Inc., 1934,1936), p. 105.
4. Norman Demuth, *Musical Trends in the 20th Century* (London: Rockliff Publishing Corp., Ltd., 1952), p. 242.
5. René Leibowitz, *Schoenberg and His School* (New York: Philosophical Library, 1949), p. 190.
6. Stravinsky and Craft, *op. cit.*, p. 136.
7. Sheldon Cheney, *The Story of Modern Art* (New York: The Viking Press, 1941), p. 474.

Chapter 13

1. Paul Hindemith, *1922*, piano suite (Mainz: B. Schott's Sohne, 1922).
2. Hindemith, *A Composer's World* (Cambridge, Mass.: Harvard University Press, 1952), p. 120.
3. Hindemith, *Das Marienleben, Introductory Remarks for the New Version* (New York: Associated Music Publishers, Inc., 1954), p. 2.
4. *Ibid.*, p. 5.
5. *Ibid.*, p. 11.
6. *Ibid.*, p. 12.

Chapter 14

1. *New York Times*, April 1, 1937, p. 20.
2. Alexander Werth, *Musical Uproar in Moscow* (London: The Turnstile Press, 1949), p. 53.
3. *Ibid.*, p. 86.

Chapter 15

1. Ralph Vaughan Williams. "Musical Autobiography," in Hubert Foss, *Ralph Vaughan Williams*, p. 24.
2. *Ibid.*, p. 23.
3. Hans Keller, "The Musical Character," in Donald Mitchell and Hans Keller, eds., *Benjamin Britten* (New York: Philosophical Library, 1953), p. 319.
4. Joseph Kerman, *Opera as Drama* (New York: Alfred A. Knopf, Inc., 1956), p. 230.
5. "Profile—Benjamin Britten," *Observer* (London), October 27, 1946. Quoted in Mitchell and Keller, p. 37.

Chapter 16

1. *New York Times*, January 12, 1925, p. 27. Quoted in Julia Smith, *Aaron Copland* (New York: E. P. Dutton & Co., Inc., 1955), p. 74.
2. Smith, *op. cit.*
3. Arthur Berger, *Aaron Copland* (New York: Oxford University Press, 1953), p. 52.
4. Paul Rosenfeld, *One Hour with American Music* (Philadelphia: J. B. Lippincott Co., 1929). p. 129.

5. *New York Times,* October 20, 1957, p. 44.
6. *Ibid.,* p. 44.
7. Nicolas Slonimsky, "Roy Harris," *Musical Quarterly,* 33(January, 1947), p. 17.
8. "Roger Sessions," in Henry Cowell, ed., *American Composers On American Music* (Palo Alto, Calif.: Stanford University Press, 1933), p. 78.
9. Three volumes of Thomson's critiques have been published: *The Musical Scene* (New York: Alfred A. Knopf, Inc., 1945); *The Art of Judging Music* (New York: Alfred A. Knopf, Inc., 1948); *Music, Right and Left* (New York: Henry Holt & Co., 1951).

Chapter 17

1. *New York Times,* October 20, 1957, p. 44.
2. Richard Goldman, "The Music of Elliott Carter," *Musical Quarterly,* 43(April, 1957), p. 161.
3. Vladimir Ussachevsky, "Notes on a Piece for Tape Recorder," *Musical Quarterly,* 46(April, 1960), p. 202.
4. "To Describe the Process of Composition Used in 'Music for Piano 21-52,'" *Die Reihe,* 3(1959), p. 41.
5. A. I. McHose, *The Contrapuntal Harmonic Technique of the 18th Century* (New York: F. S. Crofts & Co., 1947), p. 10.
6. Lejaren A. Hiller and Leonard M. Isaacson, *Experimental Music* (New York: McGraw-Hill Book Company, 1959), p. 176.
7. Nicolas Slonimsky, *Lexicon of Musical Invective* (Boston: Coleman-Ross Company, 1953), p. 113.
8. *Ibid.,* p. 47.
9. *Ibid.,* p. 231.
10. *Ibid.,* p. 136.
11. Roger Sessions, "The Problems and Issues Facing the Composer Today," *Musical Quarterly,* 46(April, 1960), p. 171.

Composers*

1860	Gustave Charpentier		Sem Dresden
	GUSTAV MAHLER		Nikolai Miaskovsky
1861	Edward MacDowell	**1882**	Zoltán Kodály
1862	CLAUDE DEBUSSY		Gian Francesco Malipiero
	Frederick Delius		IGOR STRAVINSKY
1864	RICHARD STRAUSS		Karol Szymanowski
1865	Paul Dukas		Joaquín Turina
	Alexander Glazunov	**1883**	Arnold Bax
	Carl Nielsen		Alfredo Casella
	Jean Sibelius		ANTON VON WEBERN
1866	ERIK SATIE	**1885**	ALBAN BERG
1869	Hans Pfitzner		Wallingford Riegger
	Albert Roussel		Edgar Varèse
1872	Hugo Alfvén	**1887**	Heitor Villa-Lobos
	Alexander Scriabin	**1890**	Jacques Ibert
	Ralph Vaughan Williams		Frank Martin
1873	Sergey Rachmaninoff		Bohuslav Martinu
1874	Gustav Holst	**1891**	SERGE PROKOFIEV
	CHARLES IVES	**1892**	ARTHUR HONEGGER
	ARNOLD SCHOENBERG		DARIUS MILHAUD
	Josef Suk	**1893**	Douglas Moore
1875	Reinhold Glière	**1894**	Willem Pijper
	MAURICE RAVEL	**1895**	PAUL HINDEMITH
1876	Franco Alfano		Carl Orff
	Manuel de Falla	**1896**	HOWARD HANSON
	Carl Ruggles		ROGER SESSIONS
1879	John Ireland		VIRGIL THOMSON
	Ottorino Respighi	**1897**	Henry Cowell
	Cyril Scott	**1898**	George Gershwin
1880	Ildebrando Pizzetti		ROY HARRIS
1881	BÉLA BARTÓK	**1899**	Georges Auric

*Listed by years of birth; capitalized composers are discussed in the text.

	Carlos Chávez	1910	Samuel Barber
	FRANCIS POULENC		Rolf Liebermann
	Silvestre Revueltas		Mario Peragallo
	Randall Thompson		William Schuman
1900	George Antheil		Heinrich Sutermeister
	AARON COPLAND	1911	Gian Carlo Menotti
	Ernst Krenek	1912	John Cage
	Otto Luening		Jean Françaix
	Kurt Weill	1913	Henry Brant
1901	Conrad Beck		BENJAMIN BRITTEN
	Raymond Chevreuille		Norman Dello Joio
	Marcel Poot	1915	Robert Palmer
	Edmund Rubbra		Vincent Persichetti
	Henri Sauguet		Humphrey Searle
1902	William Walton	1918	Leonard Bernstein
1903	Aram Khatchaturian		Gottfried von Einem
1904	Luigi Dallapiccola	1919	Leon Kirchner
	Dmitri Kabalevsky	1920	Bruno Maderna
	Goffredo Petrassi		Harold Shapero
	Nikos Skalkottas	1921	William Bergsma
1905	Alan Rawsthorne	1922	Lukas Foss
	Dag Wirén	1923	Peter Mennin
1906	Paul Creston	1924	Luigi Nono
	DMITRI	1925	PIERRE BOULEZ
	SHOSTAKOVICH		Giselher Klebe
1907	Henk Badings	1926	Hanz Werner Henz
	Camargo Guarnieri	1928	KARLHEINZ
1908	ELLIOT CARTER		STOCKHAUSEN
	Olivier Messiaen		

Index

Tosca, La (Puccini), 356
Toscanini, Arturo, 280
Total control, 349-350
transition, 108
Tristan und Isolde (Wagner), 7, 20-21,
    54, 205, 290, 299, 326, 349, 356
Twelve-tone music, 177-183
    Copland on, 314
    Rufer on, 179-180
    Schoenberg on, 181
Twentieth-century ballets:
    Agon, 170
    Boeuf sur le Toit, Le, 119-120
    Copland's, 311
    Création du Monde, La, 129-132
    Daphnis et Chloé, 38-39
    Firebird, The, 44
    Parade, 113
    Petrouchka, 44-45
    Pulcinella, 158
    Sacre du Printemps, Le, 3, 45-52
Twentieth-century operas:
    Dialogues des Carmélites, Les,
        144-145
    Erwartung, 66-67
    Glückliche Hand, Die, 69
    Jazz operas, 85-86
    Mamelles de Tirésias, Les, 144
    Moses und Aron, 193
    Pelléas et Mélisande, 3, 15, 20
    Peter Grimes, 299-301
    Rake's Progress, The, 166-169
    Strauss', 54
    Wozzeck, 199-202
Twentieth-century string quartets:
    Bartók No. 1, 226
    Bartók No. 2, 226
    Bartók No. 4, 227-232
    Carter No. 1, 347-348
    Debussy, 16
    Ravel, 36
    Schoenberg No. 1, 60
    Schoenberg No. 2, 61
Twentieth-century symphonies:
    Copland, Symphony No. 3, 311-314
    Hanson, Symphony No. 2, 330-332
    Harris, Symphony No. 3, 316-318
    Honegger, Symphony No. 5, 138-141
    Milhaud, Symphony No. 1, 132
    Piston, Symphony No. 4, 322-324
    Shostakovich, Symphony No. 5,

    282-286
    Sessions, Symphony No. 2, 326-328
    Vaughan Williams, Symphony No. 6,
        294-296
    Webern, Symphony, op. 21, 215-217

U

Ulysses (Joyce), 55, 106, 202
Unanswered Question, The (Ives), 81
United States, Music in the, 75-76,
    305, 337 (See American music)
University of Vienna, 209
Ussachevsky, Vladimir, Piece for Tape
    Recorder, 353

V

Valéry, Paul, 143, 152
Van Gogh, Vincent, 55
Varèse, Edgar, 89
Variations for Orchestra (Schoenberg),
    179, 185-189
    Leibowitz on, 186-187
Variations for Piano (Webern), 217-218
Variations on Sunday School Tunes
    (Thomson), 334
Vaughan Williams, Ralph, 41, 44,
    290-296
    compositions, 292-296
    Fantasia on a Theme by Thomas
        Tallis, 292-293
    on his music, 289
    Symphony No. 6, 294-296
Verdi, Guiseppe, 289, 299
Verklaerte Nacht (Schoenberg), 59-60
Verlaine, Paul, 12, 33
Vienna, 55, 175, 198, 209
Viñes, Ricardo, 143
Vivaldi, Antonio, 162

W

Wagner, Richard, 3-9, 62, 67, 112, 289,
    332, 356
    influence on Debussy, 14, 24
    music dramas, 5, 20, 53, 56
    Tristan und Isolde, 7, 20-21, 54, 205,
        290, 299, 326, 349, 356
Walküre, Die (Wagner), 15, 59
Wallpaper music, 112-114
Walton, Sir William, 297